LONDON

The Information Capital

LONDON
The Information Capital

100 maps and graphics that will change how you view the city

James Cheshire

Oliver Uberti

PENGUIN BOOKS

PENGUIN BOOKS

UK | USA | Canada | Ireland | Australia
India | New Zealand | South Africa

Penguin Books is part of the Penguin Random House group of companies
whose addresses can be found at global.penguinrandomhouse.com.

First published in Great Britain by Particular Books 2014
Published in Penguin Books 2016
001

Designed by Oliver Uberti
Set in Whitney (Hoefler & Co.) with a cameo by London's own Founder's Caslon (ITC)
Printed and bound in Italy by Graphicom srl

A CIP catalogue record for this book is available from the British Library

ISBN: 978-0-141-97879-6

Contents

THE GRAPHICS

Where We Are

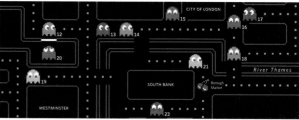

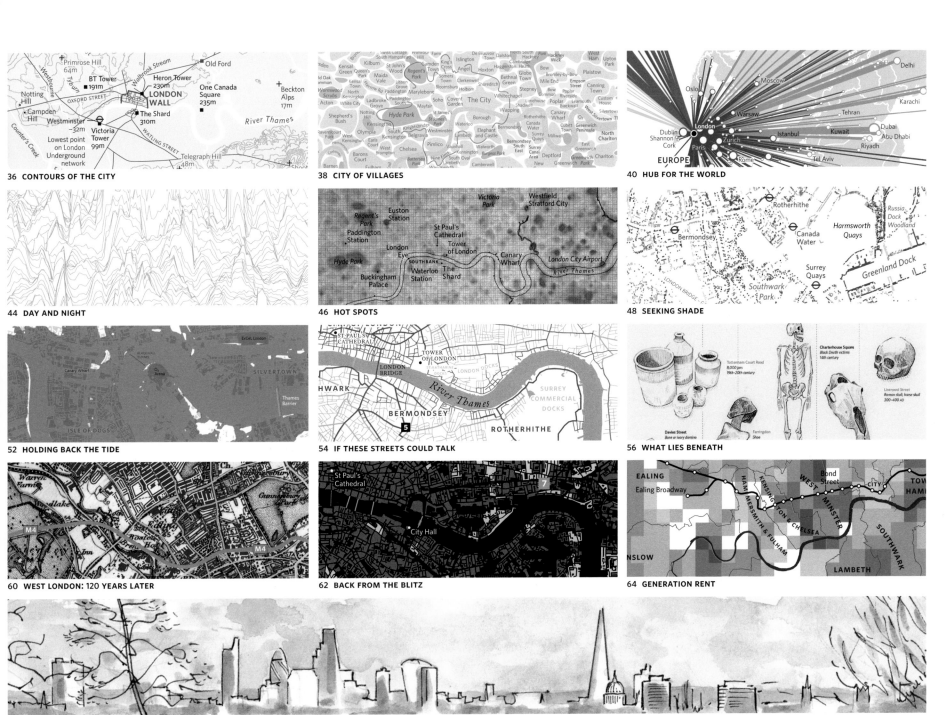

36 CONTOURS OF THE CITY

38 CITY OF VILLAGES

40 HUB FOR THE WORLD

44 DAY AND NIGHT

46 HOT SPOTS

48 SEEKING SHADE

52 HOLDING BACK THE TIDE

54 IF THESE STREETS COULD TALK

56 WHAT LIES BENEATH

60 WEST LONDON: 120 YEARS LATER

62 BACK FROM THE BLITZ

64 GENERATION RENT

68 13 VIEWS WORTH PROTECTING

Who We Are

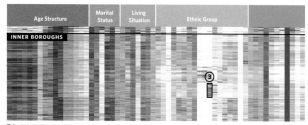

Where We Go

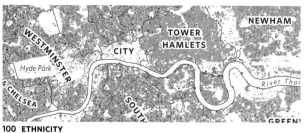

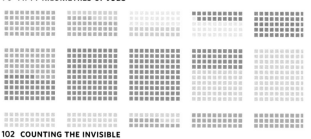

80 SIMILARITIES ATTRACT

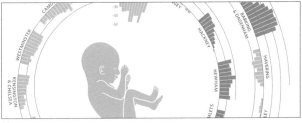
82 LIFE AND DEATH

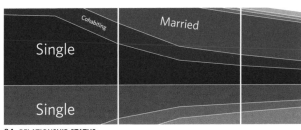
84 RELATIONSHIP STATUS

92 THE COLOUR OF VOTES

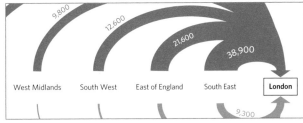
94 MOVING IN, THEN ON

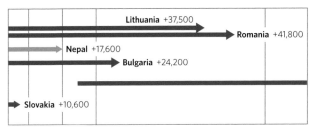
96 INCREASINGLY EASTERN

104 GREETINGS FROM LONDON

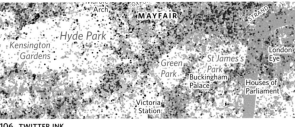
106 TWITTER INK

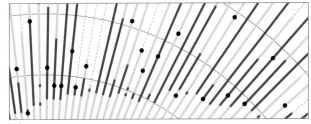
108 WHO LONDON INSPIRED

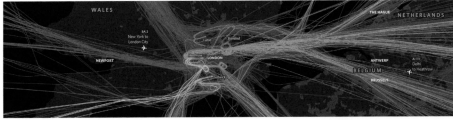
116 UNTANGLED ON ARRIVAL

120 THAMES GATEWAY

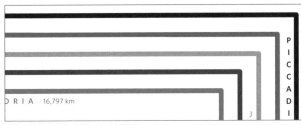
130 AROUND THE WORLD IN 10 LINES

132 DISRUPTED

134 THE TUBE CHALLENGE

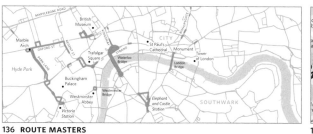

136 ROUTE MASTERS

138 MENTAL MAPS

148 BORIS'S BEST BIKERS

1,603 1,584 1,460
1,298 1,179 1,156

150 EXHAUSTING RIDES

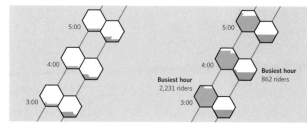

5:00 5:00
4:00 4:00
Busiest hour Busiest hour
2,231 riders 862 riders
3:00 3:00

152 CABLE CAR TO NOWHERE

How We're Doing

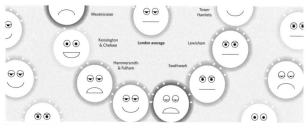

Westminster Tower Hamlets
Kensington & Chelsea London average Lewisham
Hammersmith & Fulham Southwark

162 ISLINGTON HAS ISSUES

HAMMERSMITH & FULHAM KENSINGTON & CHELSEA WESTMINSTER CITY TOWER HAMLETS NEWHAM SOUTHWARK GREENWICH

164 A TALE OF TWO CITIES

172 CAUSES OF DEATH

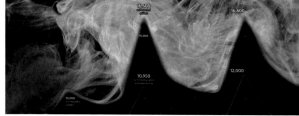

16,500 16,800
15,000
10,950 12,000
10,000

174 QUIT RATES

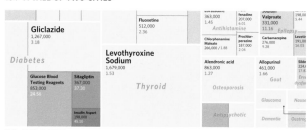

Loratadine 363,000 Sodium fenadine 207,000 1.45 Valproate 198,000 5.44
Fluoxetine 512,000 2.36 331,000 11.16 Epilepsy
Gliclazide 1,267,000 3.18 Antihistamine Carbamazepine
Chlorphenamine Maleate 266,000 / 1.88 Prochlorperazine 187,000 2.04 276,000 9.28 191,000 16.03
Diabetes Levothyroxine Sodium 1,679,000 1.53 Alendronic acid 863,000 1.27 Allopurinol 461,000 1.66 224/ 17.8 Gout
Glucose Blood Testing Reagents 853,000 24.50 Sitagliptin 367,000 37.30 Thyroid Osteoporosis Glaucoma Nause
Insulin Aspart 198,000 Antipsychotic Dementia Oestro

176 PILL BOXES

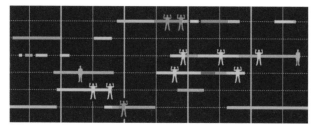

184 YOU CAN'T HIDE

186 SOUND THE ALARM!

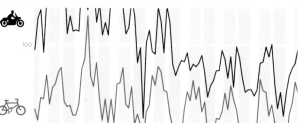

100

188 SAFER DRIVERS

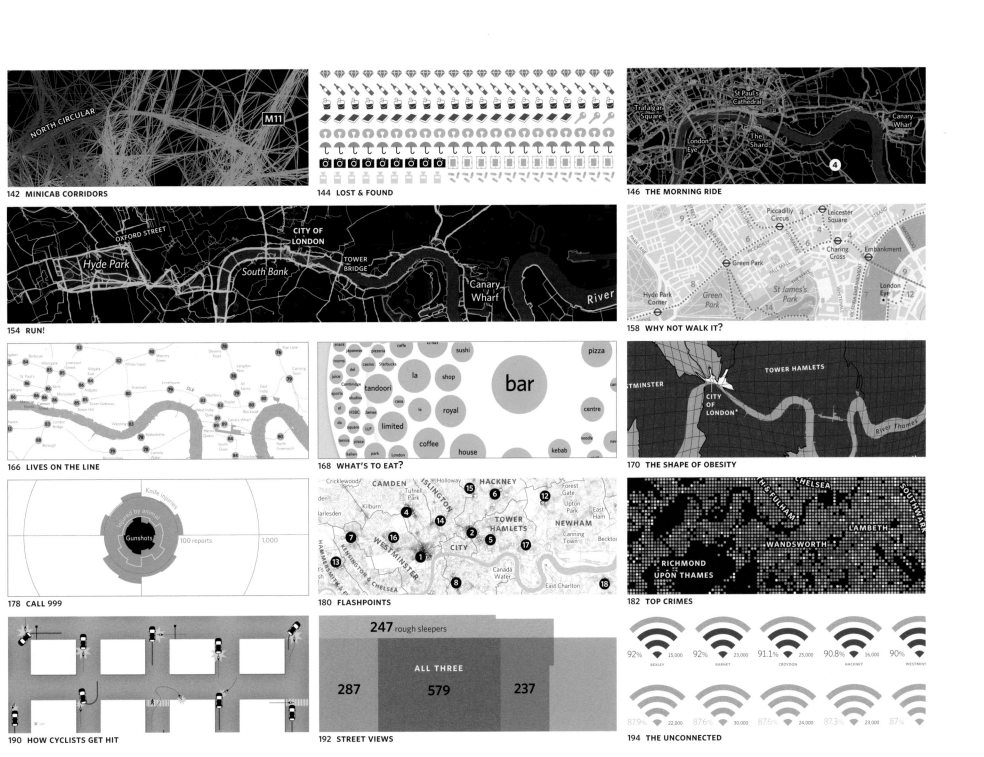

142 MINICAB CORRIDORS

144 LOST & FOUND

146 THE MORNING RIDE

154 RUN!

158 WHY NOT WALK IT?

166 LIVES ON THE LINE

168 WHAT'S TO EAT?

170 THE SHAPE OF OBESITY

178 CALL 999

180 FLASHPOINTS

182 TOP CRIMES

190 HOW CYCLISTS GET HIT

192 STREET VIEWS

194 THE UNCONNECTED

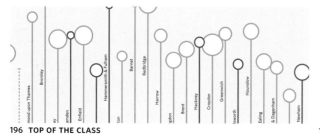

196 **TOP OF THE CLASS**

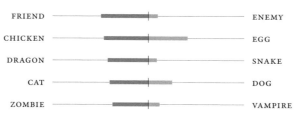

FRIEND — ENEMY
CHICKEN — EGG
DRAGON — SNAKE
CAT — DOG
ZOMBIE — VAMPIRE

198 **IN THEIR WORDS**

What We Like

210 **A TRUE ZOO**

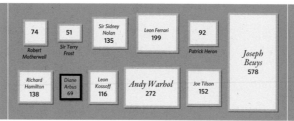

74	51	Sir Sidney Nolan 135	Leon Ferrari 199	92	
Robert Motherwell	Sir Terry Frost			Patrick Heron	Joseph Beuys 578
Richard Hamilton 138	Diane Arbus 69	Leon Kossoff 116	Andy Warhol 272	Joe Tilson 152	

212 **ALL THE TATE'S TREASURES**

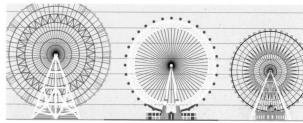

214 **FOLLOWING THE LEADER**

Arts architecture, art, poetry

Transport TfL, Tube, trains   Tube strike

224 **THE BUZZ ABOUT TOWN**

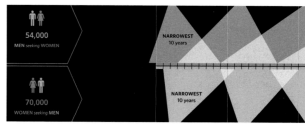

54,000
MEN seeking WOMEN

70,000
WOMEN seeking MEN

NARROWEST 10 years

NARROWEST 10 years

226 **LOOKING FOR LOVE**

222 **WHO SAYS PRINT IS DEAD?**

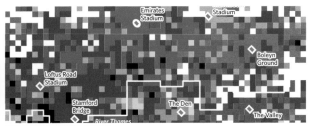

202 THE FOOTBALL TRIBES

204 THINGS TO DO

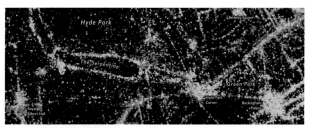

206 PHOTOGENIC FEATURES

216 FASHION CYCLES

218 THEY CAME, THEY SAW, THEY SPENT

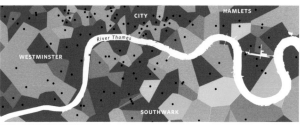

220 SHOP WINDOW

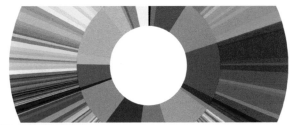

228 HAPPY TIMES

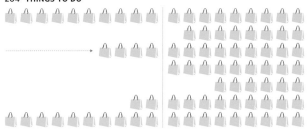

232 BOOKS, COFFEE, ETC.

Acknowledgements

Without those working tirelessly with London's data in its universities, museums, businesses and local government, London would not be 'The Information Capital'. We are tremendously fortunate to have received the support and expertise from some of the best through their data, graphics and advice. This book would not have been possible without them.

When it comes to mapping 21st-century London, Oliver O'Brien is unsurpassed. We are extremely grateful to him for being part of this project from the start. His data, expertise, fact-checking and much welcome feedback have been integral to ensuring the graphics here are the best they can be.

We are indebted to those at University College London (UCL) who have been particularly generous with their time and expertise. From the Centre for Advanced Spatial Analysis (CASA) we would like to thank Shlomit Flint for her fascinating insights into one small area of east London; Ed Manley for his 'Tube flows' and 'Minicab Corridors' graphics and his continued support throughout the project; Joan Serras for the bus data used in 'Route Masters'; Hannah Fry for her detailed comments and enthusiasm for our work; Steven Gray, Robin Edwards, Flora Roumpani, Duncan Smith, and Camilo Vargas for their help with data queries. At the UCL Department of Geography, we extend our thanks to Muhammad Adnan, Alistair Leak and Guy Lansley for their Twitter data wizardry; to Matt Disney for wrangling the NDVI satellite imagery; and to Peter Wood for his thorough read-through and helpful feedback. Thanks to Matt Ashby from UCL SECReT for his

violent crime graphic and to Anna Mavrogianni and colleagues from the UCL Bartlett Faculty of the Built Environment for their urban heat island research.

At the London School of Hygiene and Tropical Medicine, we would like to thank Daniel Lewis for helpful comments on our drafts and also Anna Goodman for her collaboration on the Boris Bikes data. Thanks to Luke Sibieta and Ellen Greaves from the Institute of Fiscal Studies for their help with our 'Top of the Class' graphic. We are also particularly grateful to the team at City University - Aidan Slingsby, Alexander Kachkaev, Jo Wood and Jason Dykes – for their brilliant Flickr map behind 'Photogenic Features'; to Jon Reades (Kings College London) for his 'Week in the Life of the Underground' graphic; to Kiril Stanilov (University of Cambridge) for his painstakingly digitised historic street and land use data; to Alex Singleton (University of Liverpool) for the London Output Area Classification; and to George MacKerron (University of Sussex) for the 'Happy Times' graphic. Thanks also to André Bruggmann (University of Zurich) for his help with the network analysis and the word frequency counts required on a number of graphics and to Jack Harrison (Ordnance Survey) for his work gathering the road accident data.

We extend our gratitude to Adam Towle of the Greater London Authority and Cass Cities for not only sporting the red laces in the Introduction, but also for his help and enthusiasm on a number of graphics in this book, not least the map of London's localities he created. Thanks also to ultimate Londoner, Matt Brown, for the (mostly true) ghost stories and for sharing tag data from Londonist. We would also like to thank Ken Titmuss for his stories in 'If These Streets Could Talk'. We are also grateful to Jay Carver, Marit Leenstra and Rose Malik at Crossrail for granting us access to their finds for 'What Lies Beneath'. Thank you to Ben Payne, Alistair Hall and the great people at Ministry of Stories for sharing their words with us; to EDITD and Francesco Franchi for sharing their fashion wheels and Ferris wheels; and to Malcolm Linskey of Taxi Trade Promotions for sharing his 'Knowledge'. Thanks to Neil Stewart for providing the Booth Map from the LSE Library and Christopher Fleet at the National Library of Scotland for the 19th Century Ordnance Survey Map. We are grateful to Gareth Rees and Louise Crow at MySociety for providing the Freedom of Information data from *whatdotheyknow.com*; Fiona Scott for providing data and comments for our 'Fifty Kilometres of Jobs' graphic and Julian Harrap Architects LLP for use of their photo collage; Fredrik Lindahl at FlightRadar24 for the allowing us to use the flight track data; Anke and Lars at FleetMon for the Thames Estuary shipping data; Paul Mach for all the Strava data; and Laurence Holloway at Lovestruck for providing our data on dating. Thank you to Guy Simpson for the London Coffee Guide and Helen Wilson at the Booksellers Association for the list of independent bookshops in London. Special thanks to Junko Tateishi and Kazuko Minagawa at Bandai Namco for granting us permission to bring Pac-Man to London.

FROM JAMES: I would like to thank the Economic and Social Research Council for their funding of the Big Open Data: Mining and Synthesis (BODMAS) project. Without it I would not have had the resources to undertake the open data research behind many of the book's graphics, nor would I have had the opportunity to make a hugely enjoyable academic visit to Sara Fabrikant and colleagues at the University of Zurich in order to learn more about cartographic representations of data.

Thanks in large part to the energy of Mike Batty, CASA has become home to some of the best brains in London and has provided the perfect base for producing a book such as this. I would also like to thank Andrew Hudson-Smith for supporting my BODMAS application as well as Martin Zaltz-Austwick and Adam Dennett for arranging cover for my teaching. From the UCL Department of Geography, I'm particularly grateful to Paul Longley for his on-going academic mentorship.

Special thanks go to Rob, William, Lydia, Kat, Chris, Kat, Holly, Jill, Allen and Mali who heard me talk about little else for a year. Thanks to Letty for being a great friend and for sorting the prescription drugs.

No words (or graphics!) can express my heartfelt gratitude to Isla for being with me every step of the way. I could not have embarked on this project without her. Lastly, I would like to thank my parents for their support and encouragement; without it, I would not have the confidence to pursue my ambitions.

FROM OLIVER: This book may be about London, but for me it bears testament to the comforts of another city: Ann Arbor, Michigan in the US. Every page of this book was designed there, either in my studio or at my favourite haunts, namely Literati Bookstore, 826Michigan, Zingerman's and The Espresso Bar. Without design assistance from Corinn Lewis and the love and support of my mother, brother, Sophie, Barrington, Jenny, Amy, Casey, Vince, Phil and Erin, my psyche surely would have crumbled. I would be remiss not to thank my friends and mentors at *National Geographic* – David, Susan, Maggie, Juan, Fernando, John, Sean and Bill – whose influence appears on all of these pages.

Finally, we both must thank our agent Luigi Bonomi for his enthusiasm from day one and for putting us in touch with the team at Particular Books/Penguin who shared our passion for the project. We are grateful to Helen Conford and Cecilia Stein for their editorial guidance, Jim Stoddart for advice on the cover design and James Blackman for his expertise on printing, binding and colour production. We feel lucky to have been paired with a team that believes books can and should be beautiful objects.

'I can never understand why Londoners fail to see that they live in the most wonderful city in the world.'

—Bill Bryson, *Notes from a Small Island*

Bill Bryson published these words in 1995,
when London was only at the beginning of its most recent
ascendancy. It was a time before London had its own mayor,
before it built landmarks like the London Eye and Tate Modern,
before the energy of the 2012 Olympics.

In the years since, there have been dark times,
not least the terrorist attacks of July 2005 and ongoing issues
of social equality that reignited in the summer riots of 2011.
Despite these setbacks, there is a real sense that London is
recognising its strengths, and for the second time in its history,
has over 8 million reasons to feel optimistic.

Hello!

Welcome to London, or as its residents might say:

¡Bienvenido a Londres!
Landana sbāgatama!
Witamy w Londynie!
Mirë se vini në Londër!
Välkommen till London!
Laṇṭan varavēṟkiṟōm!
Kalós ílthate sto Londíno!
Londra'ya hoşgeldiniz!
Rondon e yōkoso!
Kaabo si London!

To view the capital's linguistic diversity in greater detail, see pp. 104–105.

SOURCE: 2011 CENSUS, ONS

kem cho · kem cho · kem cho · kem cho · kem cho · salut · kem cho · kem cho · kem cho · kem cho · cześć · kem cho · kem cho · kem cho · kem cho · kem cho · kem cho · kem cho · kem cho · vanakkam · kem cho · kem cho · kem cho · kem cho · kem cho · kem cho · kem cho · kem cho · kem cho · vanakkam · kem cho · kem cho · kem cho · vanakkam · vanakkam · kem cho · kem cho · cześć · kem cho · cześć · vanakkam · kem cho · kem cho · haye · sat sri akal · cześć · kem cho · ni hao · cześć · cześć · cześć · cześć · kem cho · haye · cześć · cześć · cześć · kem cho · sat sri akal · cześć · ni hao · sat sri akal · cześć · kem cho · ol · sat sri akal · sat sri akal · cześć · cześć · haye · sat sri akal · sat sri akal · cześć · cześć · cześć · sat sri akal · sat sri akal · sat sri akal · cześć · cześć · cześć · sat sri akal · sat sri akal · cześć · konnichiwa · sat sri akal · cześć · cześć · cześć · cześć · sat sri akal · sat sri akal · cześć · cześć · cześć · sat sri akal · sat sri akal · cześć · cześć · cześć · sat sri akal · sat sri akal · sat sri akal · cześć · cześć · sat sri akal · sat sri akal · cześć · cześć · cześć · sat sri akal · sat sri akal · cześć · cześć · hola · sat sri akal · sat sri akal · sat sri akal · cześć · cześć · sat sri akal · sat sri akal · cześć · cześć · hola · sat sri akal · sat sri akal · cześć · cześć · guten tag · sat sri akal · cześć · cześć · guten tag

haye dorood kem cho merhaba merhaba merhaba assalam-o-alekum cześć
salut kem cho kem cho cześć cześć merhaba merhaba merhaba cześć assalam-o-alekum merhaba
cześć dorood merhaba merhaba cześć cześć assalam-o-alekum assalam-o-alekum
cześć cześć shalom bonjour merhaba cześć merhaba merhaba cześć assalam-o-alekum assalam-o-alekum
kem cho cześć ciao hola hola cześć sholem aleykhem assalam-o-alekum
kem cho cześć cześć bonjour merhaba hola merhaba sholem aleykhem assalam-o-alekum cześć
cześć marhaban bonjour merhaba merhaba merhaba sholem aleykhem cześć cześć cześć
cześć dorood bonjour salaam hola merhaba merhaba kem cho cześć kem cho assalam-o-alekum
olá marhaban bonjour bonjour bonjour hola salaam merhaba merhaba merhaba cześć salaam
cześć cześć bonjour bonjour salaam geia sou merhaba merhaba merhaba merhaba salaam salaam
olá marhaban bonjour bonjour salaam salaam merhaba merhaba merhaba merhaba salaam kem cho
marhaban marhaban konnichiwa bonjour bonjour merhaba merhaba merhaba salaam salaam salaam kem cho
olá olá marhaban marhaban bonjour salaam salaam bonjour merhaba salaam salaam salaam kem cho
marhaban marhaban marhaban salaam salaam merhaba salaam salaam salaam salaam
marhaban marhaban marhaban marhaban salaam bonjour hola merhaba salaam salaam salaam salaam salaam
haye marhaban marhaban marhaban marhaban salaam salaam salaam salaam salaam salaam
marhaban marhaban hola bonjour marhaban ni hao bonjour salaam salaam salaam salaam salaam labas
marhaban hola bonjour bonjour marhaban bonjour bonjour salaam salaam salaam salaam labas
cześć cześć bonjour bonjour bonjour ni hao hola bonjour salaam ni hao salaam salaam
bonjour bonjour ciao ni hao hola bonjour hola salaam salaam
bonjour bonjour bonjour marhaban olá salaam hola hola salaam namaste
bonjour bonjour bonjour marhaban bonjour olá hola hola hola bonjour salaam salaam
bonjour marhaban bonjour bonjour olá hola hola hola ni hao ni hao
bonjour bonjour bonjour marhaban hola hola hola bonjour olá namaste
hej marhaban bonjour ciao hola olá hola hola hola bonjour namaste
bonjour marhaban bonjour olá olá olá hola hola bonjour namaste
cześć bonjour bonjour ciao bonjour hola olá olá hola hola cześć cześć bonjour
cześć bonjour hola haye bonjour olá olá olá hola bonjour bonjour merhaba
cześć hola assalam-o-alekum bonjour olá olá hola bonjour hola vanakkam cześć bonjour

River Thames

INTRODUCTION

This book could not have been made ten years ago. Computers weren't powerful enough. Data weren't as detailed or freely available. Technologies like Twitter and smartphones did not exist. And, well, Oliver and I did not know each other.

His world of design and my world of mapping first united in 2010 when he was working at *National Geographic*. I was studying for a Ph.D. that focused on the geographic patterns of millions of surnames in Europe and beyond. Oliver contacted me for help producing a map of the most popular surnames in the US. When the resulting graphic was short-listed for the 'Information is Beautiful' awards in 2012, Oliver flew to London for the event and stopped by my office at University College London's Centre for Advanced Spatial Analysis to say hello. On that day, the collaboration for this book was born: What if we took all the data we could find – on happiness, house prices, art, violent crime, life expectancy – and created a new visual guide to London for the twenty-first century?

All cities can be captured in maps that depict street layouts or the locations of landmarks, but London is a city *defined* by them. Its maps are special. They were drawn by pioneers such as Charles Booth, who revealed the full extent of the city's poverty, and Phyllis Pearsall, who mapped 23,000 streets in her hugely popular *A to Z* guide. But the map Londoners are probably most familiar with belongs to Henry Beck. His 1931 Tube map eschewed geographic accuracy for a more diagrammatic display of the city's Underground lines. Instantly recognizable the world over, it remains one of the most beloved representations of the capital. Its multicoloured lines have become part of the urban fabric alongside London's red buses and black cabs. Remove maps from London and you damage the city itself.

The UK tops this list of the world's most 'open' countries. To determine these rankings, the World Wide Web Foundation and Open Data Institute analyzed the data-sharing capacity of each country's government, businesses and citizens; the extent of published datasets; and their political, economic and social impact.

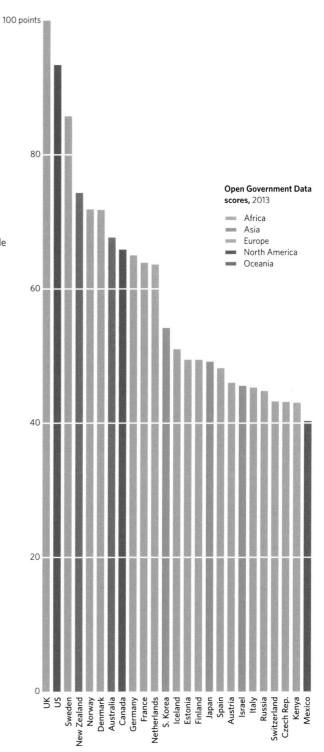

Open Government Data scores, 2013

- Africa
- Asia
- Europe
- North America
- Oceania

The Information Capital

Referring to London as *the* information capital is a bold claim. We think it is justified for two reasons: London not only generates a huge volume of data, it *shares* an unprecedented amount with its citizens to use as they wish. These data are known as 'open data' and in recent years, the UK government has made their dissemination a national priority. Open data initiatives exist in other cities, not least in Europe and North America, but what gives London an information edge is the belief that data can not only record social change but also instigate it.

Back in 2009, a now legendary (in the data world at least) exchange over

SOURCE: WEB FOUNDATION, OPEN DATA BAROMETER 2013 GLOBAL REPORT

dinner is said to have taken place between Gordon Brown, then Prime Minister, and Sir Tim Berners-Lee, inventor of the World Wide Web. Brown asked Berners-Lee how the government should make best use of the Web. Berners-Lee said that it should put all of its data online. Much to his surprise, the Prime Minister replied, 'Yeah, let's do it.' Since then, London and, in turn, many UK cities have created online data stores, sites where anyone can go to download data on everything from unemployment to cycle ridership. Berners-Lee went on to co-found the Open Data Institute, a London-based non-profit facilitating positive change through the dissemination of data around the globe.

Thanks to the subsequent development of an 'Open Government License', the public can now 'copy, publish, distribute, transmit and adapt' the work of many Great British institutions, not least the Office for National Statistics (ONS) and Ordnance Survey, Great Britain's national mapping agency. The ONS administers the census programme for England and Wales, releasing data at the finest geographic scales possible. Using data from the 2011 Census, for example, we were able to plot the ethnicities of Londoners within 25,000 small areas, each home to around 250 people (see pp. 100–101).

In 1995, Ordnance Survey finished digitizing 230,000 paper maps, making Great Britain the first country to store all its most detailed maps electronically. Their 1,200 employees continue to survey and record the changing landscape, a task that requires up to 4,000 data edits per day. Not all of Ordnance Survey's data are open, but those that are cover a huge range of uses and applications, including every building outline in this book.

The final reason for London's openness – alongside all the data from social media and transport networks – are the Freedom of Information Requests (FOIs) overseen by the Information Commissioner's Office (see right). FOIs came into

Freedom of Information requests on *whatdotheyknow.com*
January 2008 – June 2014

○ ○ ○ ○
1 500 1,000 1,500 2,000

▓ Successful
▓ Unsuccessful or outstanding

Since its launch in 2008, *whatdotheyknow.com* has fielded more than 210,000 FOI requests for information from 15,000 authorities. Here we show the forty London authorities that receive the most requests.

Transport for London
Metropolitan Police Service
Westminster City Council
Camden Council
Lambeth Council
Newham Council
Tower Hamlets Council
Hackney Council
Islington Council
Croydon Council
Barnet Council
Haringey Council
Brent Council
Southwark Council
Greenwich Council
Wandsworth Council
Harrow Council
Hammersmith and Fulham Council
Hillingdon Council
Bexley Council
Royal Borough of Kensington and Chelsea
Lewisham Council
Barking and Dagenham Council
Ealing Council
Bromley Council
Waltham Forest Council
Enfield Council
Richmond upon Thames Council
Hounslow Council
Redbridge Council
Merton Council
Havering Council
Sutton Council
Kingston upon Thames Council
City of London Corporation
Greater London Authority
City of London Police
Common Council of the City of London
West London Mental Health NHS Trust
University College London

Jan–Mar Apr–Jun

2,025 requests
985 fulfilled

2009   2010   2011   2012   2013   2014

Jul-Sept Oct-Dec Jan-Mar Apr-Jun Jul-Sept Oct-Dec Jan-Mar Apr-Jun Jul-Sept Oct-Dec Jan-Mar Apr-Jun Jul-Sept Oct-Dec Jan-Mar Apr-Jun Jul-Sept Oct-Dec Jan-Mar Apr-Jun Jul-Sept Oct-Dec Jan-Mar Apr-Jun

force with the Freedom of Information Act 2000. Since then, they have been used by all sections of society, from members of the public wondering how their taxes are spent to journalists fishing for major scandals. Each request has to be made in writing, a process made much simpler by *whatdotheyknow.com*. Launched in 2008, the site now handles 20% of all requests to the UK central government. As we show on page 23, use is increasing.

Once a request has been made, the relevant agency is legally obligated to respond within twenty working days. If there's an unexplained delay – as there was with our request to Transport for London for data on, appropriately, Tube delays – then an internal review can be requested. If the review doesn't speed things along, the case goes before the 'Information Commissioner', who has powers to solicit a response. Not all requests can be fulfilled though. Organizations may deny requests that reveal sensitive information or prove unreasonably time-consuming for staff to complete. But without FOIs, we wouldn't have been able to produce our graphics on Tube delays, police helicopters and the London Fire Brigade, among others.

In addition to these 'official' sources of data, Londoners volunteer much more through the likes of fitness apps, social media and a user-generated mapping platform called OpenStreetMap (OSM), which is like Wikipedia for roads and buildings. Its founder and fellow Londoner, Steve Coast, placed the first OSM data point in Regent's Park in 2004 (see p. 27). Since then, OSM's thousands of active users have created a comprehensive map of London and much of the planet. The result is a living map that constantly evolves in sync with the world it seeks to represent as users add new information about anything that interests them, from new road junctions through to their favourite coffee shop, even the trees in their neighbourhood (see pp. 48–49).

OpenStreetMap echoes many of London's great mapping endeavours: it began

AREA ENLARGED

Index of Multiple Deprivation by decile, 2010

MOST DEPRIVED

LEAST DEPRIVED

Today, London uses an Index of Multiple Deprivation to identify poorer areas in the capital. A century earlier, Charles Booth's 'poverty map' coloured streets 'according to the general condition of the inhabitants'. More colours meant the street contained 'a fair proportion of each of the classes represented by the respective colours'.

Booth's poverty map, 1889

LEAST DEPRIVED

Upper-middle and Upper classes. Wealthy.

Middle-class. Well-to-do.

Fairly comfortable. Good ordinary earnings.

Mixed. Some comfortable, others poor.

Poor. 18s. to 21s. a week for a moderate family.

Very poor, casual. Chronic want.

Lowest class. Vicious, semi-criminal.

MOST DEPRIVED

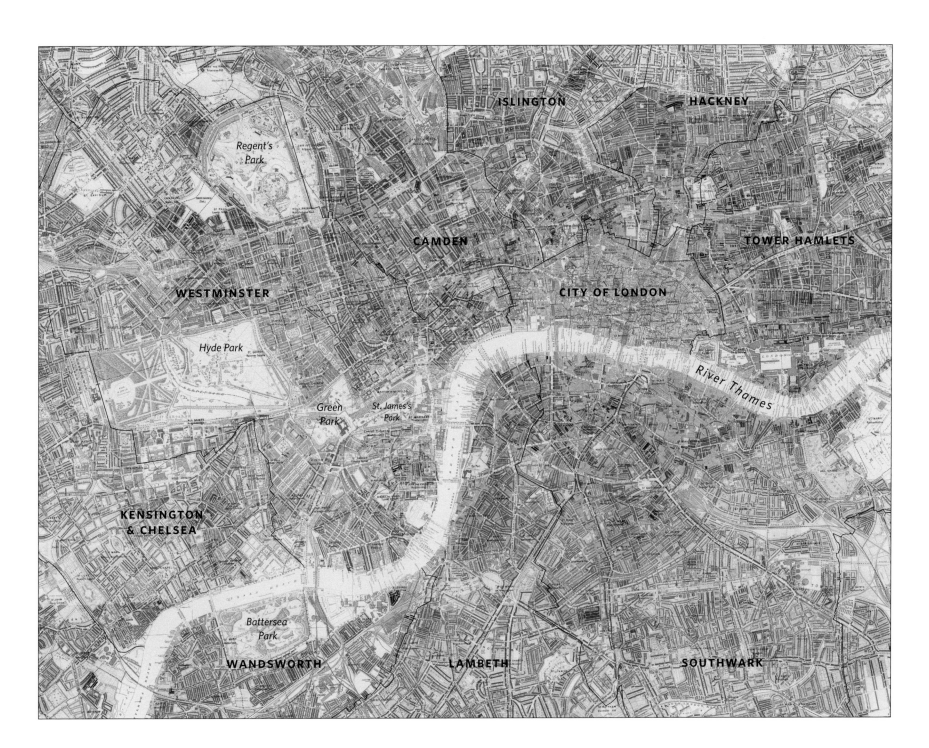

ISLINGTON

HACKNEY

Regent's Park

CAMDEN

TOWER HAMLETS

WESTMINSTER

CITY OF LONDON

Hyde Park

River Thames

Green Park

St. James's Park

KENSINGTON & CHELSEA

Battersea Park

WANDSWORTH

LAMBETH

SOUTHWARK

The founder of OpenStreetMap placed its first point in Regent's Park.

with boots on the ground. Charles Booth looked to those who walked London most – policemen and school board inspectors – to provide the data on his maps of poverty (see p. 25); and Phyllis Pearsall is said to have walked all 23,000 streets in her *A-Z*. With the exception of Oliver's hikes to all thirteen of London's Protected Vistas (see pp. 68-73), we spent more time pounding the keyboard than the pavements. For this book, we were largely recipients rather than producers of data. This created a paradox. While more of London's data are available than ever before, the bar was set a little higher for us to make full use of them. To sift through spreadsheets millions of rows long, computer programming and data mining are now essential skills for cartographers. That said, the need to tell a story

alongside the graphics remains of utmost importance. For us, it was not enough to write scripts to generate patterns from data points. We tried to go the next step to help you understand what the patterns mean. If open data are to have the societal impact Berners-Lee envisions, this step is crucial.

Mapping the paths of London's shipping lanes (pp. 120–123) or jogging routes (pp. 154-7) required some of most technologically advanced plots ever produced for the capital, but technology is no substitute for pen and paper. Before we wrote a line of computer code or bent a single Bezier curve, we sketched up and talked through our approaches with the mantra 'just because we can, doesn't mean we

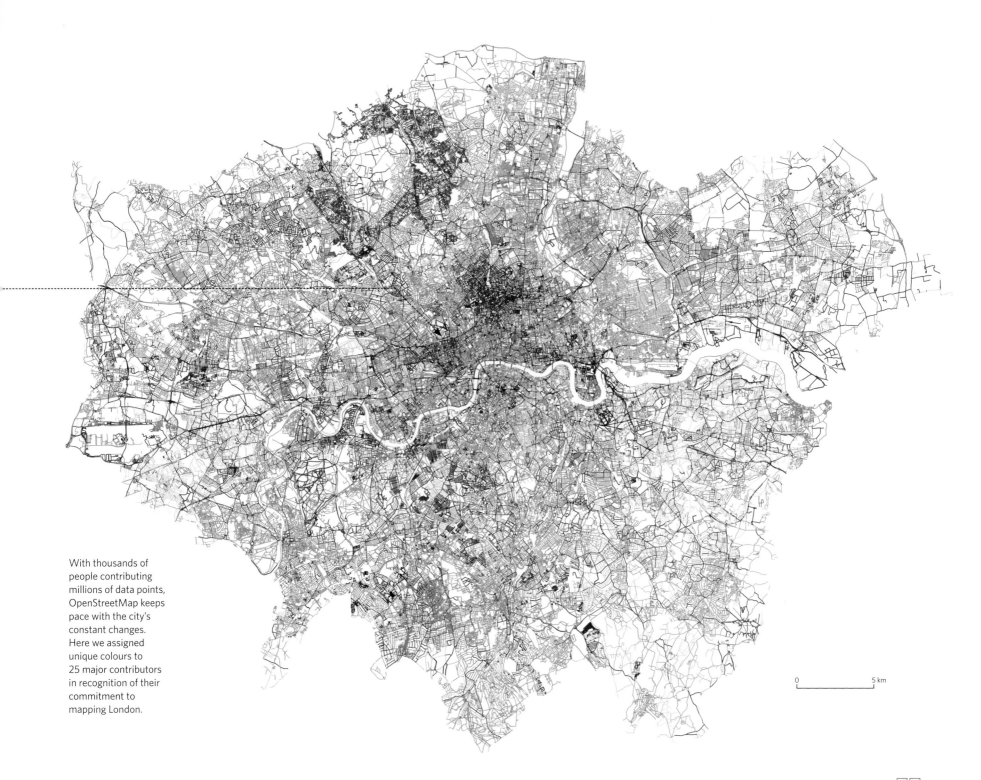

With thousands of
people contributing
millions of data points,
OpenStreetMap keeps
pace with the city's
constant changes.
Here we assigned
unique colours to
25 major contributors
in recognition of their
commitment to
mapping London.

0   5 km

SOURCES: OLIVER O'BRIEN, UNIVERSITY COLLEGE LONDON; OSM

Adam Towle, an architect on the Greater London Authority Regeneration team (with red laces) shows us Queen Elizabeth Olympic Park on a 160m^2 map in City Hall.

should'. To this end, you will find several 'low-tech' graphics in here, too. Perhaps the lowest-tech element of this book, however, is the book itself. Why print a book of maps when you can make them interactive online? Digital maps gain interactivity at the expense of tangibility and, we think, engagement. We wanted to create an object you could sit with, pore over, share with your friends (in person) and then discuss. Plus, print is still a pretty incredible technology. You can simply see more at a glance on a printed page than you can pinching, tapping and scrolling on a smartphone screen.

To see the power of print up close, head over to City Hall, the headquarters of the Greater London Authority. One of the largest printed maps of London has been pasted to its ground floor. Commissioned in time for the 2012 Olympics and produced from aerial photos taken by Ordnance Survey, it shows the expanse of the capital in amazing detail (above). Instead of panning and zooming, you can walk over to your house or stand on your favourite landmark. It is also a statement of power; if visitors to City Hall were to question the extent of the Mayor's influence, then they can be sent to the ground floor and shown it!

Our efforts continue a conversation that reached a crescendo during the 1850s, when London was already on its way to becoming the information capital. If you had walked its streets then, you may have passed Florence Nightingale using her coxcomb plots to lobby for better sanitary conditions in military hospitals or

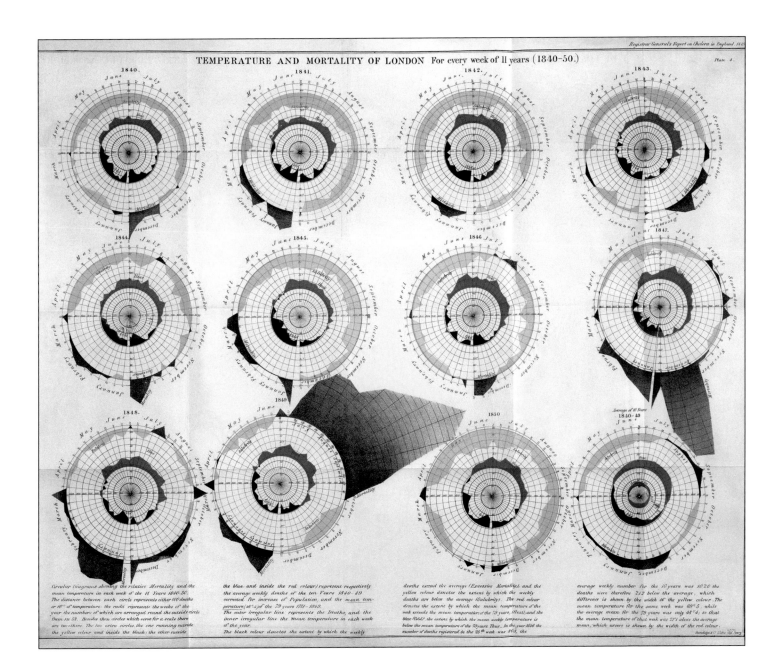

In these diagrams, epidemiologist and statistician William Farr plotted cycles of temperature and deaths from cholera from 1840-50. He noted that the circular form and colours make 'the diagram represent the facts in a striking manner to the eye'. At the time, Farr believed cholera was spread by miasma, or 'bad air', from the Thames. Although this hypothesis was incorrect, Farr left an important legacy. He set up the first national system for collecting statistics; he advocated a data-driven approach to public health; and he pioneered the graphic representation of such information.

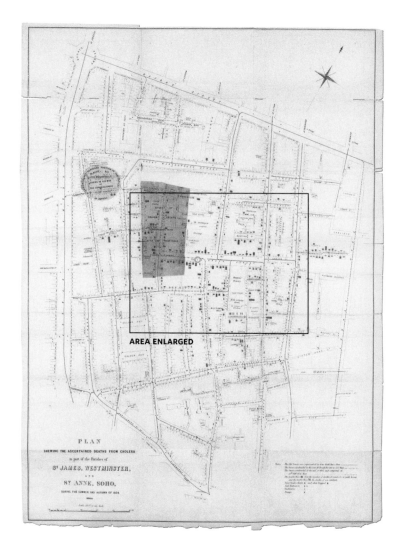

bumped into epidemiologist William Farr collecting data on the city's latest cholera mortalities. Farr was a great pioneer in the use and communication of statistics. He created polar area charts to support the theory that cholera was spread through 'bad air' blown in from the Thames (see p. 29). In spite of his data-driven approach to public health and creation of a national system for collecting statistics, his contribution is often obscured by another data visualization: John Snow's 'Ghost Map' (see right), which proved that the source of cholera was not the air as Farr posited, but London's water supply. Though much less colourful than Farr's graphic, it was – and remains – ruthlessly efficient at communicating the information. Snow grasped what Farr had missed: geography matters.

John Snow's *'Plan Showing the Ascertained Deaths from Cholera in Part of the Parishes of St. James, Westminster and St. Anne, Soho, during the summer and autumn of 1854'*, with the infamous Broad Street water pump at its centre, was the showpiece of a report that argued that cholera is a waterborne disease. This map inspired a revolution not only for medicine but also for the future of information design.

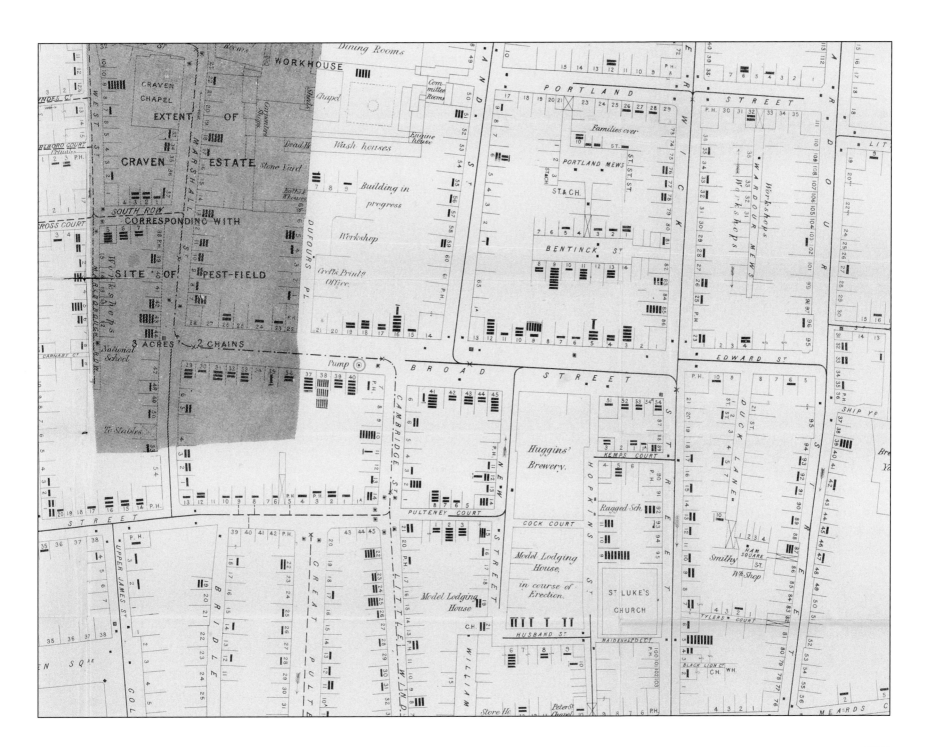

Using This Book

*'Most A-Zs are half dead, because documenting a city as alive
as London will always be an impossible task.'*

—Craig Taylor, author of *Londoners*

This book is not an atlas. We have not sought to present a single, definitive
picture of the city. Instead, we have selected 100 or so facets based on two simple
questions: do we find it interesting and do we think you will too? In a city as diverse
as London, there are many more graphics we would have loved to produce, but we
had to draw the line somewhere or the book would have never been published.

As you read, please remember that each graphic marks a point in time.
We have used the most current data available as of Spring 2014. Therefore, we
encourage you to view the graphics as snapshots rather than graven definitions.
Ultimately, we hope they will inspire conversations – and new graphics – about
the city's future.

We collated our graphics around five themes: *where we are, who we are, where
we go, how we're doing* and *what we like*. The structure is non-linear and the graphics
stand alone, so jump around the book as you might on a day out in the city.

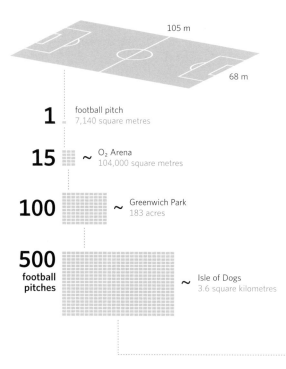

1 football pitch
7,140 square metres

15 ~ O₂ Arena
104,000 square metres

100 ~ Greenwich Park
183 acres

500
football
pitches
~ Isle of Dogs
3.6 square kilometres

London is surprisingly
vast. What appears to
be a short stroll between
Waterloo and Tower
Bridges will take the
better part of an hour to
walk. In terms of area,
the Isle of Dogs, the
peninsula enclosed by the
Thames' iconic meander,
could hold 500 football
pitches on it. The entire
boundary of Greater
London? 220,000 pitches.

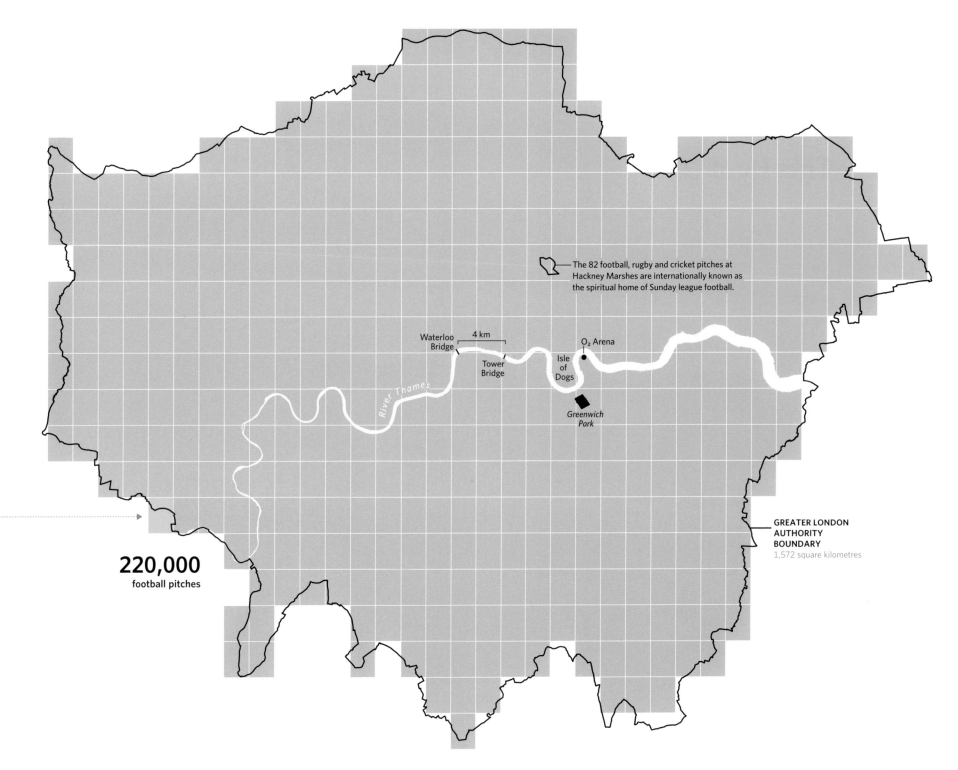

The 82 football, rugby and cricket pitches at Hackney Marshes are internationally known as the spiritual home of Sunday league football.

Waterloo Bridge

4 km

Tower Bridge

O₂ Arena

Isle of Dogs

River Thames

Greenwich Park

220,000
football pitches

GREATER LONDON AUTHORITY BOUNDARY
1,572 square kilometres

1 WHERE WE ARE

THE CHILTERNS

To St Albans

M25

To Lincoln and York

To Stevenage

Crews Hill

LEA VALLEY

M25

Amersham
150m

Highest point
on London
Underground
network

Bushey Heath
153m

Brockley
Hill
136m

Stanmore Hill
152m

Pole
Hill
91m

Harold
Hill

Mill Hill

ERMINE STREET

M25

WATLING STREET

Harrow-on-the-Hill

Highgate Hill
136m

Stamford Hill

River Lea

River Roding

Dollis Hill
78m

Parliament Hill
98m

Hackney Brook

M25

Horsenden Hill
85m

Primrose Hill
64m

Fleet

Westbourne

Old Ford

Castlebar Hill
51m

Hanger Hill
65m

Tyburn

BT Tower
191m

Walbrook Stream

Heron Tower
230m

LONDON
WALL

One Canada
Square
235m

Beckton
Alps
17m

Notting
Hill

OXFORD STREET

Stamford Brook

Campden
Hill

Westminster
−32m

Lowest point
on London
Underground
network

The Shard
310m

Victoria
Tower
99m

WATLING STREET

River Thames

Counter's Creek

Falcon Brook

Telegraph Hill
48m

Shooters Hill
133m

QUEEN
ELIZABETH II
BRIDGE

Herne Hill
43m

Hilly Fields
51m

The Thames shown
here is narrower and
deeper than it was
when the Romans
settled in the area.

River Crane

Richmond Hill
45m at Richmond Gate

Effra River

One Tree Hill
91m

King
Henry's
Mound
56m

Spankers
Hill
42m

Coombe
Hill
54m

Beaulieu
Heights
116m

Crystal
Palace
Transmitter
219m tall

Ravensbourne

GREATER LONDON
AUTHORITY
BOUNDARY

M25

River Wandle

Londinium, 300 A.D.

+ Elevated point

— Roman road

London, 2014

● Town

■ Building

— Motorway

0   5 km

Croydon

Addington
Hills
146m

River Darent

Breakneck Hill
144m

PILGRIMS' WAY

THE NORTH

3 6

M25

Winey
Hill
72m

Caterham-on-the-Hill

Westerham Heights
245m

Highest point
in London

Sevenoaks

To Chichester

Box Hill
224m

To Brighton

To Lewes

To Silchester

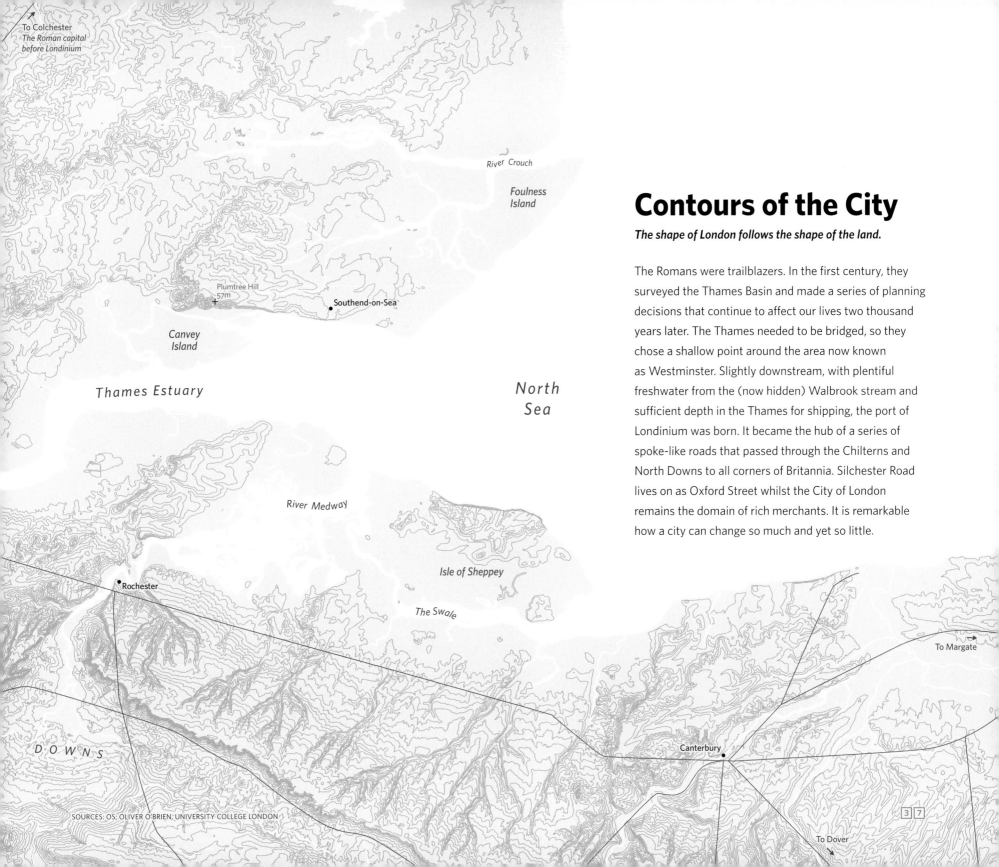

To Colchester
The Roman capital before Londinium

River Crouch

Foulness Island

Plumtree Hill
+57m

Southend-on-Sea

Canvey Island

Thames Estuary

North Sea

River Medway

Isle of Sheppey

The Swale

Rochester

DOWNS

To Margate

Canterbury

To Dover

Contours of the City

The shape of London follows the shape of the land.

The Romans were trailblazers. In the first century, they surveyed the Thames Basin and made a series of planning decisions that continue to affect our lives two thousand years later. The Thames needed to be bridged, so they chose a shallow point around the area now known as Westminster. Slightly downstream, with plentiful freshwater from the (now hidden) Walbrook stream and sufficient depth in the Thames for shipping, the port of Londinium was born. It became the hub of a series of spoke-like roads that passed through the Chilterns and North Downs to all corners of Britannia. Silchester Road lives on as Oxford Street whilst the City of London remains the domain of rich merchants. It is remarkable how a city can change so much and yet so little.

SOURCES: OS; OLIVER O'BRIEN, UNIVERSITY COLLEGE LONDON

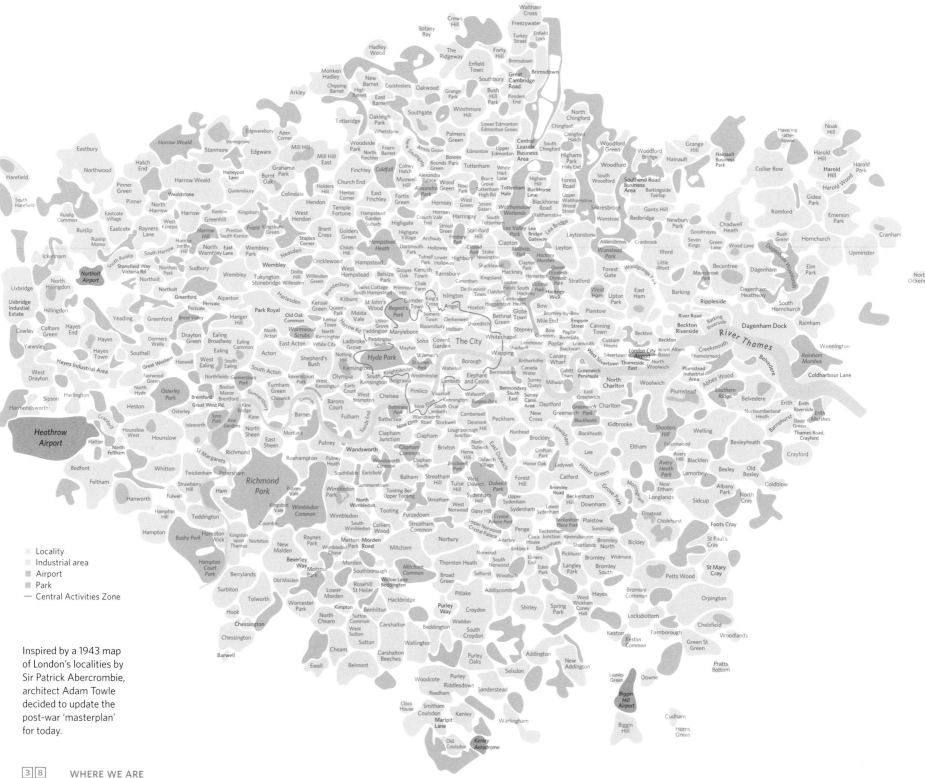

Legend:
- Locality
- Industrial area
- Airport
- Park
— Central Activities Zone

Inspired by a 1943 map of London's localities by Sir Patrick Abercrombie, architect Adam Towle decided to update the post-war 'masterplan' for today.

What we talk about when we talk about London

Ask any two Londoners to define their city for you and you will probably get three different answers. So let's be clear. In this book, we're talking about a region known as the Greater London Authority (GLA). Created by the London Government Act 1963, it spans thirty-two boroughs plus the City of London, a 2,000-year-old city-within-a-city.

The GLA boundary forms the distinctive shape you see on the cover and throughout this book. To many people, however, its rounded arms and deckled edges – and the boroughs within them – are entirely arbitrary. They are social, economic and political creations designed to help govern the city. As individuals, we experience London with much more personal geographies.

In the map to the left, Adam Towle, an architect at City Hall, shows that we can further divide the GLA into a 'City of Villages' – 770 amoeba-shaped places where we live, work and play. They bear testament to the palimpsestic nature of London with names originating from a range of sources, including historic villages

(Ealing), an anchorage for Danish invaders (Greenwich) and a 17th-century public house (Angel). As London has filled the spaces between its villages, their boundaries have blurred. Does spending the day in Camden Town now entail staying south of its lock or is there a more fluid boundary between Camden and Chalk Farm or Kentish Town? London's villages combine to form a city greater than the sum of its parts, but what keeps them unique?

We fumble for an answer because the extent and complexity of London varies in the minds of those who experience it. While no set of graphics could truly capture this diversity, many of the villages' unique characteristics appear throughout this book. As Peter Ackroyd writes in his biography of the city, 'London goes beyond any boundary or convention . . . It is illimitable.' In this sense, we use the GLA boundary not to limit our definition but as a lens through which we can focus the millions, if not billions, of data points available. At times we will zoom in on specific parts of the capital or zoom out for a wider perspective. Often we will return to London's distinctive administrative outline if only because it's a helpful tool for making comparisons and getting oriented.

In this chapter, we provide a few ways to visualize how London has evolved from an outpost of the Roman Empire to a truly global city. Its most rapid growth has been within the past 200 years, and it is still experiencing unprecedented demand from those who want to call it home. In the face of change, London remains sensitive to its past, preserving centuries-old views of St Paul's Cathedral and the street layout in the city centre. Perhaps the greatest continuity, though, is offered by the river flowing west to east past London's landmarks and acting as an enduring reminder of the city's link to nature. If you ever feel lost, look for 'Father Thames'.

SOURCES: ADAM TOWLE, GREATER LONDON AUTHORITY; ONS

Hub for the World

The sun never sets on an LHR luggage tag.

In terms of international air traffic, London is the centre of the world. Each year, a million flights set a course for 51°N, 0°W. Four of the six busiest airports in the UK share these coordinates. Each one services at least five continents, exchanging Londoners and British culture to places as far flung as Lagos, Brunei and Mauritius. But with nearly 70 million passengers and more than 200 destinations, Heathrow rules.

Built in the 1930s as a private airport, the 'Great West Aerodrome' expanded to its current size over the next fifty years. It has long since hit capacity. By travelling further afield, Gatwick, Stansted, Luton and London City Airport are bearing some of the load. Still, to meet projected demand, they're going to need reinforcements. Heathrow hopes to build a third runway. Mayor of London Boris Johnson envisions a new, larger airport in the middle of the Thames Estuary (see p. 119). If they build it, this airborne empire will have a new king.

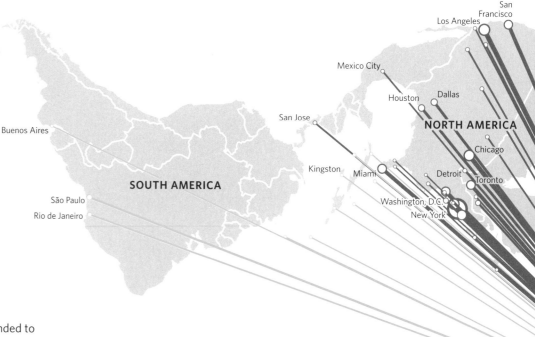

69.5
million passengers
per year

LHR

Heathrow is not only the busiest airport in the UK, it handles more international traffic than any other airport globally. To do so requires a staff of more than 76,000 working around the clock. To see how flights descend into Heathrow, turn to page 116.

Number of passengers in thousands, August 2012

- More than 200
- 150–199
- 100–149
- 50–99
- Less than 50

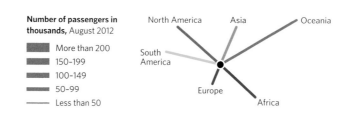

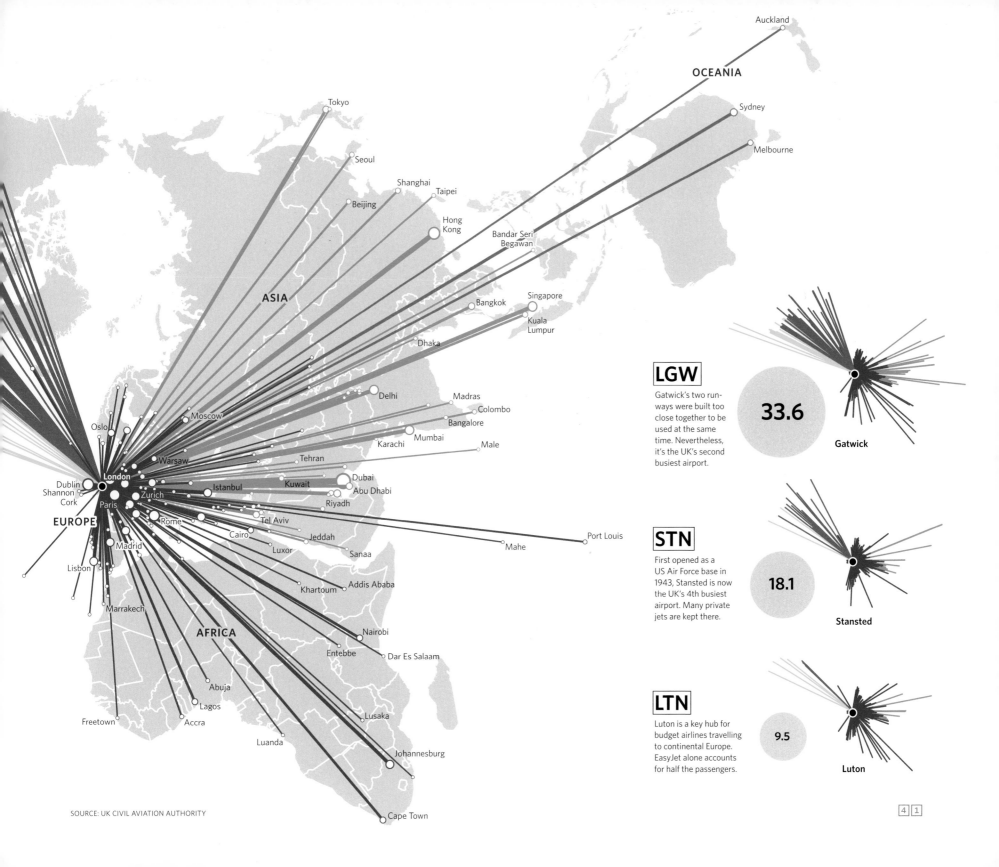

OCEANIA

Auckland
Sydney
Melbourne

ASIA

Tokyo
Seoul
Shanghai
Taipei
Beijing
Hong Kong
Bandar Seri Begawan
Bangkok
Singapore
Kuala Lumpur
Dhaka
Delhi
Madras
Colombo
Bangalore
Mumbai
Karachi
Male
Moscow
Tehran
Dubai
Kuwait
Abu Dhabi
Istanbul
Riyadh
Tel Aviv
Warsaw
Oslo
Zurich
London
Dublin
Shannon
Cork
Paris
Rome
EUROPE
Madrid
Lisbon
Marrakech
Cairo
Jeddah
Luxor
Sanaa
Khartoum
Addis Ababa
Port Louis
Mahe

AFRICA

Nairobi
Entebbe
Dar Es Salaam
Abuja
Lagos
Accra
Freetown
Luanda
Lusaka
Johannesburg
Cape Town

LGW

Gatwick's two runways were built too close together to be used at the same time. Nevertheless, it's the UK's second busiest airport.

33.6

Gatwick

STN

First opened as a US Air Force base in 1943, Stansted is now the UK's 4th busiest airport. Many private jets are kept there.

18.1

Stansted

LTN

Luton is a key hub for budget airlines travelling to continental Europe. EasyJet alone accounts for half the passengers.

9.5

Luton

SOURCE: UK CIVIL AVIATION AUTHORITY

From Home to Work

High-paying jobs draw workers from far, far away

In this depiction of daily commutes, London shines like the Sun in the constellation of Southern England. Like all stars, it has an immense gravitational pull. Whether by car, train or tube, thousands travel into the capital each day from all directions. Including this 'commuter belt' beyond the Greater London Authority boundary makes the capital one of the largest metropolitan areas in the EU with a population of more than 13 million.

Half of London's workforce make their journey by public transport, compared with only 9% in the rest of the country. Still, most need thirty minutes or more to get to work. Elsewhere in the UK, only 20% have commutes that long. Why do so many live so far away?

For one, London salaries go further in satellite towns like Banbury. As of May 2014, a five-bedroom converted barn there was going for the price of two-bedroom flats along the Underground's Central Line (see pp. 66–7). It's only a matter of time before faster trains propel commuters into even wider orbits.

Commuting times in minutes by region of workplace
October–December 2009

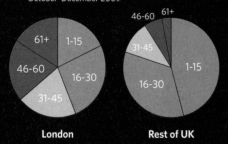

London

Rest of UK

WALES

Carmarthen

Haverfordwest

Llanelli

SWANSEA

NEWPORT

CARDIFF

Barry

Bristol Channel

Barnstaple

Taunton

E

EXETER

PLYMOUTH

St. Austell

TRURO

Penzance

Falmouth

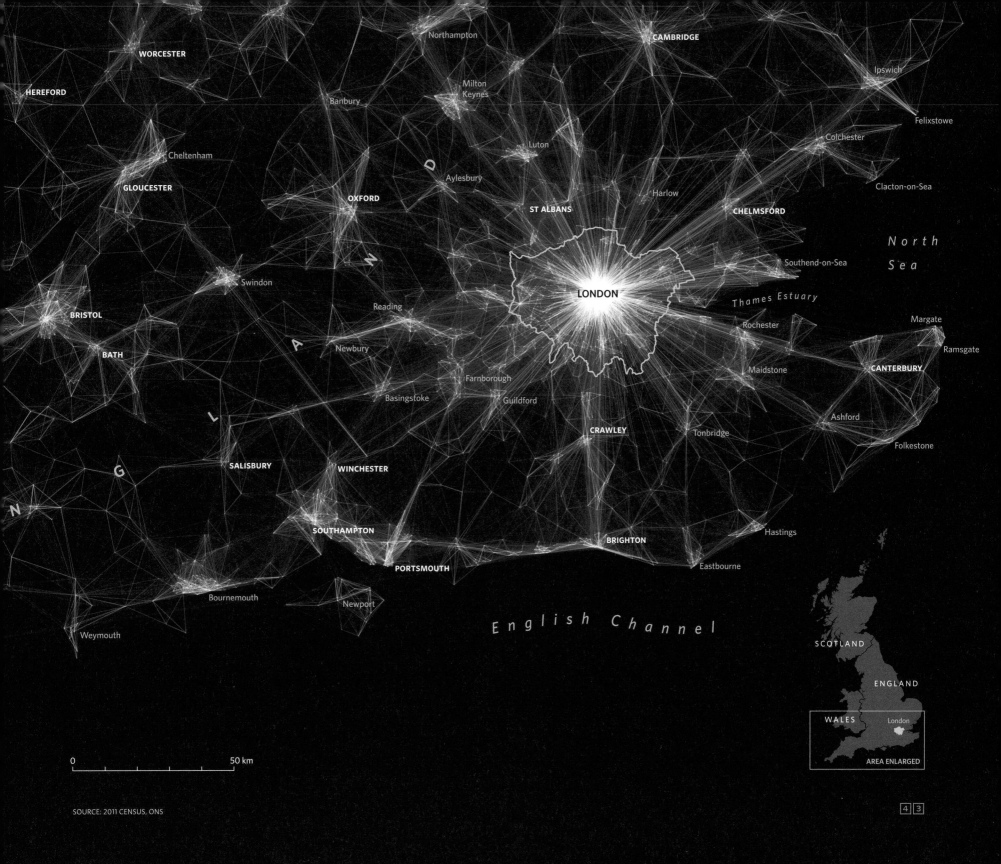

WORCESTER

HEREFORD

Northampton

CAMBRIDGE

Ipswich

Milton
Keynes

Banbury

Felixstowe

Cheltenham

Luton

Colchester

GLOUCESTER

D

Aylesbury

Harlow

Clacton-on-Sea

OXFORD

ST ALBANS

CHELMSFORD

N

Swindon

North
Sea

Southend-on-Sea

LONDON

BRISTOL

Reading

A

Thames Estuary

Rochester

Margate

Newbury

BATH

Farnborough

Maidstone

Ramsgate

L

Basingstoke

Guildford

CANTERBURY

Ashford

SALISBURY

WINCHESTER

CRAWLEY

Tonbridge

Folkestone

G

N

SOUTHAMPTON

Hastings

BRIGHTON

PORTSMOUTH

Eastbourne

Bournemouth

Newport

English Channel

Weymouth

SCOTLAND

ENGLAND

WALES

London

AREA ENLARGED

SOURCE: 2011 CENSUS, ONS

Day and Night

Commuters send the City's population off the charts.

London is a city of extremes. Just look at the difference in its daytime and nighttime populations. Using data from the 2011 Census, the top map shows the number of people by place of employment; the bottom one, by place of residence. In one corner of the City of London, the population spikes from 222 residents by night to in excess of 127,000 by day. How do they all fit? The only way is up in the rising number of skyscrapers (see pp. 68–73). By late evening, the pattern reverses. Workers head home and the City becomes eerily quiet.

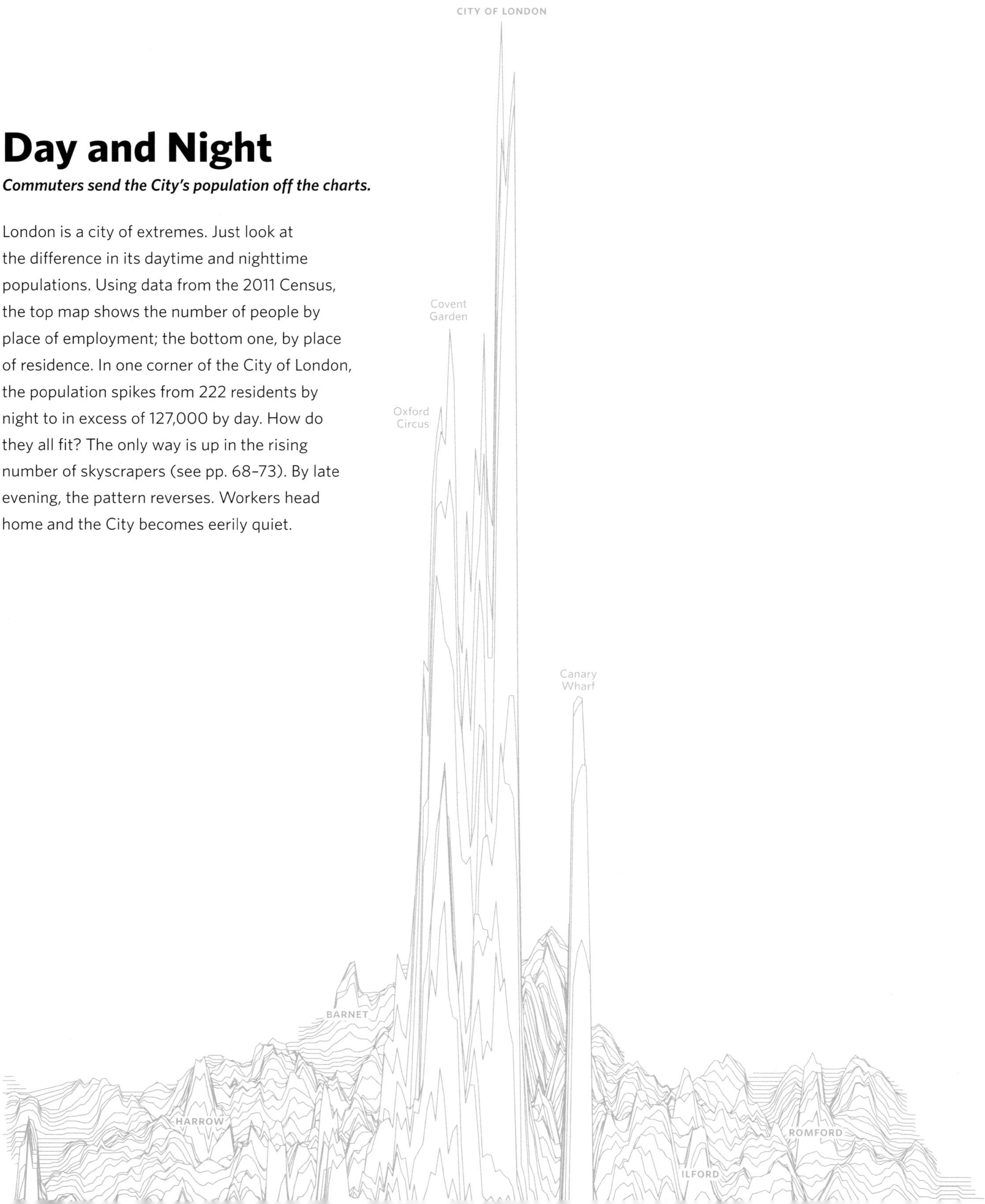

CITY OF LONDON

Canary Wharf

Covent Garden

Oxford Circus

BARNET

HARROW

ROMFORD

ILFORD

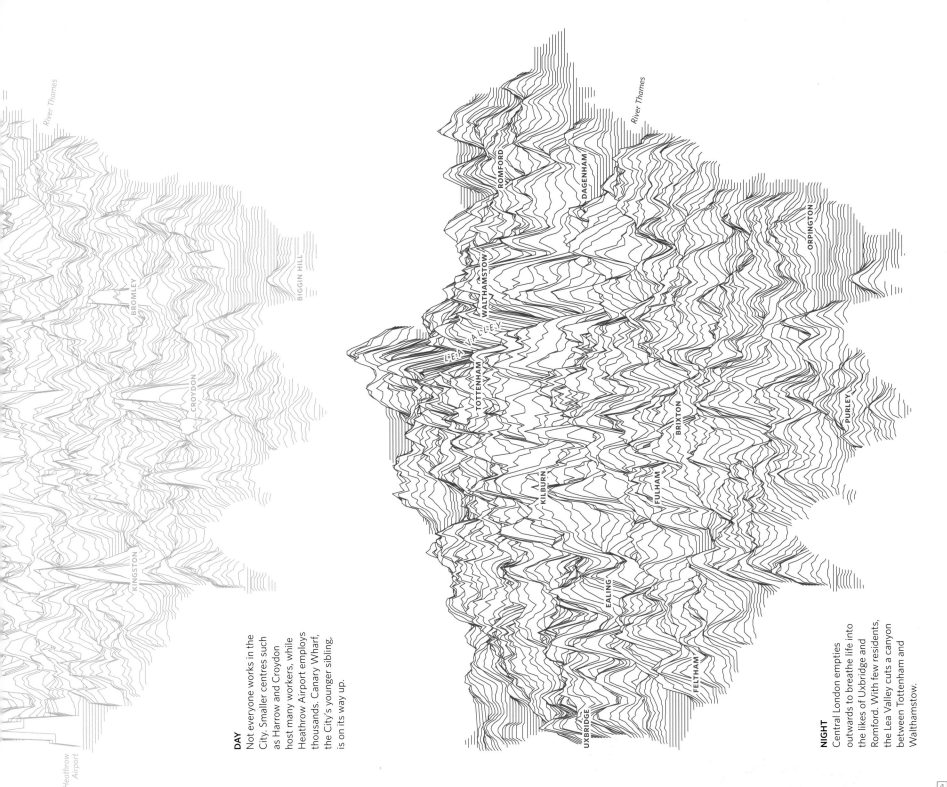

River Thames

Heathrow Airport

KINGSTON

CROYDON

BROMLEY

BIGGIN HILL

DAY
Not everyone works in the
City. Smaller centres such
as Harrow and Croydon
host many workers, while
Heathrow Airport employs
thousands. Canary Wharf,
the City's younger sibling,
is on its way up.

ROMFORD

DAGENHAM

ORPINGTON

WALTHAMSTOW

River Thames

LEA VALLEY

TOTTENHAM

BRIXTON

PURLEY

KILBURN

FULHAM

EALING

UXBRIDGE

FELTHAM

NIGHT
Central London empties
outwards to breathe life into
the likes of Uxbridge and
Romford. With few residents,
the Lea Valley cuts a canyon
between Tottenham and
Walthamstow.

WHERE WE ARE

M25/M11 Junction
This junction shows the warmth of roads compared to surrounding countryside.

BARNET

ENFIELD

King George's Reservoir

ROMFORD

Alexandra Palace

HARROW

Hampstead Heath

Wembley Stadium

Victoria Park

Westfield Stratford City

UXBRIDGE

Regent's Park

Euston Station

St Paul's Cathedral

Paddington Station

Tower of London

EALING

London Eye

Canary Wharf

London City Airport

Hyde Park

SOUTHBANK

Waterloo Station

The Shard

River Thames

Temperatures at Heathrow hit an all time high in August 2003 when they soared to 37.9°C (100.2°F).

Buckingham Palace

Battersea Park

Greenwich Park

Heathrow Airport

Richmond Park

Parks are the coolest places to be on a midsummer night.

CRYSTAL PALACE

Bushy Park

BROMLEY

0   5 km

CROYDON

Hot Spots

If the climate continues to warm, Londoners will feel the heat.

London's abundance of concrete, glass and tarmac can turn an often cool city into a summer hot-house. It's what climatologists call the Urban Heat Island Effect. These dry, exposed surfaces accumulate energy from the sun during the day and then release it slowly overnight, which can lead to extreme temperature differences between the city and surrounding countryside. In this infrared image, all that released heat appears as bubbling lava, oozing eastwards through the River Thames. Purple blotches indicate cooler areas like parks and woodland. Elevated temperatures, particularly in the summer, can amplify energy usage (as people crank up their air conditioners) and instances of health problems like heatstroke. On the hottest days of the year it's actually good to get off the island.

Tilbury
Docks

Northfleet
Power
Station

With their cooling towers and limited green space, the Tilbury Docks and Northfleet Power Station glow bright on this map.

Surface temperatures
12 July 2006

- 27°C
- 25
- 23
- 21
- 19
- 17
- 15
- 13°C

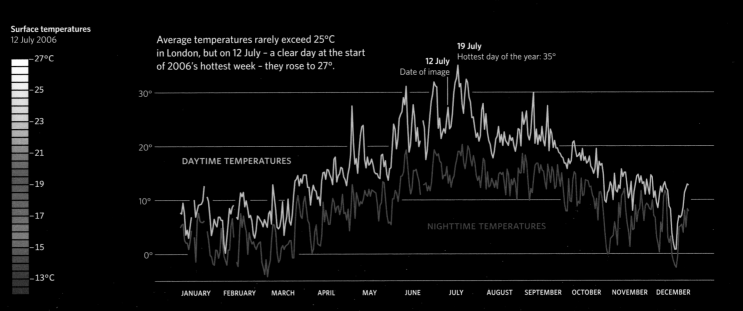

Average temperatures rarely exceed 25°C in London, but on 12 July – a clear day at the start of 2006's hottest week – they rose to 27°.

19 July
Hottest day of the year: 35°

12 July
Date of image

30°

DAYTIME TEMPERATURES

20°

10°

NIGHTTIME TEMPERATURES

0°

JANUARY   FEBRUARY   MARCH   APRIL   MAY   JUNE   JULY   AUGUST   SEPTEMBER   OCTOBER   NOVEMBER   DECEMBER

SOURCES: THE LUCID PROJECT; WEATHERSPARK.COM (CHART DATA)

Seeking Shade

Natural remedies exist for the Urban Heat Island Effect. They're called trees.

Strip away the roads, rails and buildings from the Borough of Southwark and what've you got? A forest. With nearly 600 'street trees' per square kilometre, it's one of London's leafiest boroughs. Only Islington has a higher density. As a whole, the city maintains more than half a million of these all-natural air filters. After planting 10,000 during his first term, the Mayor of London hopes to increase tree cover by five per cent by 2025. Emphasizing 'Right Place Right Tree', the London Trees and Woodland Framework recommends he plant broadleaf trees like maples, planes and limes, which shade people and property in summer whilst admitting sunlight in winter. Come spring, apple, pear and cherry trees offer another benefit: flowers.

Genuses with more than 1,000 public trees in the London Borough of Southwark, 2010

Maple	Plane	Cherry	Lime	Ash	Birch	Rowan	Hawthorn	Pear	Oak	Apple	Locust	Horse-chestnut	Poplar	Cypress	Willow	Other
7,271	6,409	4,223	3,904	3,077	2,340	2,254	1,776	1,575	1,467	1,305	1,159	1,153	1,142	1,102	1,027	

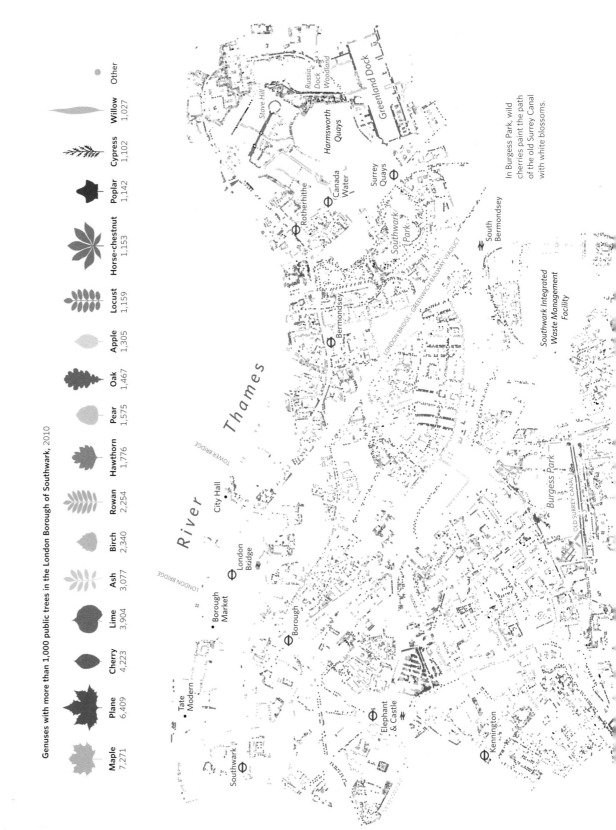

In Burgess Park, wild cherries paint the path of the old Surrey Canal with white blossoms.

A hybrid of the American sycamore and oriental plane became prevalent during the Industrial Revolution because its thick leaves and flaky bark could survive London's soot-clogged air. Today, Southwark's most popular species is known as the London Plane.

There's more than one tree on One Tree Hill, but only 'The Oak of Honor' has a fence around it. A sign at its base says it was planted in 1905 'to perpetuate the original oak tree that stood near this spot, and under which Queen Elizabeth I is said to have rested on Mayday 1602'.

Privately-owned trees are not included in the open data.

Honor Oak Park

One Tree Hill

The Oak of Honor

Nunhead

Queens Road Peckham

Nunhead Cemetery

Peckham Rye Common

Peckham Rye Park

Camberwell Old Cemetery

Peckham Rye

Dulwich and Sydenham Hill Golf Club

Sydenham Hill

East Dulwich

Dulwich Park

Dulwich College

North Dulwich

Bel Air Park

West Dulwich

Denmark Hill

Street trees
per square kilometre
2011

600–710
500–599
400–499
300–399
200–299
130–199

Barking and Dagenham **133**

Southwark **542**

Islington **704**

SOURCES: TOM CHANCE, OSM, SOUTHWARK COUNCIL; OLIVER O'BRIEN, UNIVERSITY COLLEGE LONDON; GLA

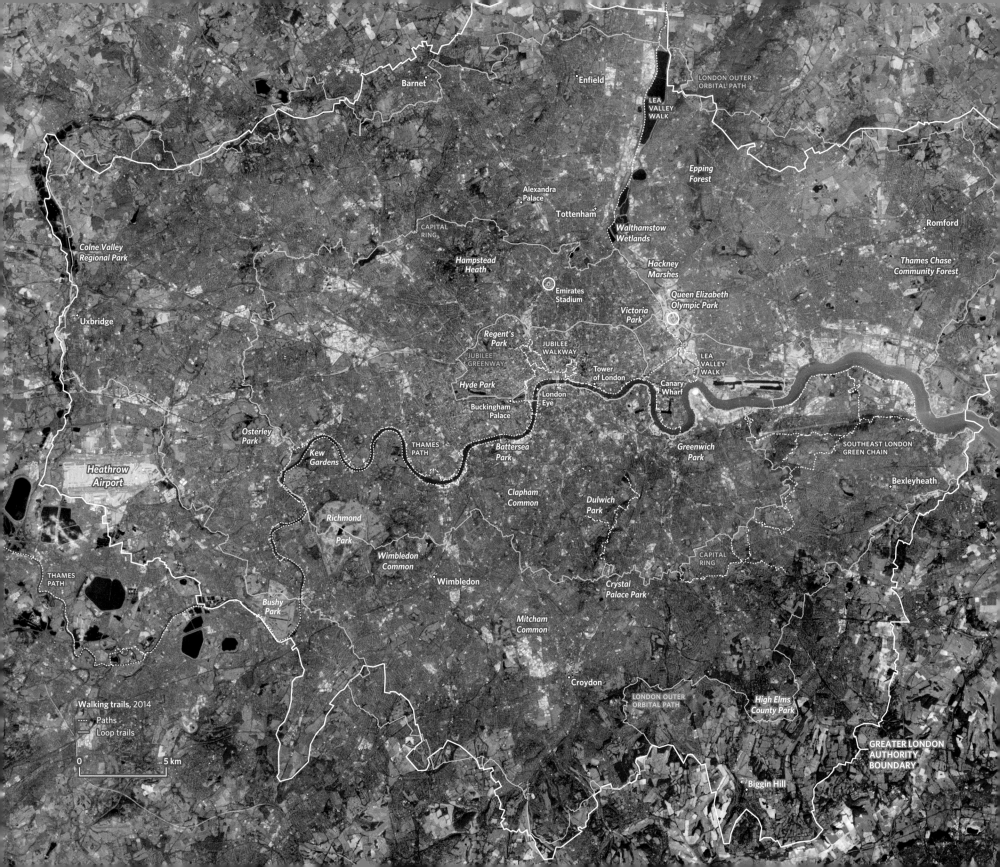

Barnet

Enfield

LONDON OUTER
ORBITAL PATH

LEA
VALLEY
WALK

*Epping
Forest*

Romford

Alexandra
Palace

Tottenham

*Walthamstow
Wetlands*

*Thames Chase
Community Forest*

*Colne Valley
Regional Park*

CAPITAL
RING

*Hampstead
Heath*

*Hackney
Marshes*

Emirates
Stadium

*Queen Elizabeth
Olympic Park*

Uxbridge

*Victoria
Park*

*Regent's
Park*

JUBILEE
WALKWAY

JUBILEE
GREENWAY

LEA
VALLEY
WALK

Tower of London

Hyde Park

Canary
Wharf

London
Eye

SOUTHEAST LONDON
GREEN CHAIN

*Osterley
Park*

Buckingham
Palace

THAMES
PATH

*Battersea
Park*

*Greenwich
Park*

**Heathrow
Airport**

*Kew
Gardens*

Bexleyheath

*Clapham
Common*

*Dulwich
Park*

*Richmond
Park*

*Wimbledon
Common*

CAPITAL
RING

THAMES
PATH

Wimbledon

*Crystal
Palace Park*

*Bushy
Park*

*Mitcham
Common*

*High Elms
County Park*

Croydon

LONDON OUTER
ORBITAL PATH

Walking trails, 2014

· · · · · Paths
———— Loop trails

0   5 km

Biggin Hill

**GREATER LONDON
AUTHORITY
BOUNDARY**

The Urban Wild

Greater London is greener than you may think.

Londoners refer to the ring of woodland and open space encircling the Greater London Authority as a 'green belt', a restraining device set up in 1935 to keep the city's buildings from sprawling into the countryside. Within this green binding, however, London offers a patchwork of parks, reserves, World Heritage Sites and waterways that could be stitched together into something more: a national park.

Measuring 1,600 square-kilometres, Greater London National Park (as proposed by geographer Daniel Raven-Ellison) would be the seventh-largest in the UK and make London the world's first National Park city. 'There is this idea that a National Park has to be remote and rural,' says Raven-Ellison, 'but cities are incredibly important habitats too. An amazing 13,000 species of wildlife can be found in London's open spaces.' It's all possible because much of the infrastructure is already in place, including a 245-kilometre orbital footpath that, like a line of thread, weaves its way along the outer fringe.

In this false-colour satellite image taken on 14 March 2014, near-infrared, red and green wavelengths combine to make dense green vegetation appear red. Look closely and you'll see crimson specks within Olympic Stadium and Emirates Stadium, home of Arsenal Football Club (circled). Richmond Park still appears a bit brown because the trees were not yet in leaf.

SOURCE: NASA; MATHIAS DISNEY, UNIVERSITY COLLEGE LONDON;
WALKING LONDON (PATHS). SHAREGEO OPEN (GREEN BELT)

GREEN BELT

M25

M25

GREATER LONDON BOUNDARY

M25

0   10 km

Holding Back the Tide

It took a few floods to re-learn how to live with Father Thames.

If the Thames Barrier didn't exist, here's what could happen to the city. First, heavy rainfall swells the river. Then high tide or a storm surge pushes the excess water back upriver and over embankments. The threat isn't new. For most of London's history, these banks were uninhabited marshes that absorbed rising waters. But the Victorians seem to have buried that knowledge when they built up the Embankments in the early 19th century. On 7 January 1928, nature reasserted its power. The river burst its banks, drowning fourteen and leaving thousands homeless. Lesson learned? Not quite. It wasn't until a North Sea surge inundated Silvertown in 1953 that plans for a new defence system began.

CAMDEN TOWN

ISLINGTON

Regent's Park

SOMERS TOWN

BLOOMSBURY

CITY

St Paul's Cathedral

MAYFAIR

King's College

VICTORIA EMBANKMENT

Trafalgar Square

Tate Modern

Green Park

St James's Park

London Eye

Waterloo Station

SOUTHWARK

The Shard

KENSINGTON

BROMPTON

Buckingham Palace

Houses of Parliament

Westminster Abbey

VICTORIA EMBANKMENT

Lambeth Palace

Elephant and Castle

WESTMINSTER

EARLS COURT

WEST KENSINGTON

CHELSEA

Tate Britain

ALBERT EMBANKMENT

KENNINGTON

WALWORTH

WEST BROMPTON

CHELSEA EMBANKMENT

River Thames

Stamford Bridge Chelsea F. C.

WALHAM GREEN

Battersea Park

New Covent Garden Market

PARSONS GREEN

Victoria Park

BOW

BETHNAL
GREEN

STEPNEY

POPLAR

ExCeL London

ROTHERHITHE
TUNNEL

Tower
of London

BLACKWALL
TUNNEL

London City
Airport

City Hall

Canary Wharf

O₂
Arena

SILVERTOWN

BERMONDSEY

ROTHERHITHE

Thames
Barrier

Southwark
Park

ISLE OF DOGS

Burgess
Park

DEPTFORD

River Thames

GREENWICH

Greenwich
Park

HOW THE THAMES BARRIER WORKS
On days with high flooding risk, ten steel gates, each 15 metres tall, rotate up from the riverbed at low tide to prevent water from flowing upriver. They remain in this closed position until the tide recedes.

Of all the barrier closures since its completion in 1982, one-fifth occurred in early 2014 when 250 millimetres of rain fell in two months.

0 ————————— 1 km

■ Areas with a 1% risk of flooding per year

SOURCES: ENVIRONMENT AGENCY; OS (BUILDINGS)

If These Streets Could Talk

You can't turn a corner in London without stepping through time.

In 1685, London's street plan didn't look too different from the one laid down by the Romans. Then when the population rose to six million in the following centuries, new streets were built as the city spread and became a stomping ground for many famous names.

Many Londoners have heard of John Snow, the physician-turned-epidemiologist who ended a cholera outbreak in 1854 by tracing its source to a water pump on what is now Soho's Broadwick Street. They might also know of William Caslon, who designed the serif fonts on this map at his type foundry on Chiswell Street. But what about Lord Rowton, Robert Adam or The Old Nichol slum? Ken 'Old Map Man' Titmuss can tell you all about them and he'll show you around town for a tenner. 'My walks celebrate everyday London and the many unsung local heroes,' he says. Here he shares six of his lesser-known stories from the streets.

Historic Streets
— 1685
— 1880

1 STRATFORD PLACE

This cul-de-sac takes you back to 1236 A.D. when the City of London constructed a conduit here to divert water from the River Tyburn to the City. Around 1553, a hunting lodge was built to house the Lord Mayor and his Aldermen when they rode out to inspect the conduits. Once the New River aqueduct opened in 1613, the Tyburn conduit fell out of use and the lodge was demolished. Edward Stratford leased the site in 1771 and built a grand house that is now home to the Oriental Club.

2 CHANDOS STREET

Follow this street until it curves and you will find a house with two Doric columns. Completed in 1771, it's the first London house designed by the Scottish neoclassical architect Robert Adam and his brother John. The house owes its unusual shade of grey to the Adam brothers' choice of stone from the Craigleith Quarry near Edinburgh, where they grew up. When it was first put up for sale there were no buyers. Now its current tenant, the Royal Society of Medicine, hires out the house for weddings.

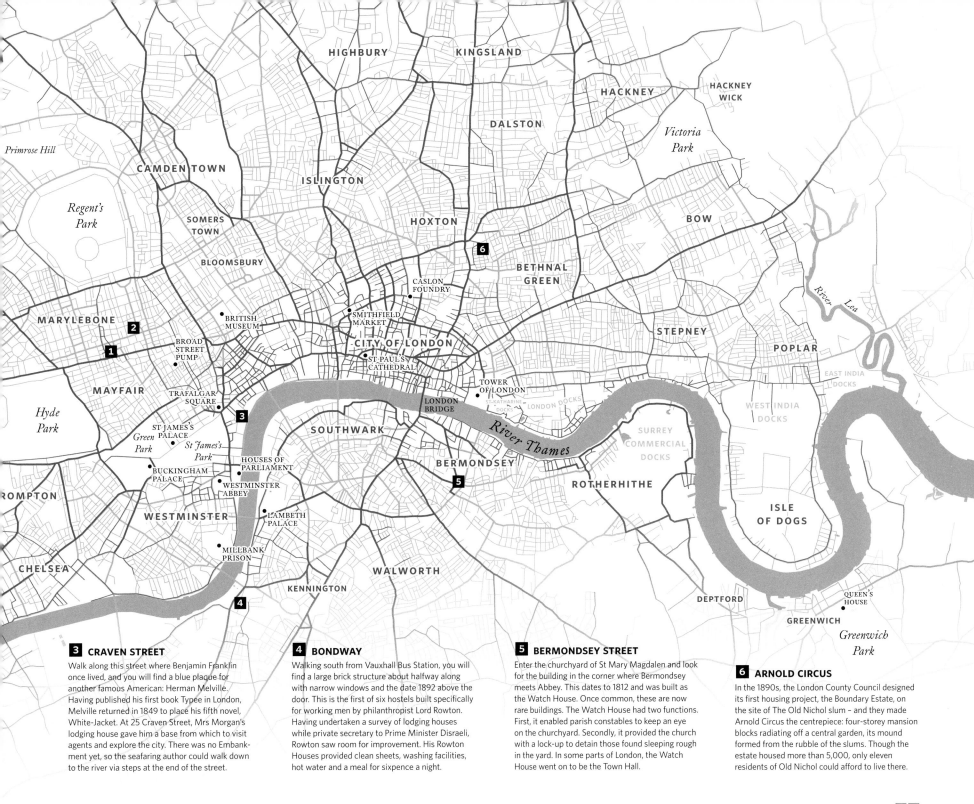

HIGHBURY
KINGSLAND
HACKNEY
HACKNEY WICK
DALSTON
Victoria Park
HACKNEY
CAMDEN TOWN
Primrose Hill
ISLINGTON
SOMERS TOWN
HOXTON
BOW
Regent's Park
BLOOMSBURY
6
BETHNAL GREEN
CASLON FOUNDRY
STEPNEY
MARYLEBONE
2
• BRITISH MUSEUM
• SMITHFIELD MARKET
POPLAR
1
BROAD STREET PUMP
CITY OF LONDON
EAST INDIA DOCKS
MAYFAIR
ST PAUL'S CATHEDRAL
• TOWER OF LONDON
WEST INDIA DOCKS
TRAFALGAR SQUARE •
Hyde Park
3
LONDON BRIDGE
ST KATHARINE DOCKS
LONDON DOCKS
SURREY COMMERCIAL DOCKS
St James's PALACE •
Green Park
• St James's Park
SOUTHWARK
River Thames
BERMONDSEY
ISLE OF DOGS
HOUSES OF PARLIAMENT
ROTHERHITHE
• BUCKINGHAM PALACE
5
• WESTMINSTER ABBEY
ROMPTON
WESTMINSTER
• LAMBETH PALACE
• MILLBANK PRISON
CHELSEA
WALWORTH
4
KENNINGTON
DEPTFORD
QUEEN'S HOUSE
GREENWICH
Greenwich Park
River Lea

3 CRAVEN STREET

Walk along this street where Benjamin Franklin once lived, and you will find a blue plaque for another famous American: Herman Melville. Having published his first book Typee in London, Melville returned in 1849 to place his fifth novel, White-Jacket. At 25 Craven Street, Mrs Morgan's lodging house gave him a base from which to visit agents and explore the city. There was no Embankment yet, so the seafaring author could walk down to the river via steps at the end of the street.

4 BONDWAY

Walking south from Vauxhall Bus Station, you will find a large brick structure about halfway along with narrow windows and the date 1892 above the door. This is the first of six hostels built specifically for working men by philanthropist Lord Rowton. Having undertaken a survey of lodging houses while private secretary to Prime Minister Disraeli, Rowton saw room for improvement. His Rowton Houses provided clean sheets, washing facilities, hot water and a meal for sixpence a night.

5 BERMONDSEY STREET

Enter the churchyard of St Mary Magdalen and look for the building in the corner where Bermondsey meets Abbey. This dates to 1812 and was built as the Watch House. Once common, these are now rare buildings. The Watch House had two functions. First, it enabled parish constables to keep an eye on the churchyard. Secondly, it provided the church with a lock-up to detain those found sleeping rough in the yard. In some parts of London, the Watch House went on to be the Town Hall.

6 ARNOLD CIRCUS

In the 1890s, the London County Council designed its first housing project, the Boundary Estate, on the site of The Old Nichol slum – and they made Arnold Circus the centrepiece: four-storey mansion blocks radiating off a central garden, its mound formed from the rubble of the slums. Though the estate housed more than 5,000, only eleven residents of Old Nichol could afford to live there.

SOURCE: KEN TITMUSS; KIRIL STANILOV, UNIVERSITY OF CAMBRIDGE (STREET DATA)

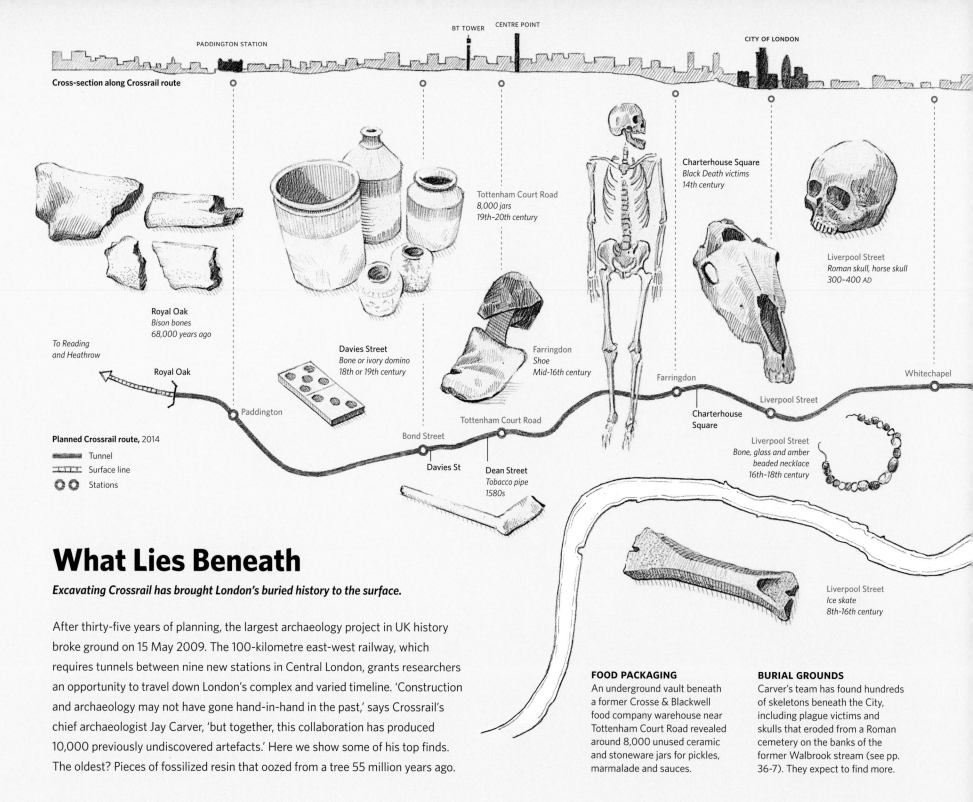

Cross-section along Crossrail route

PADDINGTON STATION

BT TOWER

CENTRE POINT

CITY OF LONDON

Tottenham Court Road
8,000 jars
19th–20th century

Charterhouse Square
Black Death victims
14th century

Liverpool Street
Roman skull, horse skull
300–400 AD

Royal Oak
Bison bones
68,000 years ago

To Reading
and Heathrow

Davies Street
Bone or ivory domino
18th or 19th century

Farringdon
Shoe
Mid-16th century

Royal Oak

Whitechapel

Paddington

Farringdon

Liverpool Street

Planned Crossrail route, 2014

Tunnel

Surface line

Stations

Bond Street

Tottenham Court Road

Charterhouse
Square

Liverpool Street
Bone, glass and amber
beaded necklace
16th–18th century

Davies St

Dean Street
Tobacco pipe
1580s

Liverpool Street
Ice skate
8th–16th century

What Lies Beneath

Excavating Crossrail has brought London's buried history to the surface.

After thirty-five years of planning, the largest archaeology project in UK history broke ground on 15 May 2009. The 100-kilometre east-west railway, which requires tunnels between nine new stations in Central London, grants researchers an opportunity to travel down London's complex and varied timeline. 'Construction and archaeology may not have gone hand-in-hand in the past,' says Crossrail's chief archaeologist Jay Carver, 'but together, this collaboration has produced 10,000 previously undiscovered artefacts.' Here we show some of his top finds. The oldest? Pieces of fossilized resin that oozed from a tree 55 million years ago.

FOOD PACKAGING
An underground vault beneath a former Crosse & Blackwell food company warehouse near Tottenham Court Road revealed around 8,000 unused ceramic and stoneware jars for pickles, marmalade and sauces.

BURIAL GROUNDS
Carver's team has found hundreds of skeletons beneath the City, including plague victims and skulls that eroded from a Roman cemetery on the banks of the former Walbrook stream (see pp. 36-7). They expect to find more.

SOURCE: CROSSRAIL. SKETCHES: OLIVER UBERTI

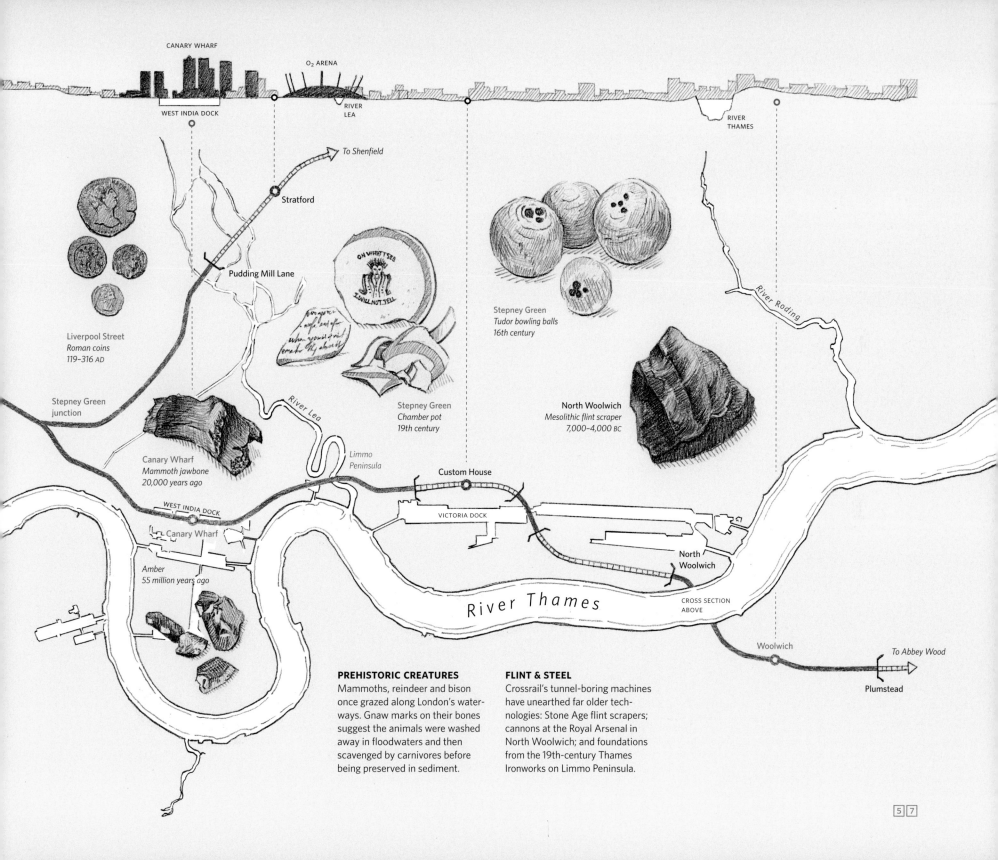

CANARY WHARF

O₂ ARENA

WEST INDIA DOCK

RIVER
LEA

RIVER
THAMES

To Shenfield

Stratford

Pudding Mill Lane

Liverpool Street
Roman coins
119–316 AD

Stepney Green
junction

River Lea

Canary Wharf
Mammoth jawbone
20,000 years ago

WEST INDIA DOCK

Canary Wharf

Amber
55 million years ago

Limmo
Peninsula

Stepney Green
Chamber pot
19th century

OH WHAT SEB
I WILL NOT JELL

Stepney Green
Tudor bowling balls
16th century

North Woolwich
Mesolithic flint scraper
7,000–4,000 BC

Custom House

VICTORIA DOCK

River Roding

North
Woolwich

CROSS SECTION
ABOVE

River Thames

Woolwich

To Abbey Wood

Plumstead

PREHISTORIC CREATURES
Mammoths, reindeer and bison
once grazed along London's waterways. Gnaw marks on their bones
suggest the animals were washed
away in floodwaters and then
scavenged by carnivores before
being preserved in sediment.

FLINT & STEEL
Crossrail's tunnel-boring machines
have unearthed far older technologies: Stone Age flint scrapers;
cannons at the Royal Arsenal in
North Woolwich; and foundations
from the 19th-century Thames
Ironworks on Limmo Peninsula.

Ghosts of London Past

Two thousand years of history haunts the city's streets and structures.

Phasmophobic? Then you may want to make like Pac-Man and avoid the ghosts on this map. Otherwise follow the dots to tour centuries of paranormal activity, including victims of Jack the Ripper, the Tower executioner and the Blitz. For extra points, grab some cherries at Borough Market or a cocktail at Apples & Pears.

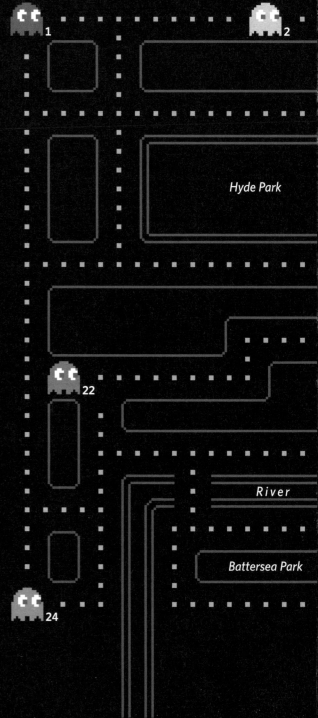

Hyde Park

River

Battersea Park

1 Phantom Bus
A spectral No. 7 troubles the corner of Cambridge Gardens and St Marks Road.

2 Crocker's Folly
Former landlord Frank Crocker still stalks the abandoned pub, having supposedly taken his own life at the inn's failure.

3 The Volunteer
This pub is haunted by the Duke of Norfolk, whose mansion once stood on this site.

4 Langham Hotel
At least seven different ghosts have been attributed to room 333.

5 British Museum
The museum's tube station closed in 1933. It's now cursed by the wailing of Egyptian voices.

6 The Dolphin
Hit by a Zeppelin bomb in WWI, this pub's stopped clock can sometimes be heard ticking.

7 Farringdon
One of London's oldest stations harbours a screaming ghost, said to be murdered orphan Anne Naylor.

8 Sadler's Wells
The ghost of clown Grimaldi haunts a theatre box.

9 The Sutton Arms
A mischievous red-headed ghost has been sighted at this pub near the setting of the Sherlock Holmes tale, *The Red Headed League.*

10 Bethnal Green
Cries of those who perished in a wartime crush are still heard by Underground staff.

11 Bow Bells
The ladies' toilet at this pub flushes of its own accord.

12 50 Berkeley Square
London's most famous haunted house is said to have literally scared people to death.

13 Covent Garden
Actor William Terriss haunts the station, having been murdered nearby.

14 Peacock Theatre
Inside, you can hear the clicks and squeaks of a phantom dolphin, star of a Paul Raymond show in the 1960s.

15 Amen Court
A ghastly canine haunts this street, a shade of a former prisoner in Newgate Gaol.

16 Mitre Square
The ghost of Jack the Ripper victim Catherine Eddowes appears here, bearing her wounds.

17 Aldgate
The ghostly figure of a woman nursed a worker who'd received an electric shock. He later recovered.

18 Tower of London
More than a dozen phantoms dwell here, including Anne Boleyn, the Two Princes and a bear.

19 The Grenadier
Said to be among London's most haunted pubs, paranormal activity peaks in September.

20 Green Park
A black figure and pained voices have been witnessed near the park's 'Death Tree'.

21 The George
This 17th-century inn is haunted by a tech-hating landlady who might break your phone.

 Pubs

 Transport

Houses & theatres

Parks & streets

22 Brompton Cemetery
A phantom squirrel is often heard scrabbling around the northern end of the Colonnades.

23 Elephant and Castle
The tube station is haunted by ghostly girls.

24 Fulham Palace
The Great Hall of this ancient building echoes with the sound of persecuted Protestants.

25 Burgess Park
The sounds of ghostly children playing on boats can be heard along the old Surrey Canal.

26 Queen's House
One of the most famous ghost photos ever captured depicts a shrouded figure on the Tulip staircase.

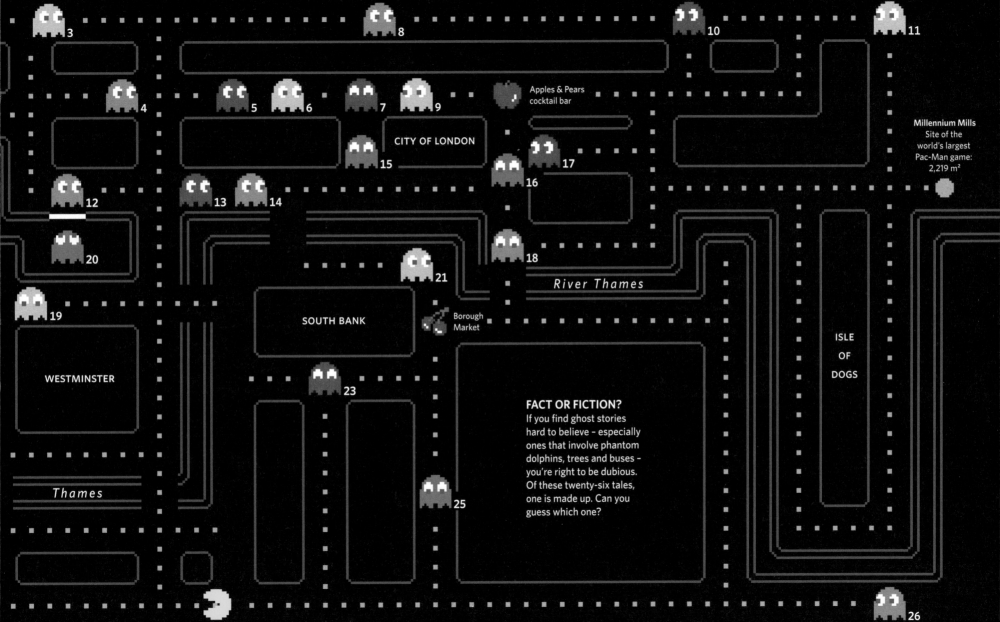

3

8

10

11

4

5 6 7 9

Apples & Pears
cocktail bar

Millennium Mills
Site of the
world's largest
Pac-Man game:
2,219 m²

CITY OF LONDON

15

17

16

12

13 14

20

18

21

19

SOUTH BANK

Borough
Market

WESTMINSTER

23

River Thames

ISLE
OF
DOGS

Thames

25

FACT OR FICTION?
If you find ghost stories
hard to believe – especially
ones that involve phantom
dolphins, trees and buses –
you're right to be dubious.
Of these twenty-six tales,
one is made up. Can you
guess which one?

26

West London: 120 Years Later

The city has changed as much as the way we map it.

Once meticulous and highly skilled draftsmen using paper and ink, cartographers now map London with complex spatial databases of contemporary building geometry to centimetre accuracy. By overlaying this modern map form over its corresponding area from the late 19th-century Ordnance Survey One-Inch series, we can see the westward expansion of the capital. Gradually, houses and streets filled in the fields between the trunk roads built to trade with the historic city centre on the north of the Thames. Development reached its peak in the first half of the 20th century as the population boomed. London's appetite for growth persists, this time to the east where city planners are converting industrial areas into housing and parkland.

AREA ENLARGED

Development since 1895

- ▮▮▮ Buildings
- ▬▬ Motorways
- ▬▬ Primary roads
- ▬▬ Major roads
- ▬▬ Railways
- ▬▬ Airport runways

0   1 km

Much of London's growth has used existing development as its template. Perhaps the greatest exception to this was the construction of Heathrow Airport. The hamlet of Heathrow with its farmsteads and market gardens was paved over to make way for one of the world's busiest airports (see pp. 40–41).

SOURCES: THE NATIONAL LIBRARY OF SCOTLAND (1892-1908 MAP); KIRIL STANILOV, UNIVERSITY OF CAMBRIDGE (1895 DATA); OS (2014 BUILDINGS)

Back from The Blitz

A new East London has risen from the rubble of 'Black Saturday'.

When Hitler's *Luftwaffe* began bombing London on 7 September 1940, they set their sights on the Docklands. The plan: disable the docks – and supply chain hubs like Beckton Gas Works and the Royal Arsenal – disable a nation. The 'lightning strike' lasted 57 days, killed 430, wounded 1,600 and left the East End ablaze. Fast-forward seven decades. The port has moved downriver (see pp. 120–121). In its stead, shops, flats, parks and skyscrapers abound. Here we contrast areas damaged during the Blitz's first twenty-four hours (yellow) with the city we know today.

1 *5:50 p.m.*
Frances Street, Woolwich
DAMAGE HM War Dept.
Military College of Science
NOW Barracks

2 *5:59 p.m.*
Milborne Street, Hackney
DAMAGE Workrooms,
offices and store of a slipper
manufacturer
NOW Medium block of flats

3 *6:01 p.m.*
Well Street, Hackney
DAMAGE Both decks of
passenger bus No. EXV 246
NOW Parade of shops

4 *6:02 p.m.*
**St. Catherine's Church,
Lewisham**
DAMAGE Fire consumes the
nave and roof
NOW Church

5 *6:10 p.m.*
Stebondale St, Cubitt Town
DAMAGE 39 six-room houses
and four shops
NOW Recreation ground

6 *6:14 p.m.*
Glengall Grove, Millwall
DAMAGE The store at Walter
Voss and Co. Manufacturing
Chemists laboratories
NOW Low rise flats

7 *6:24 p.m.*
Cable Street, Stepney
DAMAGE Confectionery and
fancy goods buildings
NOW Cable Street Studios

8 *7:25 p.m.*
Union Road, Millwall
DAMAGE Machine rooms,
workshops, offices, and store
at a beer retailer
NOW Medium block of flats

9 *8:56 p.m.*
Bessemer Road, Camberwell
DAMAGE Entrance, casualty
ward of Kings College Hospital
NOW Hospital

10 *9:10 p.m.*
Hillside Road, Tulse Hill
DAMAGE Tennis net at the
Artizans Company, builder of
working-class housing
NOW Tennis courts

11 *11:59 p.m.*
Benledi Street, Poplar
DAMAGE 57 buildings;
Fire Brigade rescues four
severely injured people
NOW Flats, park

12 *12:44 a.m.*
Old Kent Road, Southwark
DAMAGE Four seats at the
Astoria, an Art Deco cinema
NOW Parade of shops

SOURCES: NATIONAL ARCHIVES; GUARDIAN DATASTORE

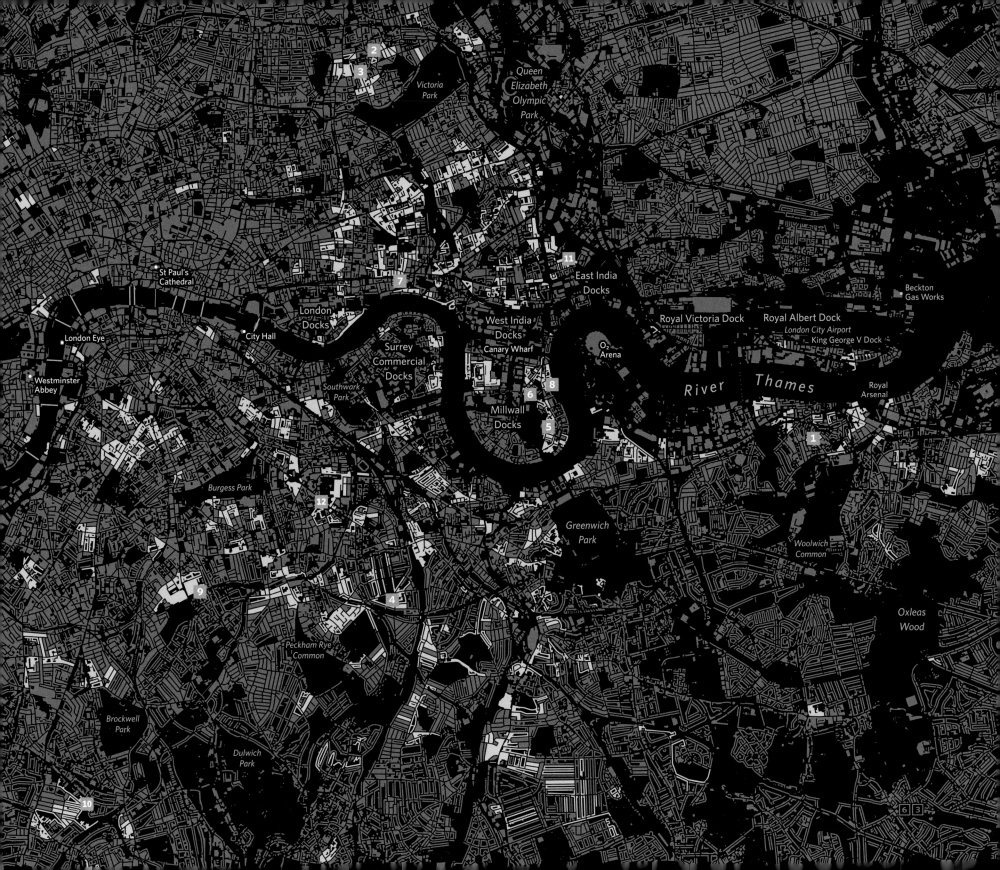

2

3

Victoria Park

Queen
Elizabeth
Olympic
Park

11

East India
Docks

7

Beckton
Gas Works

St Paul's
Cathedral

London
Docks

West India
Docks

Royal Victoria Dock   Royal Albert Dock

London City Airport

City Hall

Surrey
Commercial
Docks

Canary Wharf

O₂
Arena

King George V Dock

London Eye

8

River   Thames

Royal
Arsenal

Westminster
Abbey

*Southwark
Park*

6

Millwall
Docks

5

1

Burgess Park

12

*Greenwich
Park*

*Woolwich
Common*

9

4

*Oxleas
Wood*

*Peckham Rye
Common*

*Brockwell
Park*

*Dulwich
Park*

10

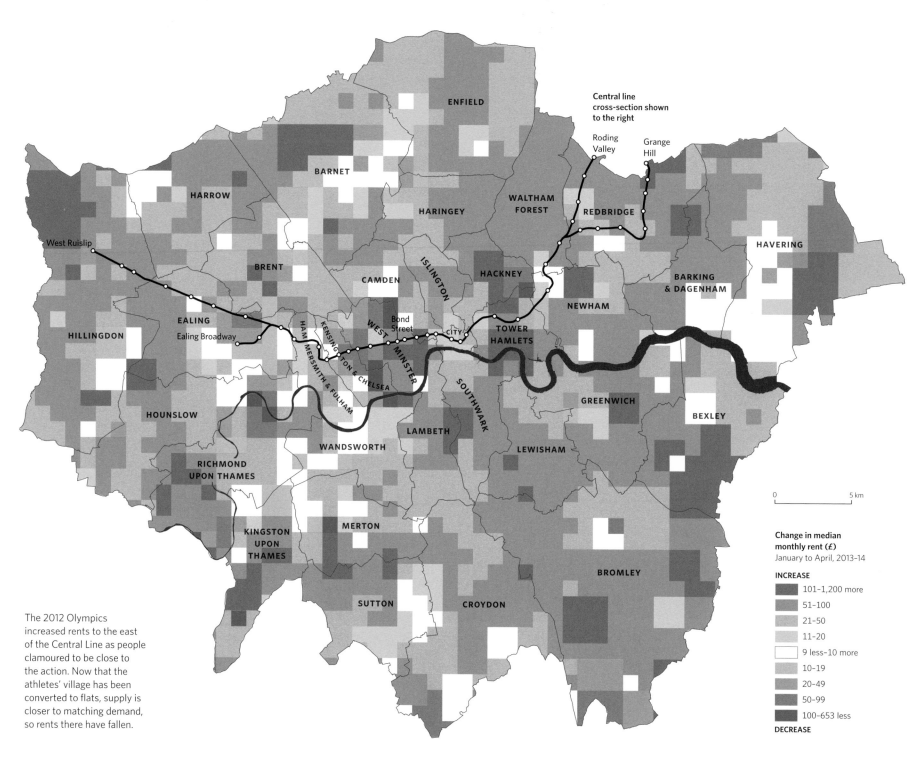

Central line
cross-section shown
to the right

Roding
Valley

Grange
Hill

West Ruislip

Ealing Broadway

Bond
Street

City

The 2012 Olympics
increased rents to the east
of the Central Line as people
clamoured to be close to
the action. Now that the
athletes' village has been
converted to flats, supply is
closer to matching demand,
so rents there have fallen.

ENFIELD

HARROW

BARNET

HARINGEY

WALTHAM
FOREST

REDBRIDGE

HAVERING

BRENT

CAMDEN

ISLINGTON

HACKNEY

BARKING
& DAGENHAM

HILLINGDON

EALING

KENSINGTON & CHELSEA

WEST
MINSTER

TOWER
HAMLETS

NEWHAM

HAM
MERSMITH & FULHAM

HOUNSLOW

SOUTHWARK

GREENWICH

BEXLEY

LAMBETH

RICHMOND
UPON THAMES

WANDSWORTH

LEWISHAM

KINGSTON
UPON
THAMES

MERTON

BROMLEY

SUTTON

CROYDON

0   5 km

**Change in median
monthly rent (£)**
January to April, 2013-14

INCREASE

101–1,200 more

51–100

21–50

11–20

9 less–10 more

10–19

20–49

50–99

100–653 less

DECREASE

Generation Rent

London has become a city of renters.

London has so much to offer that people the world over are looking to bed down wherever they can. With such huge demand, prices are rising. Here we show where average rents for two-bedroom flats have increased (or decreased) between 2013 and 2014. After tax, the median income for those in London is about £500 per week, so for those at the limits of what they can afford, a small increase can make a big difference. It's not all bad news though. Some areas are getting cheaper (9%). And thanks to ever more sophisticated property search engines, it's never been easier to seek out a bargain.

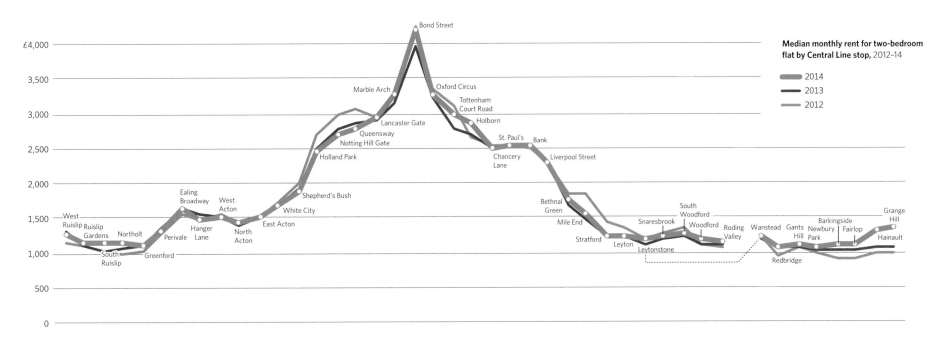

Median monthly rent for two-bedroom flat by Central Line stop, 2012-14

— 2014
— 2013
— 2012

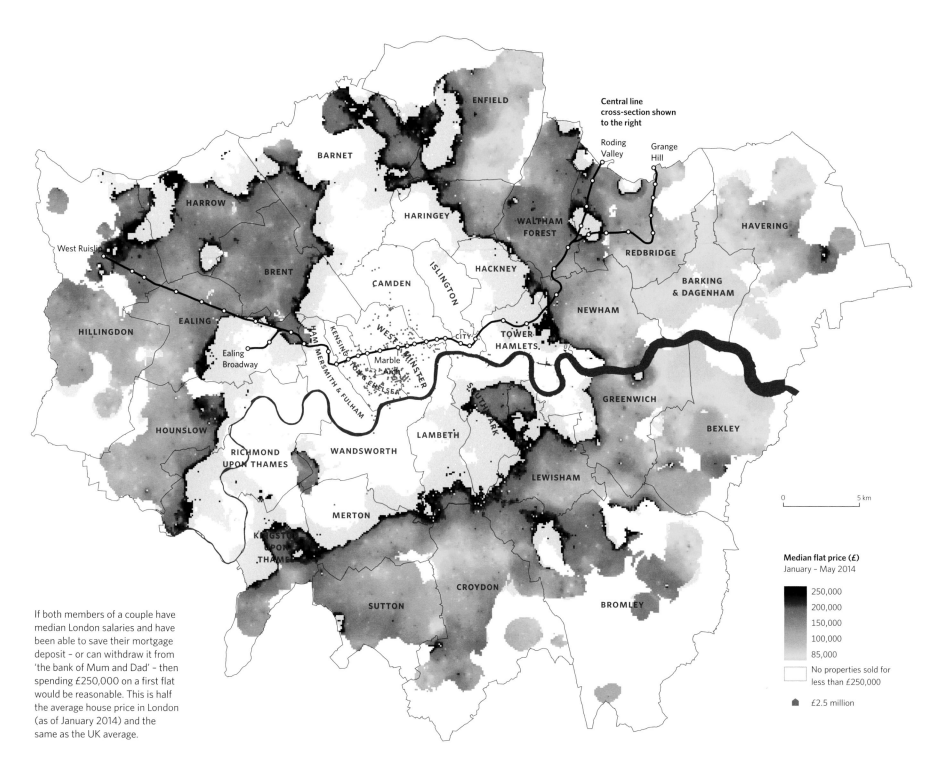

Central line
cross-section shown
to the right

Roding
Valley

Grange
Hill

ENFIELD

BARNET

HARROW

HARINGEY

WALTHAM
FOREST

HAVERING

West Ruislip

BRENT

CAMDEN

ISLINGTON

HACKNEY

REDBRIDGE

BARKING
& DAGENHAM

HILLINGDON

EALING

NEWHAM

Ealing
Broadway

HAMMERSMITH & FULHAM

KENSINGTON & CHELSEA

WESTMINSTER

CITY

TOWER
HAMLETS

Marble
Arch

HOUNSLOW

RICHMOND
UPON THAMES

WANDSWORTH

LAMBETH

SOUTHWARK

GREENWICH

BEXLEY

LEWISHAM

MERTON

KINGSTON
UPON
THAMES

CROYDON

BROMLEY

SUTTON

0   5 km

If both members of a couple have
median London salaries and have
been able to save their mortgage
deposit – or can withdraw it from
'the bank of Mum and Dad' – then
spending £250,000 on a first flat
would be reasonable. This is half
the average house price in London
(as of January 2014) and the
same as the UK average.

Median flat price (£)
January – May 2014

250,000
200,000
150,000
100,000
85,000

No properties sold for
less than £250,000

£2.5 million

(Un)Affordable Flats

When it comes to property, only the wealthy are burning a hole in their pockets.

London has more billionaires than any other city, so not everyone is concerned about the cost of housing. Nearly 500 flats sold for over £2.5 million in 2013 alone. This map shows what is left for the rest of us.

Central living is out of the question. As price increases spread like wildfire across the capital, only smaller and more fractured areas of affordability remain. With global demand fanning the flames, there is little more Londoners can do than to stick it out as 'Generation Rent' or move to one of the stars in London's constellation of commuter towns (see pp. 42–3).

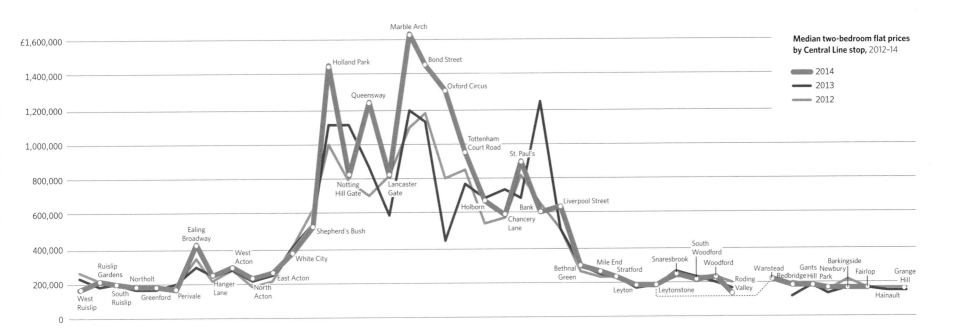

Median two-bedroom flat prices by Central Line stop, 2012–14

- 2014
- 2013
- 2012

13 Views Worth Protecting

Will the skyline of the future honour its past?

It started with a Gherkin. Then the Cheesegrater, the Walkie-Talkie and the Shard. Now there's talk of 230 new skyscrapers with names like The Blades, The Stage and The Quill. Many Londoners fear these new towers – especially those funded by foreign investors – will eclipse their ancestors: the Palace of Westminster and St Paul's Cathedral. Fortunately, the London Plan has identified 27 cherished views, including thirteen 'Protected Vistas' that cannot be obstructed. We visited all of them and recorded what we saw in case things don't go according to plan.

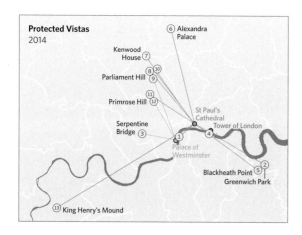

Protected Vistas
2014

⑥ Alexandra Palace

Kenwood House ⑦

Parliament Hill ⑧ ⑩ ⑨

⑪ Primrose Hill ⑫

St Paul's Cathedral

Tower of London

Serpentine Bridge ③ ①

Palace of Westminster

④

Blackheath Point ⑤ ②

Greenwich Park

⑬ King Henry's Mound

① St Paul's from Westminster Pier

The London Plan protects four types of view: panoramas (2, 5), river prospects, linear views and townscapes. Linear views like the one from Westminster Pier (1) frame landmarks in a 'keyhole'. Townscapes celebrate classic vantages like Serpentine Bridge (3) and Queen's Walk (4).

② St Paul's from Greenwich Park

⑤ St Paul's from Blackheath Point

③ Westminster from Serpentine Bridge

④ Tower of London from Queen's Walk

⑥ St Paul's from Alexandra Palace

⑦ St Paul's from Kenwood House

⑧ St Paul's from Parliament Hill

⑩ St Paul's from Hampstead Heath

These seven panoramas look south towards Central London and include either the Palace of Westminster or St Paul's Cathedral. Notice how The Shard photobombs St Paul's. Residents in Hampstead sure do.

⑪ St Paul's from Primrose Hill

THE ORIGINAL 'KEYHOLE'

⑬ St Paul's from King Henry's Mound

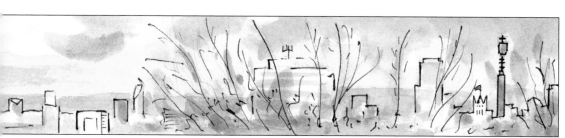

⑨ Westminster from Parliament Hill

⑫ Westminster from Primrose Hill

2 WHO WE ARE

DNA of the City

Census variables reveal London's genetic code.

The 2011 Census questionnaire for England contained fifty-six questions that solicited a broad spectrum of answers. Multiply these by 3.27 million households in London and that's a lot of data for one city. It took the Office for National Statistics (ONS) the best part of two years to release headline figures, covering the likes of gender, religion, ethnicity and employment. To convey the magnitude of their task, we have taken 207 variables from 16 of these categories and shown their values in all 649 London wards, grouped here by borough. Instead of numbers, we used colours. More intense colours correspond to higher values and reveal areas with, for example, more Buddhists than another. 134,343 blocks may seem like a lot, but it's only a fraction of the data collected. To include everything would require a plot 305 times this size, large enough to fill the floor of a Tube carriage!

SOURCE: 2011 CENSUS, ONS

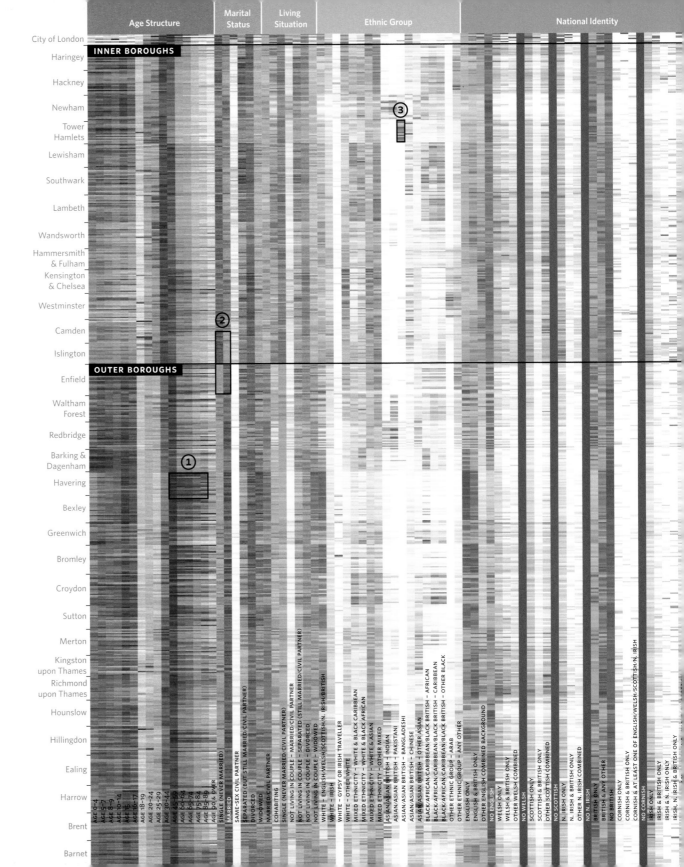

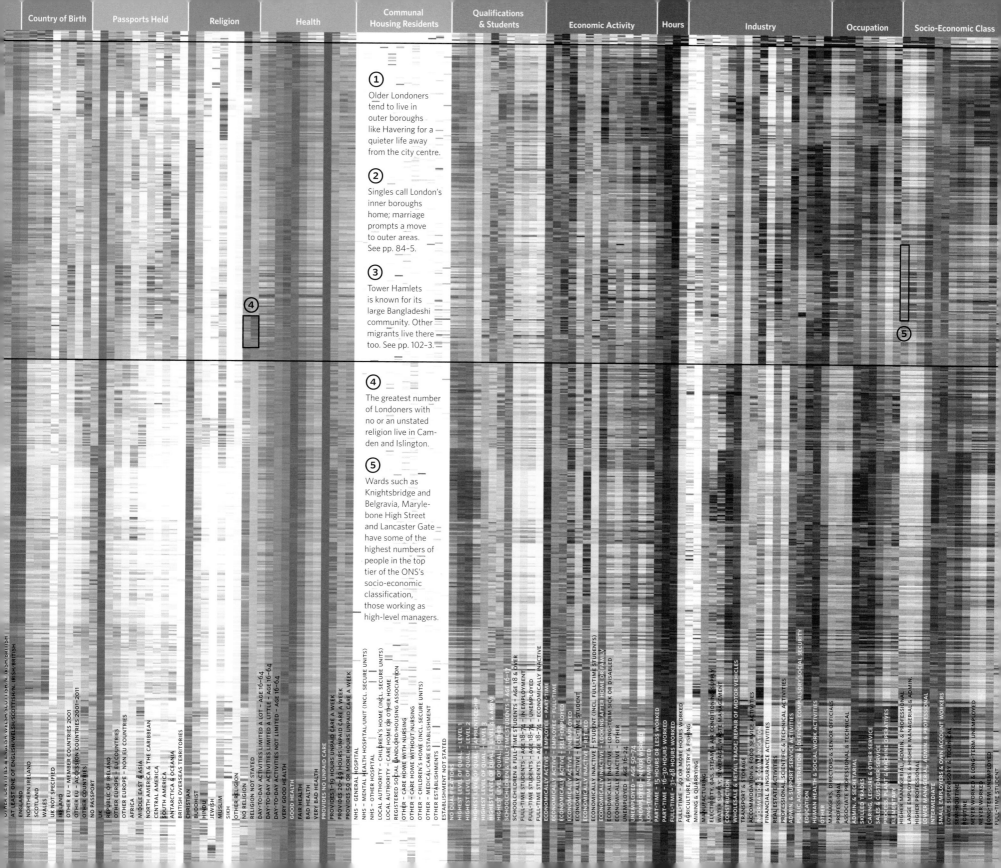

Country of Birth | Passports Held | Religion | Health | Communal Housing Residents | Qualifications & Students | Economic Activity | Hours | Industry | Occupation | Socio-Economic Class

① Older Londoners tend to live in outer boroughs like Havering for a quieter life away from the city centre.

② Singles call London's inner boroughs home; marriage prompts a move to outer areas. See pp. 84–5.

③ Tower Hamlets is known for its large Bangladeshi community. Other migrants live there too. See pp. 102–3.

④ The greatest number of Londoners with no or an unstated religion live in Camden and Islington.

⑤ Wards such as Knightsbridge and Belgravia, Marylebone High Street and Lancaster Gate have some of the highest numbers of people in the top tier of the ONS's socio-economic classification, those working as high-level managers.

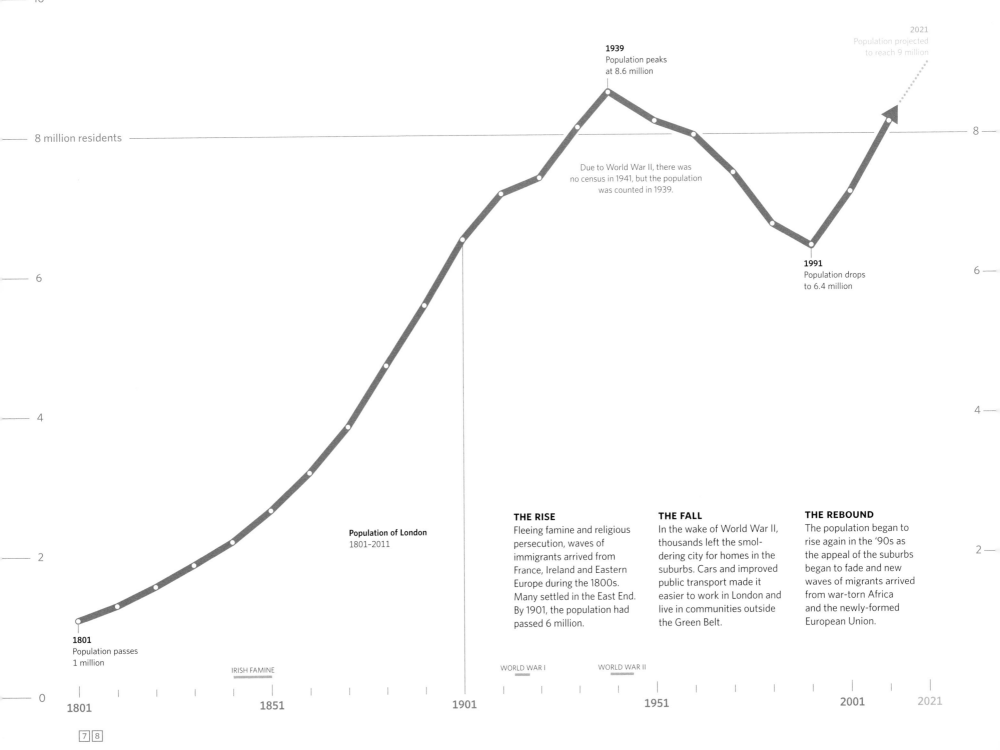

10

2021
Population projected
to reach 9 million

1939
Population peaks
at 8.6 million

8 million residents

Due to World War II, there was
no census in 1941, but the population
was counted in 1939.

1991
Population drops
to 6.4 million

6

4

Population of London
1801–2011

THE RISE
Fleeing famine and religious
persecution, waves of
immigrants arrived from
France, Ireland and Eastern
Europe during the 1800s.
Many settled in the East End.
By 1901, the population had
passed 6 million.

THE FALL
In the wake of World War II,
thousands left the smol-
dering city for homes in the
suburbs. Cars and improved
public transport made it
easier to work in London and
live in communities outside
the Green Belt.

THE REBOUND
The population began to
rise again in the '90s as
the appeal of the suburbs
began to fade and new
waves of migrants arrived
from war-torn Africa
and the newly-formed
European Union.

2

1801
Population passes
1 million

IRISH FAMINE

WORLD WAR I   WORLD WAR II

0

1801   1851   1901   1951   2001   2021

Why it's worth knowing who we are

For statisticians, Sunday 27 March 2011 was a big day. Across the UK, regardless of age, sex, income, religion or politics, households filled out census forms – answering 56 questions such as 'Who usually lives here?' and 'How many hours a week do you usually work?' – and posted them back to the Office for National Statistics (ONS). The result? The latest snapshot in a series that plays back 210 years of UK history like a stop-motion movie.

It takes minutes to fill out the census form but years for ONS to fully process and share the data collected. Like a trailer for a long-anticipated film, the first data from this national event were released in July 2012. In a decade, the population of England and Wales had grown 7.1% to 56.1 million – the most rapid increase in the history of the census. In London, growth was faster – up 12% to 8.2 million. With each subsequent data release, life in London could be seen in ever-higher definition from the passports people hold to the jobs they work.

The problem is, gathering high-quality data costs money: £482 million to be exact for the 2011 Census. With cost savings in mind, the UK's new Conservative-led coalition government questioned the census's value to tax payers. They first explored the option of cancelling it but then reconsidered. We are fortunate they did because, as the Royal Statistical Society put it, census data ensure 'that we build our schools where they are required by our children, that hospitals are equipped to deliver the services that we need, that transport links reflect the journeys we undertake. With good data we can get these things right (and can hold people to account should things go wrong).'

The biggest limitation of the census is its infrequency. A wealth of new technologies offer near-continuous supplies of data from existing government databases such as tax records or the National Health Service through to smartphones and social media. However, quantity is no substitute for quality. For example, if you were to learn that 1% of Twitter users in London tweet in Arabic, you still wouldn't know how many Londoners speak Arabic. To appear on our 'Twitter Ink' map (pp. 106–107), you needed a smartphone *and* you needed to be tweeting. It's a self-selected sample. To be included in the census, all you need is a pen and a post-box.

The census is our control. It provides the baseline to see how accurately experimental data sources can answer questions like 'Where do most of London's Arabic speakers live?' or 'How many people moved to London last year?' If we get it right, we'll be able to monitor change almost hourly as population statistics transition from static to streaming. Get it wrong and we won't really know who we are until the next census in 2021.

Similarities Attract

We are where we live.

To better understand the demographic diversity of London, the Greater London Authority (GLA) asked geographers Paul Longley and Alex Singleton to map it. This is no easy task. As the previous pages show, Londoners span the full spectrum of ethnicities, ages and occupations. Their infinite combinations don't readily fit into typical classifications. So first, Longley and Singleton ran variables from the 2011 Census through a clustering algorithm to identify eight broad groups of people with similar population and built environment characteristics (e.g. White, homeowners, students). Then they ran it again within each of those groups to get more specific. The resulting kaleidoscope (right) helps the city target local initiatives and tells new businesses where to set up shop.

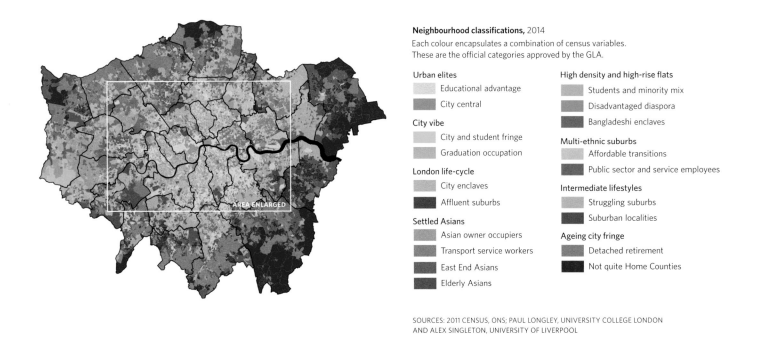

Neighbourhood classifications, 2014
Each colour encapsulates a combination of census variables.
These are the official categories approved by the GLA.

Urban elites
- Educational advantage
- City central

City vibe
- City and student fringe
- Graduation occupation

London life-cycle
- City enclaves
- Affluent suburbs

Settled Asians
- Asian owner occupiers
- Transport service workers
- East End Asians
- Elderly Asians

High density and high-rise flats
- Students and minority mix
- Disadvantaged diaspora
- Bangladeshi enclaves

Multi-ethnic suburbs
- Affordable transitions
- Public sector and service employees

Intermediate lifestyles
- Struggling suburbs
- Suburban localities

Ageing city fringe
- Detached retirement
- Not quite Home Counties

SOURCES: 2011 CENSUS, ONS; PAUL LONGLEY, UNIVERSITY COLLEGE LONDON AND ALEX SINGLETON, UNIVERSITY OF LIVERPOOL

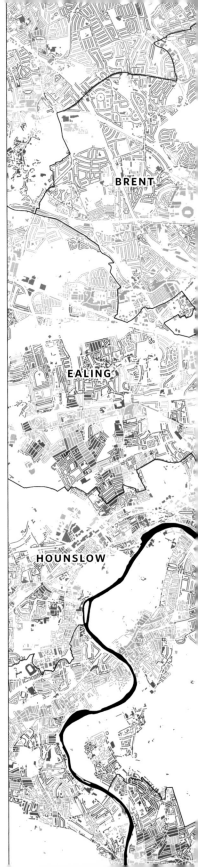

BRENT

EALING

HOUNSLOW

Life and Death

Only one explanation adds up.

London's population increased by 100,000 in 2012. Everyone wants to know why. There are four possible causes: more migrants from within the UK, more from overseas, more babies or fewer deaths. As we explain later in this chapter, internal migration (pp. 94–5) and international migration (pp. 96–7) directly accounted for a net increase of only 14,000 people, which means the city's unchecked growth is a matter of life or death. We'll give you a hint: it's not death. In fact, the causes overlap somewhat. Births outnumbered deaths 134,000 to 48,000 but more than half of those babies belonged to mothers born outside the UK. If total births in London continue to increase by 2,500 per year, the population will hit nine million in the next decade.

In these graphics, we show how the fertility and mortality rates for each borough compared to the London average over a ten-year span. Women in Inner London are having fewer babies than those in Outer London, where Barking & Dagenham had the highest fertility rate of all.

READ CLOCKWISE
2003   2012

AMOUNT ABOVE OR BELOW THE LONDON AVERAGE

Fertility rate by borough
2003–2012

ONS MEASURES FERTILITY BY THE NUMBER OF LIVE BIRTHS PER 1,000 WOMEN AGED 15-44.

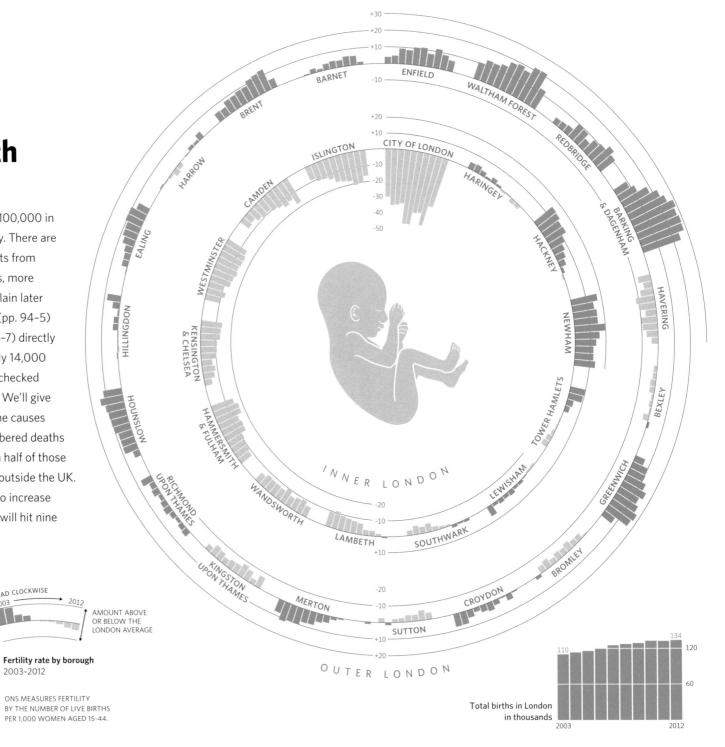

Total births in London
in thousands
2003   2012
110   134   120   60

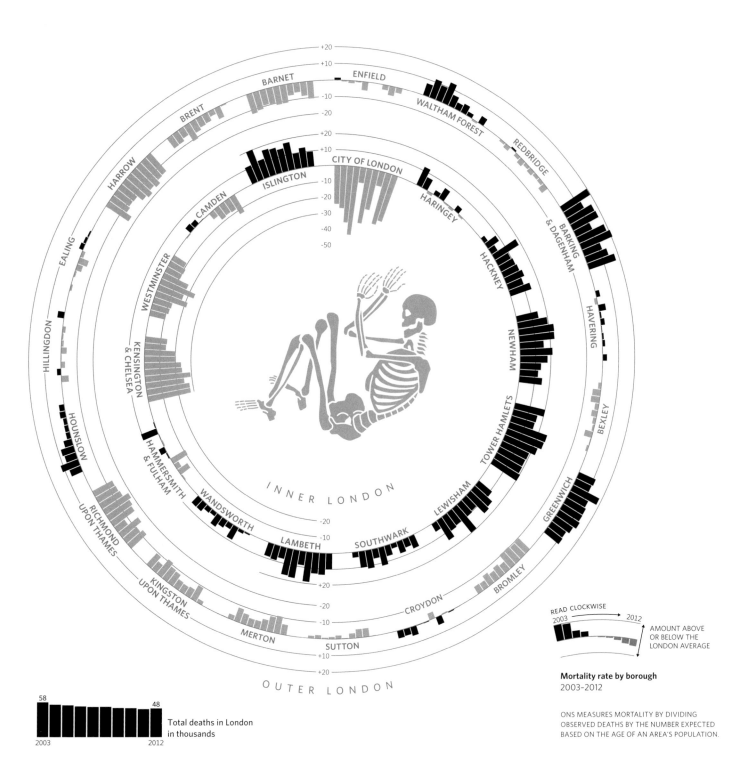

BARNET

ENFIELD

BRENT

WALTHAM FOREST

HARROW

REDBRIDGE

ISLINGTON

CITY OF LONDON

CAMDEN

HARINGEY

BARKING & DAGENHAM

EALING

WESTMINSTER

HACKNEY

HAVERING

HILLINGDON

KENSINGTON & CHELSEA

NEWHAM

INNER LONDON

BEXLEY

HOUNSLOW

HAMMERSMITH & FULHAM

TOWER HAMLETS

WANDSWORTH

LEWISHAM

GREENWICH

RICHMOND UPON THAMES

LAMBETH

SOUTHWARK

KINGSTON UPON THAMES

CROYDON

BROMLEY

MERTON

SUTTON

OUTER LONDON

+20
+10
-10
-20

+20
+10
-10
-20
-30
-40
-50

-20
-10
+20

-20
-10
+10
+20

READ CLOCKWISE

2003 → 2012

AMOUNT ABOVE
OR BELOW THE
LONDON AVERAGE

Mortality rate by borough
2003–2012

ONS MEASURES MORTALITY BY DIVIDING
OBSERVED DEATHS BY THE NUMBER EXPECTED
BASED ON THE AGE OF AN AREA'S POPULATION.

Deaths have been delayed
in wealthier boroughs like
Kensington & Chelsea and
Richmond upon Thames where
residents can afford healthier
lifestyles. Not so in eastern
boroughs like Tower Hamlets
where there have been far
more deaths than expected.

58   48

Total deaths in London
in thousands

2003   2012

Relationship Status

We age, we marry, we migrate.

Twenty-five and single? In London, you're anything but alone. According to the 2011 Census, more than half of twentysomethings go solo. Then come your thirties and that deep river of available singles your age narrows to a shallow stream. By age fifty, it's little more than a trickle.

Most will have married and settled in the leafier boroughs (see maps). Young singles – and their cohabiting friends – prefer trendier parts of the city such as Hoxton, Clapham and Peckham. Those living away from their spouse fall into two camps: pricey places in Kensington or more affordable housing near Heathrow, Wembley and Upton Park. Separated couples and divorcees cluster around Tottenham and to the east; widowed spouses stay put.

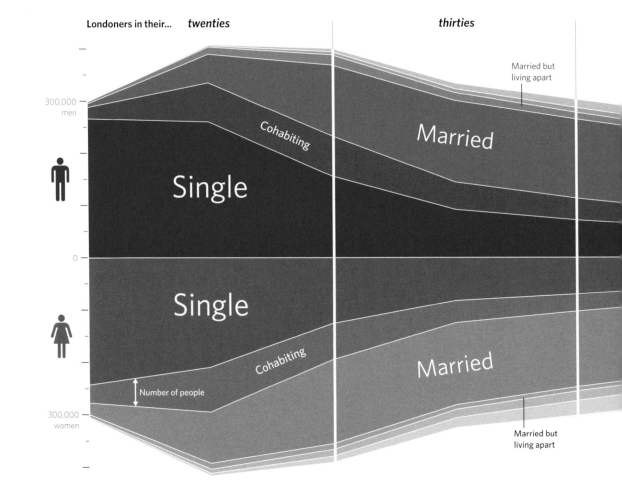

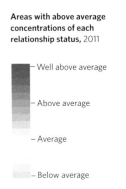

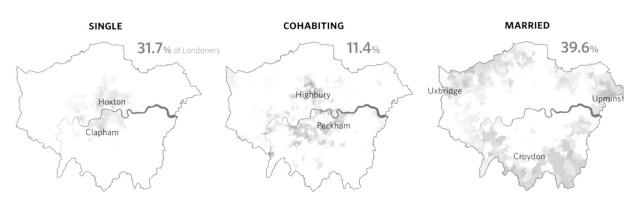

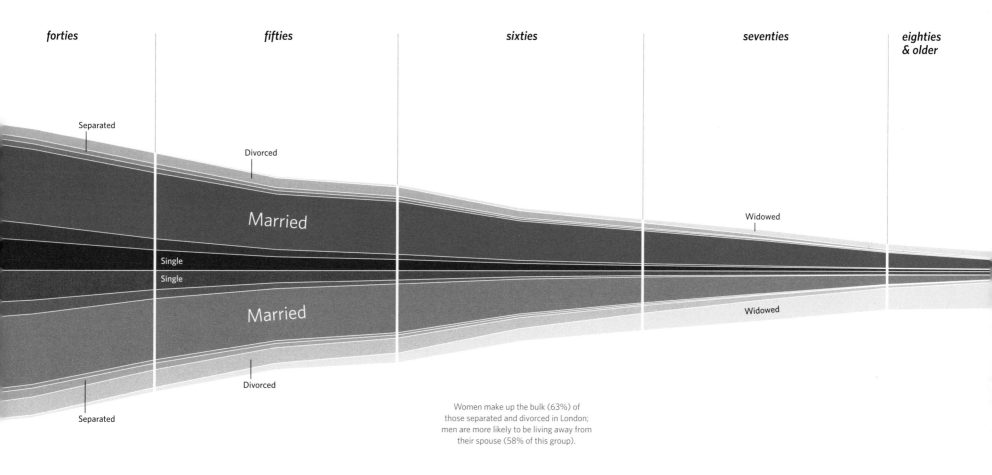

forties *fifties* *sixties* *seventies* *eighties & older*

Separated

Divorced

Married

Single

Widowed

Single

Married

Widowed

Divorced

Separated

Women make up the bulk (63%) of
those separated and divorced in London;
men are more likely to be living away from
their spouse (58% of this group).

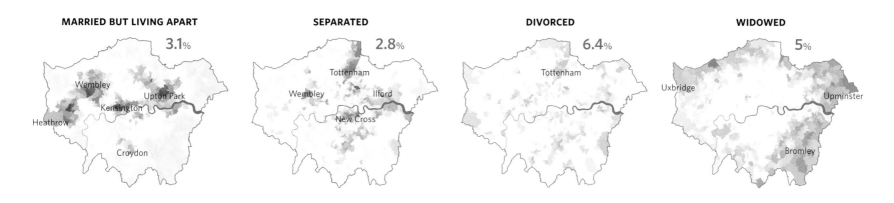

MARRIED BUT LIVING APART **3.1**%

Wembley
Upton Park
Kensington
Heathrow
Croydon

SEPARATED **2.8**%

Tottenham
Wembley Ilford
New Cross

DIVORCED **6.4**%

Tottenham

WIDOWED **5**%

Uxbridge
Upminster
Bromley

SOURCES: 2011 CENSUS, ONS; OS

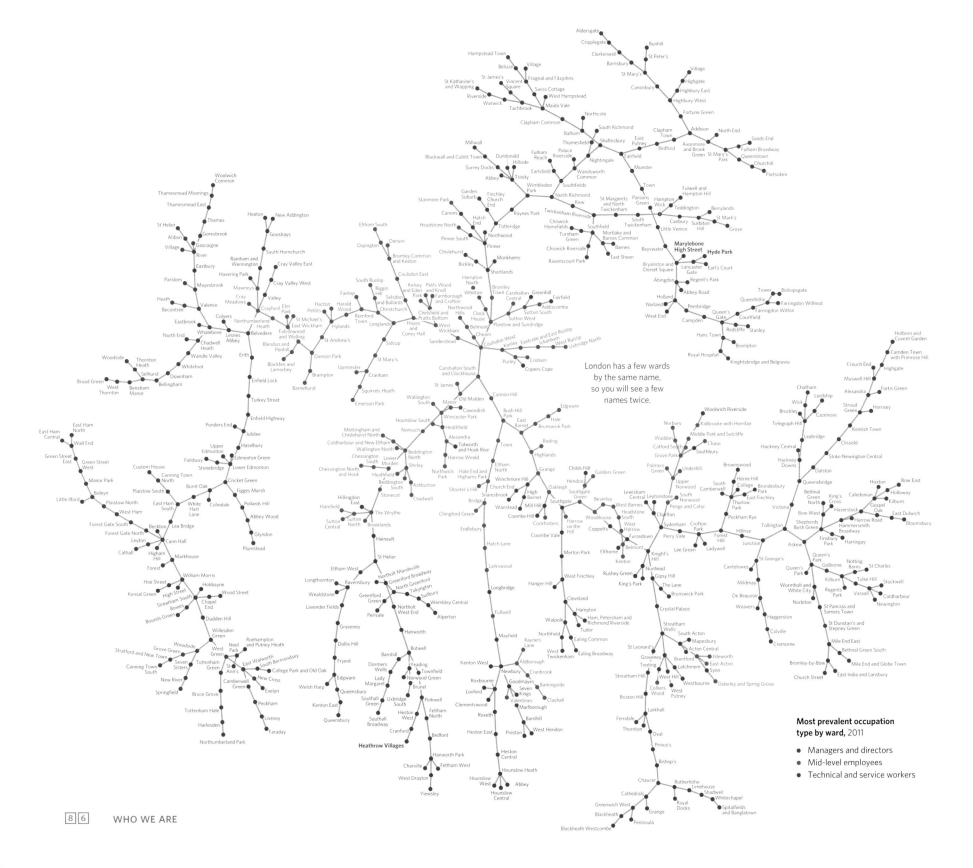

London has a few wards
by the same name,
so you will see a few
names twice.

**Most prevalent occupation
type by ward,** 2011

- Managers and directors
- Mid-level employees
- Technical and service workers

Professional Networking

It's not what you know but where you live.

Imagine London as one big company and within it, the twenty-four occupation types registered in the 2011 Census from corporate managers to machine operatives. The tree to the left then is an organizational chart, grouping areas together that have similar concentrations of workers in those twenty-four job types. Blue areas have lots of degree-level managers and directors; green areas have lots of mid-level employees; and brown areas have lots of technical and service workers. Much like at an office (or on LinkedIn), those connected to each other share the most in common.

The algorithm we used to generate this network did not factor in geography, only job types from the 2011 Census. Still, some adjacent areas on the map (below right) remain adjacent on this tree. That's because socio-economic classes tend to stick together. For example, Hyde Park and Marylebone High Street wards both have 15% of their residents working as corporate managers. Contrast those areas with Heathrow Villages. With 20% working in technical and service jobs, they're not just on opposite ends of the city. They're on opposite ends of the ladder.

On this tree, some nodes differ in colour from the rest of their branch. These areas may be changing, thereby transitioning them from one set of employment characteristics to another.

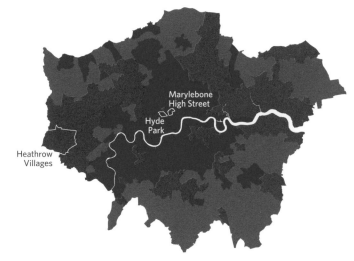

Here we transfer the colours from the network tree to the true geography of London's 649 wards. This reveals the concentration of managers and directors (blue) in Central London.

There's a Guild for That

Art scholars and educators join the butchers, bakers and candlestick makers.

A thousand years before smartphones, Londoners turned to craftsmen to get things done. Fletchers fletched arrows, Grocers sold spices 'in gross', and Cordwainers worked – or 'wained' – leather from Cordoba. Gradually they formed guilds, which began as religious, commercial or social associations in different parts of the City. Streets like Cloth Fair and Ironmonger Lane still recall the guilds, which came to be known as livery companies for the bicoloured garments – or livery – worn by members and servants. Here we have redesigned the coat of arms for all 110 'Worshipful Companies' as app icons. They are arranged by their order of precedence (see note), beginning with the 'Great Twelve'.

    Early companies like the Bonnet Makers and Heaumers vanished with their trades; others like the Horners and Fanmakers adapted their crafts to plastics and air conditioning respectively, or shifted their focus to charitable giving. After the Fanmakers in 1709, no new companies were established until the 1920s, when the Master Mariners and Air Pilots and Air Navigators became the first of the thirty-three 'modern livery companies', a group that now includes trades of today: Educators, International Bankers and Information Technologists.

THE GREAT TWELVE

Mercers	Grocers	Drapers
Fishmongers	Goldsmiths	Merchant Taylors*
Skinners*	Haberdashers	Salters
Ironmongers	Vintners	Clothworkers

*In the 15th century, the Skinners and Merchant Taylors both claimed to deserve sixth place in the order of precedence. To settle this dispute, the Lord Mayor decreed in 1484 that the two companies would alternate between sixth and seventh every year, and they have ever since.

13 Dyers Brewers Leathersellers Pewterers Barbers Cutlers Bakers Wax Chandlers Tallow Chandlers

 Armourers & Brasiers Girdlers Butchers Saddlers Carpenters Cordwainers Painter-Stainers   Curriers Masons

 Plumbers Innholders Founders Poulters Cooks Coopers Tylers & Bricklayers Bowyers Fletchers

 Blacksmiths Joiners & Ceilers Weavers** Woolmen Scriveners Fruiterers Plaisterers Stationers & Newspaper Makers Broderers

ORDER OF PRECEDENCE
The City assigns each new company a position in the order of precedence. The order for the first 48 was 'sette, ordeyned, and agreed' by the Court of Aldermen in 1515 according to each company's wealth and influence at that time. All subsequent companies have been numbered consecutively, from the Upholders (49) to the Art Scholars (110), who attained livery status in February 2014.

 49 Upholders Musicians Turners Basketmakers Glaziers Horners Farriers Paviors Loriners Apothecaries Shipwrights Spectacle Makers Clockmakers Glovers Feltmakers

** The Weavers' charter dates to 1155, making them the oldest chartered craft in the City.

Framework Knitters Needle Makers Gardeners Tin Plate Workers Wheelwrights Distillers Patten Makers   Glass Sellers Coachmakers Gunmakers Silver Wyre Drawers  Makers of Playing Cards Fanmakers Carmen Master Mariners

 Solicitors Farmers Air Pilots & Air Navigators Tobacco Blenders Furniture Makers Scientific Inst. Makers Chartered Surveyors Chartered Accountants Chartered Secretaries Builders' Merchants Launderers Marketors Actuaries Insurers Arbitrators Engineers

Fuellers Lightmongers Enviro. Cleaners Chartered Architects Constructors Information Technologists World Traders Water Conservators Firefighters Carriage Drivers Management Consultants Intl. Bankers Tax Advisers Security Professionals Educators Art Scholars

Fifty Kilometres of Jobs

A chain of high streets unites London's villages.

Shoes, jewellery, coffee, halal meats and fried chicken. Hair stylists, optometrists and immigration lawyers. Hospitals, mosques and pubs. You can find them all along Whitechapel Road in Tower Hamlets (below). Nearly 600 of these corridors line the capital. Here we show how many link together to form a chain from Uxbridge to Romford with the world's most famous, Oxford Street, at its centre. Often thought of as places of leisure, high streets double up to provide office space on their upper floors. The coloured bars below show the estimated numbers of floors available for employment; colour indicates the usage type.

Romford

Uxbridge

ENLARGED BELOW

GREATER LONDON AUTHORITY BOUNDARY

Uxbridge

① ② ③ ④

Hillingdon

⑤ ⑥ ⑦ ⑧

Kilometre 1
BUSINESSES 146
FLOORS 1,535

⑨ ⑩ ⑪ ⑫ ⑬ ⑭ ⑮ ⑯ ⑰ ⑱ ⑲ ⑳ ㉑ ㉒ ㉓ ㉔ ㉕

Southall

Ealing

Acton

Shepherd's Bush

Notting Hill

Hyde Park

Kilometre 9
BUSINESSES 238
FLOORS 1,005

Kilometre 14
BUSINESSES 240
FLOORS 5,195

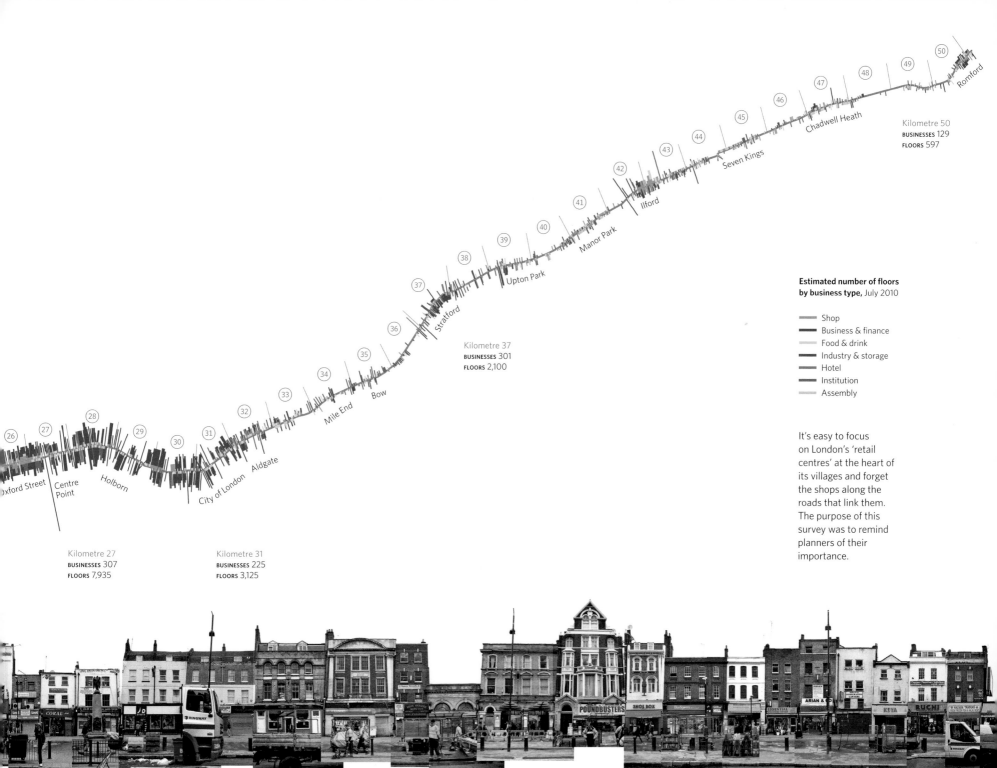

Kilometre 50
BUSINESSES 129
FLOORS 597

Romford

Chadwell Heath

Seven Kings

Ilford

Manor Park

Upton Park

Estimated number of floors by business type, July 2010

— Shop
— Business & finance
— Food & drink
— Industry & storage
— Hotel
— Institution
— Assembly

Kilometre 37
BUSINESSES 301
FLOORS 2,100

Stratford

Bow

Mile End

It's easy to focus on London's 'retail centres' at the heart of its villages and forget the shops along the roads that link them. The purpose of this survey was to remind planners of their importance.

Oxford Street

Centre Point

Holborn

City of London

Aldgate

Kilometre 27
BUSINESSES 307
FLOORS 7,935

Kilometre 31
BUSINESSES 225
FLOORS 3,125

SOURCE: GORT SCOTT ARCHITECTS. PHOTO COLLAGE: JULIAN HARRAP ARCHITECTS LLP

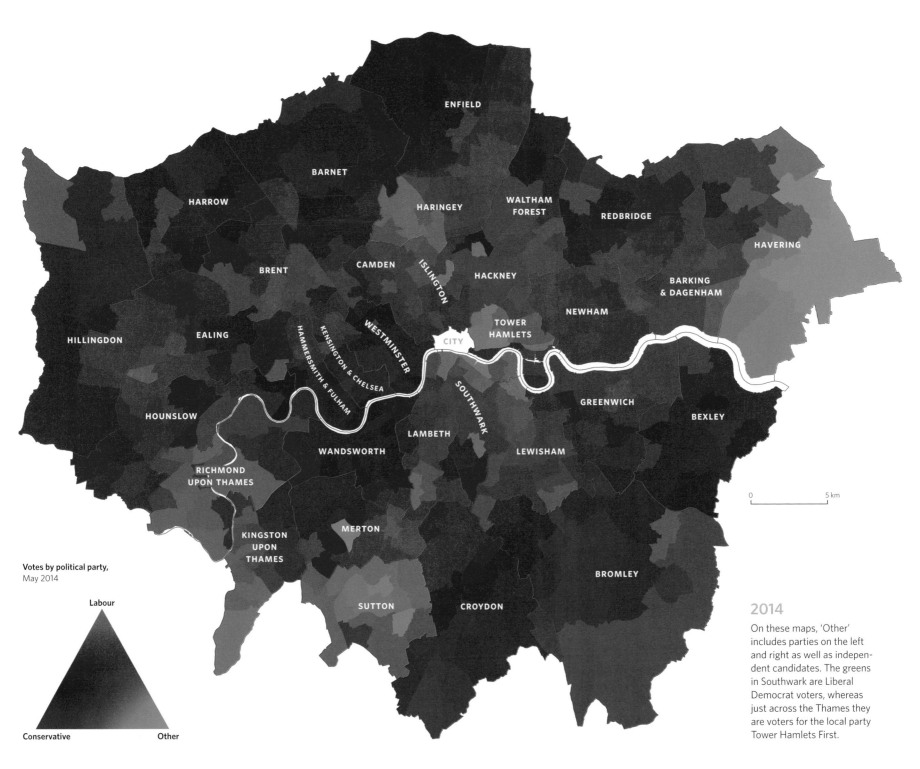

ENFIELD

BARNET

HARROW

HARINGEY

WALTHAM
FOREST

REDBRIDGE

HAVERING

BRENT

CAMDEN

ISLINGTON

HACKNEY

BARKING
& DAGENHAM

NEWHAM

HILLINGDON

EALING

HAMMERSMITH & FULHAM

KENSINGTON & CHELSEA

WESTMINSTER

CITY

TOWER
HAMLETS

HOUNSLOW

SOUTHWARK

GREENWICH

BEXLEY

LAMBETH

WANDSWORTH

LEWISHAM

RICHMOND
UPON THAMES

MERTON

KINGSTON
UPON
THAMES

SUTTON

CROYDON

BROMLEY

0   5 km

Votes by political party,
May 2014

Labour

Conservative   Other

2014

On these maps, 'Other'
includes parties on the left
and right as well as independent candidates. The greens
in Southwark are Liberal
Democrat voters, whereas
just across the Thames they
are voters for the local party
Tower Hamlets First.

The Colour of Votes

Red is rising in London's political mix.

When it comes to voting in London, things are far from black and white. The ballots for the May 2014 council elections featured more than twenty parties. To the left we show the results for Labour (red), Conservative (blue) and everyone else (green), including British National Party, Christian People's Alliance and the Trade Unionist and Socialist Coalition. For example, a very well-organized group of independent councillors from local residents' groups has kept the Borough of Havering coloured green for three straight elections (see right). Over the past few years, greens have turned to red as liberal Londoners have switched from Liberal Democrats to Labour in response to national issues that made the party less popular. The Conservative voters in Westminster and Kensington and Chelsea seem a more loyal bunch, keeping the red at bay.

2006

Support for the Labour party and its London Mayor Ken Livingstone was beginning to wane as Londoners were becoming more enamoured with Boris Johnson, the soon-to-be-elected Conservative mayor.

2010

Conservatives edged Labour nationally and locally and formed a coalition government with Liberal Democrats. Votes for the far right-wing British National Party peak in Barking and Dagenham in an area of traditional Labour supporters.

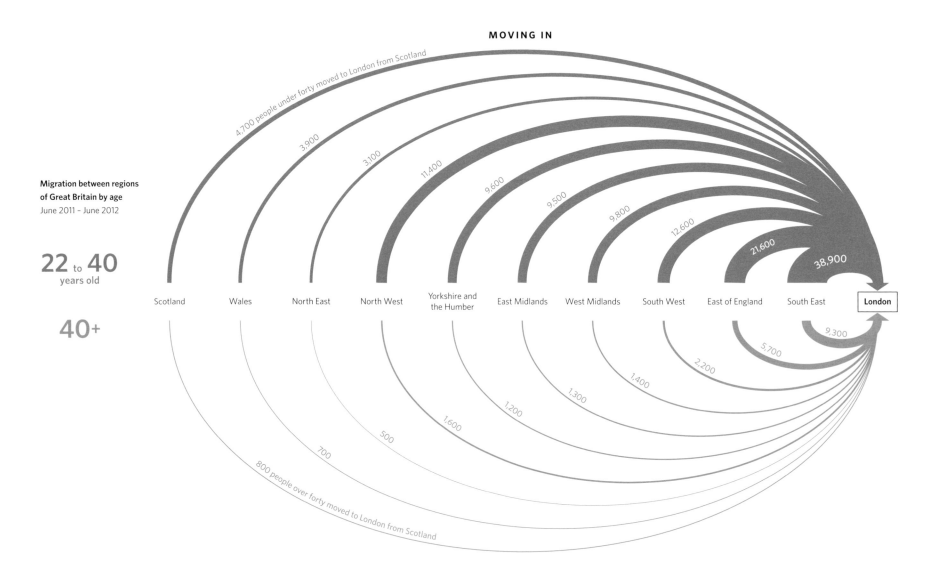

Migration between regions
of Great Britain by age
June 2011 – June 2012

22 to 40
years old

40+

4,700 people under forty moved to London from Scotland

3,900

3,100

11,400

9,600

9,500

9,800

12,600

21,600

38,900

Scotland Wales North East North West Yorkshire and the Humber East Midlands West Midlands South West East of England South East London

9,300

5,700

2,200

1,400

1,300

1,200

1,600

500

700

800 people over forty moved to London from Scotland

Moving In, Then On

London's population may be growing, but not everyone is sticking around.

Unlike parcels in the post, people have no tracking numbers to record their movements around the country. Instead, the Office for National Statistics (ONS) creates estimates by combining higher education records with patient register data. If a person registers with a new doctor in a new region, that counts as a move. Across all age groups, between 2011 and 2012, London experienced the largest turnover margin in the country: 55,000 more people left than arrived. Looking at those aged 22 or older, the arcs above show

MOVING OUT

44,600
29,300
9,000
6,100
5,600
4,600
6,500
1,300
2,400
3,200

London
South East
East of England
South West
West Midlands
East Midlands
Yorkshire and the Humber
North West
North East
Wales
Scotland

22 to 40 years old

40+

24,600
16,500
5,500
1,900
2,200
1,400
2,000
400
1,100
1,400

that young adults (purple) were more likely to migrate to another region than those over forty (orange). Many were graduates moving to the capital after finishing their studies or new families moving out in search of more affordable homes, better schools and higher quality of life. This isn't to suggest love for London was lost. According to research from the real estate agency Hamptons International, the average distance travelled by homebuyers leaving the city was only 26 commuter-friendly miles.

SCOTLAND

North East
North West
Yorkshire and the Humber
ENGLAND
East Midlands
West Midlands
East of England
WALES
London
South West
South East

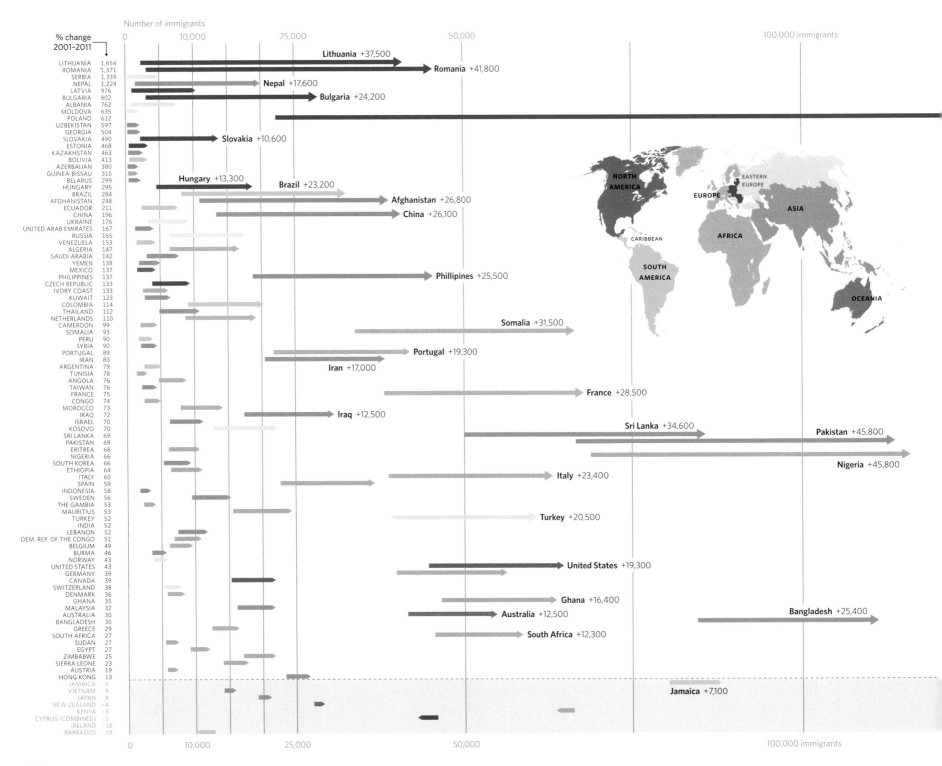

Number of immigrants

% change
2001–2011

LITHUANIA	1,654
ROMANIA	1,371
SERBIA	1,339
NEPAL	1,224
LATVIA	976
BULGARIA	802
ALBANIA	762
MOLDOVA	635
POLAND	612
UZBEKISTAN	597
GEORGIA	504
SLOVAKIA	490
ESTONIA	468
KAZAKHSTAN	463
BOLIVIA	413
AZERBAIJAN	380
GUINEA-BISSAU	315
BELARUS	299
HUNGARY	295
BRAZIL	284
AFGHANISTAN	248
ECUADOR	211
CHINA	196
UKRAINE	176
UNITED ARAB EMIRATES	167
RUSSIA	165
VENEZUELA	153
ALGERIA	147
SAUDI ARABIA	142
YEMEN	138
MEXICO	137
PHILIPPINES	137
CZECH REPUBLIC	133
IVORY COAST	133
KUWAIT	123
COLOMBIA	114
THAILAND	112
NETHERLANDS	110
CAMEROON	99
SOMALIA	93
PERU	90
SYRIA	90
PORTUGAL	89
IRAN	83
ARGENTINA	79
TUNISIA	78
ANGOLA	76
TAIWAN	76
FRANCE	75
CONGO	74
MOROCCO	73
IRAQ	72
ISRAEL	70
KOSOVO	70
SRI LANKA	69
PAKISTAN	69
ERITREA	68
NIGERIA	66
SOUTH KOREA	66
ETHIOPIA	64
ITALY	60
SPAIN	59
INDONESIA	58
SWEDEN	56
THE GAMBIA	53
MAURITIUS	53
TURKEY	52
INDIA	52
LEBANON	52
DEM. REP. OF THE CONGO	51
BELGIUM	49
BURMA	46
NORWAY	43
UNITED STATES	43
GERMANY	39
CANADA	39
SWITZERLAND	38
DENMARK	36
GHANA	35
MALAYSIA	32
AUSTRALIA	30
BANGLADESH	30
GREECE	29
SOUTH AFRICA	27
SUDAN	27
EGYPT	27
ZIMBABWE	25
SIERRA LEONE	23
AUSTRIA	19
HONG KONG	13
JAMAICA	9
VIETNAM	9
JAPAN	8
NEW ZEALAND	+4
KENYA	-3
CYPRUS (COMBINED)	-5
IRELAND	-18
BARBADOS	-19

Lithuania +37,500
Romania +41,800
Nepal +17,600
Bulgaria +24,200
Slovakia +10,600
Hungary +13,300
Brazil +23,200
Afghanistan +26,800
China +26,100
Phillipines +25,500
Somalia +31,500
Portugal +19,300
Iran +17,000
France +28,500
Iraq +12,500
Sri Lanka +34,600
Pakistan +45,800
Nigeria +45,800
Italy +23,400
Turkey +20,500
United States +19,300
Ghana +16,400
Australia +12,500
South Africa +12,300
Bangladesh +25,400
Jamaica +7,100

NORTH
AMERICA

EASTERN
EUROPE

EUROPE

ASIA

CARIBBEAN

AFRICA

SOUTH
AMERICA

OCEANIA

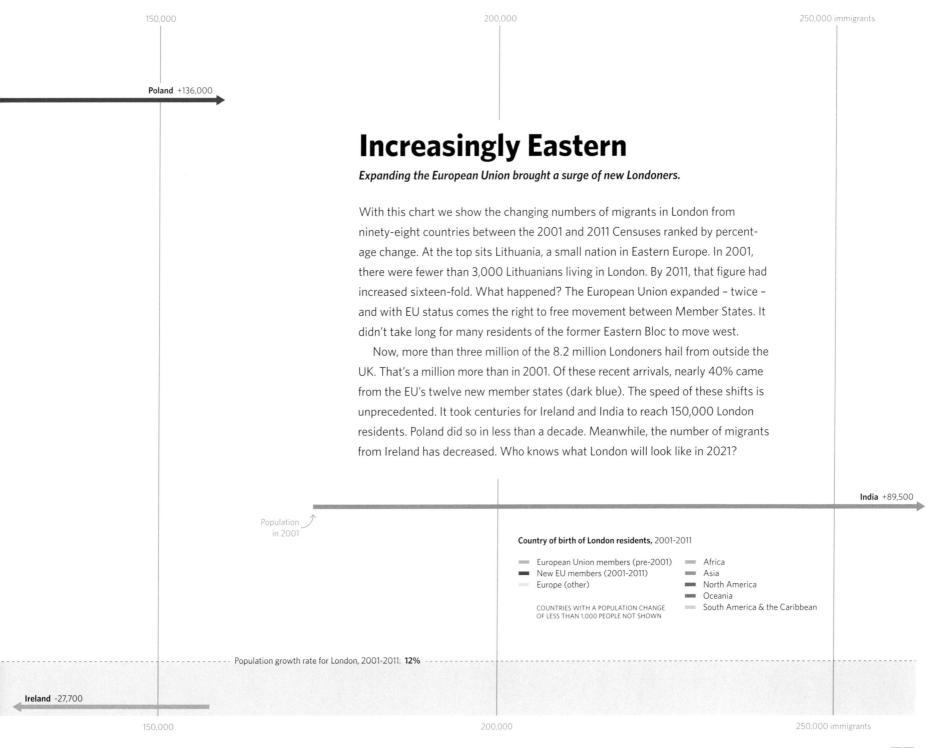

150,000   200,000   250,000 immigrants

Poland +136,000

Increasingly Eastern

Expanding the European Union brought a surge of new Londoners.

With this chart we show the changing numbers of migrants in London from ninety-eight countries between the 2001 and 2011 Censuses ranked by percentage change. At the top sits Lithuania, a small nation in Eastern Europe. In 2001, there were fewer than 3,000 Lithuanians living in London. By 2011, that figure had increased sixteen-fold. What happened? The European Union expanded – twice – and with EU status comes the right to free movement between Member States. It didn't take long for many residents of the former Eastern Bloc to move west.

Now, more than three million of the 8.2 million Londoners hail from outside the UK. That's a million more than in 2001. Of these recent arrivals, nearly 40% came from the EU's twelve new member states (dark blue). The speed of these shifts is unprecedented. It took centuries for Ireland and India to reach 150,000 London residents. Poland did so in less than a decade. Meanwhile, the number of migrants from Ireland has decreased. Who knows what London will look like in 2021?

India +89,500

Population in 2001

Country of birth of London residents, 2001-2011

▬ European Union members (pre-2001)   ▬ Africa
▬ New EU members (2001-2011)   ▬ Asia
▬ Europe (other)   ▬ North America
                                           ▬ Oceania
COUNTRIES WITH A POPULATION CHANGE   ▬ South America & the Caribbean
OF LESS THAN 1,000 PEOPLE NOT SHOWN

Population growth rate for London, 2001-2011: **12%**

Ireland -27,700

150,000   200,000   250,000 immigrants

Passports, Please

Londoners are global citizens.

For the first time, the 2011 Census asked, 'What passports do you hold?' 5.8 million Londoners ticked 'United Kingdom'; 1.7 million named another country. In the map on this page, we show where London's 5.8 million British passport holders were born. Many came from India, Bangladesh, Pakistan, Jamaica and Kenya decades ago and have since gained British or dual citizenship.

Number of British passport holders in London by country of birth, 2011

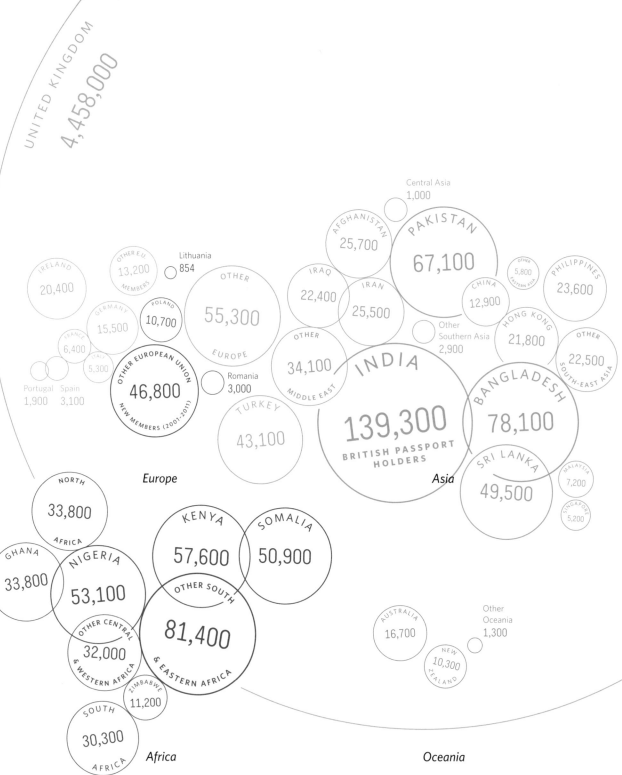

UNITED KINGDOM 4,458,000

Europe

IRELAND 20,400

OTHER E.U MEMBERS 13,200

Lithuania 854

OTHER EUROPE 55,300

GERMANY 15,500

POLAND 10,700

FRANCE 6,400

ITALY 5,300

Portugal 1,900 Spain 3,100

OTHER EUROPEAN UNION NEW MEMBERS (2001-2011) 46,800

Romania 3,000

TURKEY 43,100

Asia

Central Asia 1,000

AFGHANISTAN 25,700

PAKISTAN 67,100

IRAQ 22,400

IRAN 25,500

CHINA 12,900

OTHER EASTERN ASIA 5,800

PHILIPPINES 23,600

HONG KONG 21,800

OTHER SOUTH-EAST ASIA 22,500

Other Southern Asia 2,900

OTHER MIDDLE EAST 34,100

INDIA 139,300 BRITISH PASSPORT HOLDERS

BANGLADESH 78,100

SRI LANKA 49,500

MALAYSIA 7,200

SINGAPORE 5,200

The Americas

CANADA 8,400

UNITED STATES OF AMERICA 18,900

JAMAICA 62,800

1,700 Central America

SOUTH AMERICA 36,200

OTHER CARIBBEAN 46,000

• 23 British Overseas Territories

Africa

NORTH AFRICA 33,800

GHANA 33,800

NIGERIA 53,100

OTHER CENTRAL & WESTERN AFRICA 32,000

KENYA 57,600

SOMALIA 50,900

OTHER SOUTH & EASTERN AFRICA 81,400

ZIMBABWE 11,200

SOUTH AFRICA 30,300

Oceania

AUSTRALIA 16,700

Other Oceania 1,300

NEW ZEALAND 10,300

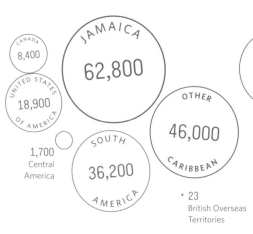

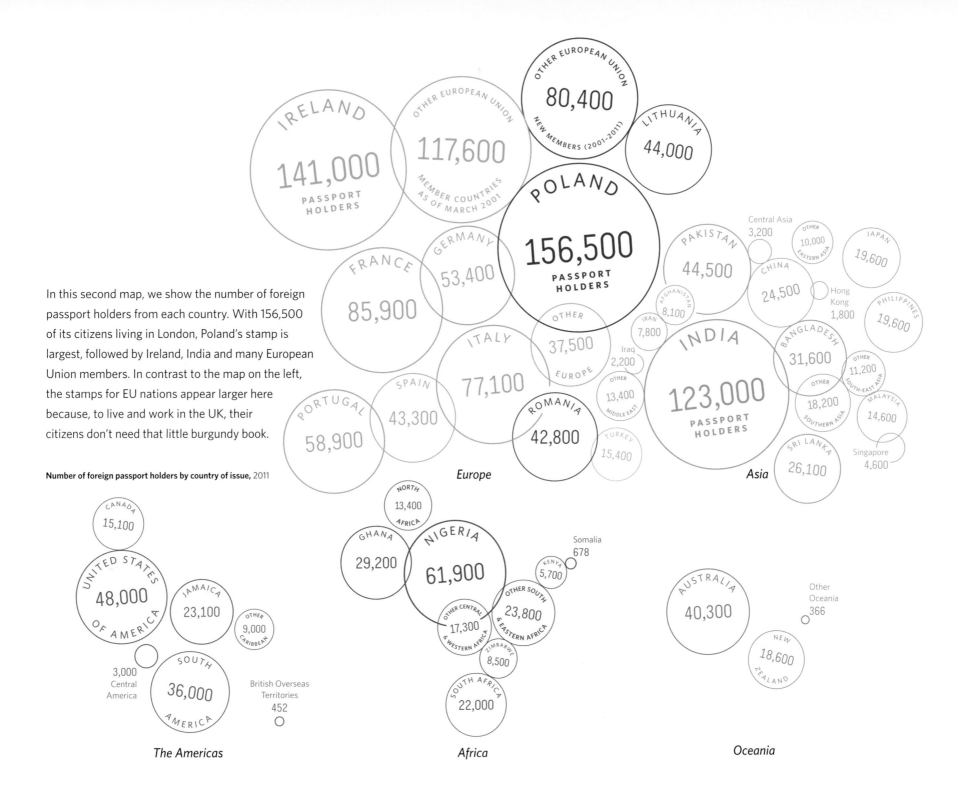

In this second map, we show the number of foreign passport holders from each country. With 156,500 of its citizens living in London, Poland's stamp is largest, followed by Ireland, India and many European Union members. In contrast to the map on the left, the stamps for EU nations appear larger here because, to live and work in the UK, their citizens don't need that little burgundy book.

Number of foreign passport holders by country of issue, 2011

IRELAND
141,000
PASSPORT HOLDERS

OTHER EUROPEAN UNION
117,600
MEMBER COUNTRIES AS OF MARCH 2001

OTHER EUROPEAN UNION
80,400
NEW MEMBERS (2001-2011)

LITHUANIA
44,000

POLAND
156,500
PASSPORT HOLDERS

GERMANY
53,400

FRANCE
85,900

OTHER
37,500
EUROPE

ITALY
77,100

SPAIN
43,300

PORTUGAL
58,900

ROMANIA
42,800

OTHER
13,400
MIDDLE EAST

TURKEY
15,400

Iraq
2,200

Iran
7,800

AFGHANISTAN
8,100

PAKISTAN
44,500

CHINA
24,500

Central Asia
3,200

OTHER
10,000
EASTERN ASIA

JAPAN
19,600

Hong Kong
1,800

PHILIPPINES
19,600

INDIA
123,000
PASSPORT HOLDERS

BANGLADESH
31,600

OTHER
18,200
SOUTHERN ASIA

OTHER
11,200
SOUTH-EAST ASIA

MALAYSIA
14,600

SRI LANKA
26,100

Singapore
4,600

Europe

Asia

CANADA
15,100

UNITED STATES OF AMERICA
48,000

JAMAICA
23,100

OTHER
9,000
CARIBBEAN

3,000
Central America

SOUTH AMERICA
36,000

British Overseas Territories
452

The Americas

NORTH AFRICA
13,400

GHANA
29,200

NIGERIA
61,900

Somalia
678

KENYA
5,700

OTHER CENTRAL & WESTERN AFRICA
17,300

OTHER SOUTH & EASTERN AFRICA
23,800

ZIMBABWE
8,500

SOUTH AFRICA
22,000

Africa

AUSTRALIA
40,300

Other Oceania
366

NEW ZEALAND
18,600

Oceania

SOURCE: 2011 CENSUS, ONS

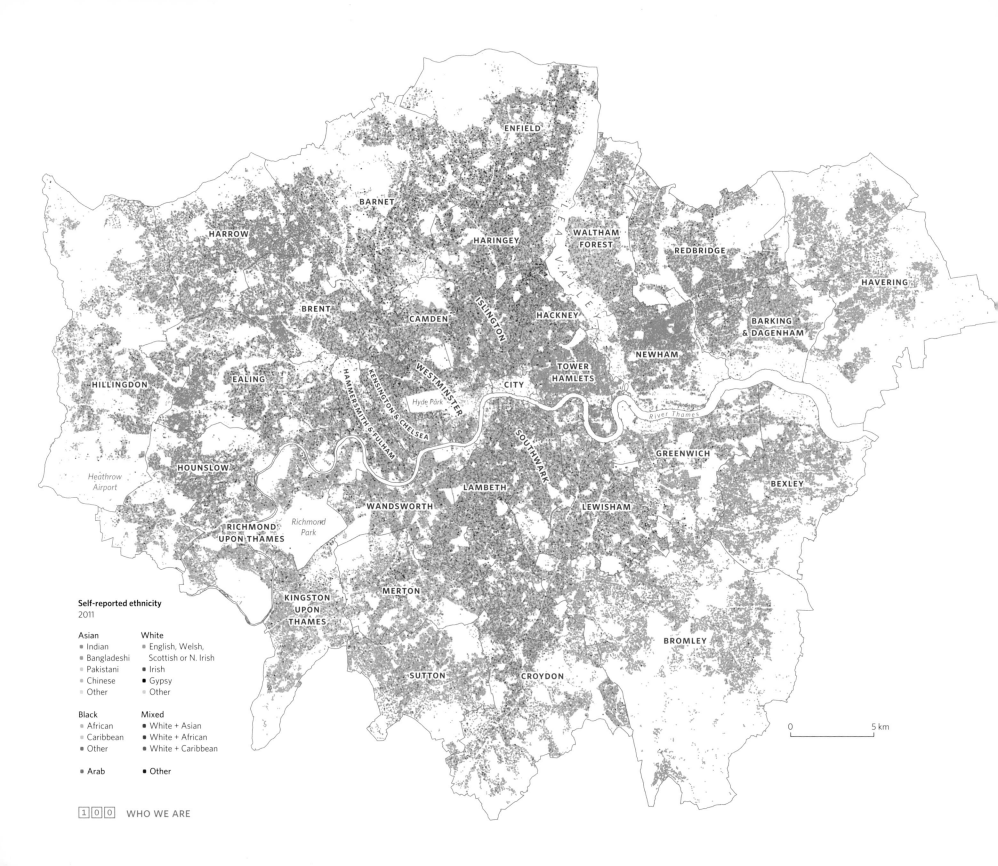

ENFIELD

BARNET

HARROW

HARINGEY

WALTHAM FOREST

REDBRIDGE

HAVERING

BRENT

CAMDEN

ISLINGTON

HACKNEY

LEA VALLEY

BARKING & DAGENHAM

NEWHAM

WESTMINSTER

HILLINGDON

EALING

HAMMERSMITH & FULHAM

KENSINGTON & CHELSEA

Hyde Park

CITY

TOWER HAMLETS

River Thames

GREENWICH

HOUNSLOW

BEXLEY

RICHMOND UPON THAMES

Richmond Park

WANDSWORTH

LAMBETH

SOUTHWARK

LEWISHAM

Heathrow Airport

KINGSTON UPON THAMES

MERTON

BROMLEY

Self-reported ethnicity
2011

Asian
• Indian
• Bangladeshi
• Pakistani
• Chinese
• Other

White
• English, Welsh, Scottish or N. Irish
• Irish
• Gypsy
• Other

Black
• African
• Caribbean
• Other

Mixed
• White + Asian
• White + African
• White + Caribbean

• Arab

• Other

SUTTON

CROYDON

0   5 km

1 0 0   WHO WE ARE

Asian

Bangladeshis cluster
in Tower Hamlets, the
first home for many
migrant communities.

Black

Many of the Jamaican
migrants who sailed in
on the *Empire Windrush*
in 1948 settled in Brixton.

Arab/Other

At the southern end of
Edgware Road you'll find
Lebanese restaurants
and Islamic banks.

White

Mixed

EthniCity

Few cities can match London's ethnic diversity.

This isn't a colour blindness test. But in a way it
could be. Fewer than 45% of Londoners consider
themselves 'White British'. Some see this statistic
as a symptom of unregulated immigration; others
see it as proof that London is and has always been
a global city. Whatever your views, there is no doubt
that generations of migrants – Irish, Jewish, Indian,
Jamaican and Polish, to name just a few – have helped
shape the city we know today.

Using data from the 2011 Census, we have counted
the number of people per self-reported ethnic group
across 25,270 small areas (each of which is home
to around 250 people). We then scattered coloured
dots within each of these areas for every twenty
people or so of the same ethnicity. Places with lots
of different coloured dots are therefore more diverse.
Patterns emerge where communities have developed
along with the amenities that serve them, such as
places of worship, specialist food shops and schools.
These in turn attract more people who value them.
In the smaller maps, we highlight some of these
communities. Those who identified themselves as
Asian tend to span from east to west, and as Black,
north to south. Unlike colour blindness, none of these
patterns are permanent. Londoners are often on the
move, so this map will never look the same again.

Counting the Invisible

In 2012, one researcher set out to document people the census couldn't see.

Over the course of a year, Shlomit Flint, a researcher at University College London, walked the streets of Whitechapel to better understand how the microdynamics of this one small, multicultural neighbourhood might influence the global city.

The 2011 Census counted about 9,000 individuals in this area. To her, that figure sounded low. So she went door-to-door from sunrise to well-past sunset, conducting a census of her own. In total, she visited 4,269 families in 47 community buildings and 1,615 privately owned flats. Having spent five years learning Arabic and Bengali to prepare for this survey, Flint gradually became part of the community. She met with local leaders, visited mosques and brought her children to the playground. In the end, she had tallied 13,000 individuals, 4,000 more than the official census. 'They think that they cover everything,' says Flint. 'I know that they only cover 70%.'

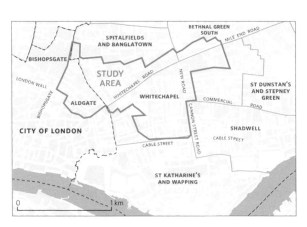

Just east of the City's wall, Whitechapel was transformed from a rural road to the bowels of Dickensian London and then to a 21st-century melting pot. With an influx of Eastern Europeans, it may be transforming yet again.

Self-reported ethnicity of families interviewed, 2012

- White British
- European Union members (pre-2001)
- E.U. accession countries (since 2001)
- Europe (other)
- Middle Eastern
- East Asian
- South Asian
- African
- Caribbean

1995

2,643 families* ■ = 1 family

2012

4,269 families

*There aren't more flats now then twenty years ago, so why are there so many more families? 'First, it's the overcrowding,' says Flint. 'In the area I examined, 40% are undocumented. In a flat that's supposed to have one family, they have actually 20 or 30 individuals.'

There were also fewer unknowns in 2012. To estimate how many families lived in the area in 1995, Flint asked the current tenants to remember from whom they bought their flat. But it wasn't always easy to determine who lived where in 1995.

WORD OF MOUTH

More than 80% of the tenants interviewed found their flats through word of mouth from family or a friend. South Asians and Africans were most likely to choose a place because of its neighbours rather than its price. 'It's very important for them to keep a separation of identity,' says Flint, 'and to live among their friends.'

Motives for choosing a flat by self-identified ethnicity, 2012

Greetings From London

You say hello. I say cześć.

London boasts over 300 different spoken languages – more than any other city in the world. The capital's *lingua franca,* of course, remains English: 78% of Londoners cited it as their 'main' language in the 2011 Census. The other 22% speak in different tongues, including Urdu, Somali and Tagalog. We celebrate the city's linguistic diversity by mapping how you'd say 'hello' in the most frequently spoken languages aside from English. Each 'hello' has been scaled to show the percentage of people in each area who use it. Bengali is now the third most spoken language in the capital, behind Polish. So next time you are heading east of the City, give *salaam* a try, or *hola* south of the river. You might just get a *labas* or *olá* in return.

LANGUAGE FAMILIES

Romance	Germanic	Balto-Slavic	Indo-Aryan	Iranian	Other	
bonjour French	guten tag German	**labas** Lithuanian	**salaam** Bengali	dorood Persian/Farsi	marhaban Arabic	ni hao Chinese
ciao Italian	hej Swedish	**cześć** Polish	**kem cho** Gujarati	Hindus who speak Bengali say *nômoshkar;* Muslims who speak Punjabi say *salaam.*	shalom Hebrew	konnichiwa Japanese
olá Portuguese	sholem aleykhem Yiddish	**privet** Russian	**namaste** Hindi & Nepalese		kamusta Tagalog/Filipino	**anyoung haseyo** Korean
salut Romanian	**Albanian**	**Hellenic**	**sat sri akal** Punjabi		**vanakkam** Tamil	haye Somali
hola Spanish	**përshëndetje** Albanian	**geia sou** Greek	**assalam-o-alekum** Urdu		**merhaba** Turkish	**kaabo** Yoruba

It is rare for a language to have only one way to say hello. We have done our best to match levels of formality and reflect the most popular usage. If in doubt, just say hi!

Percentage of people specifying this as their main language, 2011

hello | hello | hello | hello

5%   10   20

River Thames

Twitter Ink

London's online and offline worlds blend into one.

Each of the 9.4 million tweets splattered across this map tells us two things: the location from where it was sent and the home town of the person who sent it. Many of these 140-character messages were sent by visitors from countries such as Turkey or Italy. We know this because Twitter users have the option of sharing their location every time they post a message. If most of the messages in a user's account were sent from Rome, we assumed this to be their 'home'.

Tweets from international tweeters fill the air in the city centre, where visitors admire London's landmarks or do business in the City. Middle-eastern restaurants along Edgware Road light up with tweets from Kuwaitis while passengers on Turkish Airlines speckle Heathrow's Terminals 3 and 5. Grey tweets trace the path of London's railways as British commuters take to Twitter to complain of delays or to announce their arrival in the capital.

WEMBLEY

A40

EALING

TRAINS TO PADDINGTON

M4

A4

Terminals 1-3

Terminal 5

Heathrow Airport

Terminal 4

Tweets by home country
September 2012 – November 2013

- Saudi Arabia
- Kuwait
- Turkey
- Spain
- France
- Italy
- United States
- UK
- Other

Each dot represents a single tweet. Users who tweeted multiple times created multiple dots on the map. All are coloured by their home countries.

CAMDEN

London
Zoo

Regent's Park

Euston
Station

HOXTON

KINGSLAND ROAD

HOLLOWAY ROAD

Westfield
Stratford City

Victoria Park

OLD STREET

EDGWARE ROAD

TRAINS TO PADDINGTON

British
Museum

MILE END ROAD

TRAINS TO FENCHURCH STREET

MARYLEBONE

Paddington
Station

Marble
Arch

OXFORD STREET

SOHO

St Paul's
Cathedral

CITY OF LONDON

LIMEHOUSE

MAYFAIR

STRAND

NOTTING
HILL

Hyde Park

Tower
of London

Canary
Wharf

Westfield
London

*Kensington
Gardens*

*Green
Park*

*St James's
Park*

London
Eye

Tate
Modern

London
Bridge
Station

*Holland
Park*

Buckingham
Palace

Houses of
Parliament

ISLE OF DOGS

Earl's Court
Exhibition Building

Victoria
Station

Elephant
and Castle

TRAINS TO LONDON BRIDGE STATION

*River
Thames*

SOUTH
KENSINGTON

CHELSEA

KING'S ROAD

GREENWICH

*Battersea
Park*

OLD KENT ROAD

TRAINS TO VICTORIA STATION

*Greenwich
Park*

PUTNEY

Clapham Junction
Station

BRIXTON

0   3 km

SOURCES: ALISTAIR LEAK AND MUHAMMAD ADNAN, UNIVERSITY COLLEGE LONDON; TWITTER

Who London Inspired

From Mozart to Lenin, blue plaques commemorate those who called the city home.

Years before he took up painting, Vincent van Gogh came to London. He lived in Lambeth and worked at his uncle's gallery near the Strand. In a letter to his brother Theo, he said, 'I used to pass Westminster Bridge every morning and every evening and know how it looks when the sun sets behind Westminster Abbey and the Houses of Parliament.' Though he stayed only two years, the city left an impression. He returned at age 23 to teach Sunday school in Isleworth. One night after a long walk home, he wrote to Theo: 'I wished you could have seen those London streets when the twilight began to fall and the lamps were lit.'

To honour the influence the city has had on some of history's great minds, English Heritage and its predecessors have installed more than 900 blue clay roundels on buildings where they once lived or worked. As we show on the lifelines to the right, many like van Gogh went on to create defining works after walking 'those London streets'.

ARE YOU WORTHY?
The Blue Plaques Panel reviews about a hundred nominations a year. To be eligible, you must either be 100 years old or have been dead for twenty years. And:

- have resided in London
- be regarded as 'eminent' by a majority of your professional peers
- have made an important positive contribution to human welfare
  OR
- be so famous that a 'well-informed passer-by' recognizes your name

All of the above may not apply to **Vladimir Lenin** who lived here at 36 Tavistock Place in 1908, fourteen years before founding the Soviet Union.

The first blue plaque went up in 1867 at the birthplace of the poet **Lord Byron**, 24 Holles Street, where he lived until he was three. The house and plaque were torn down in 1889.

100 Londoners commemorated with blue plaques

— Lifespan
— Period in London as noted on the plaque
● Age when the listed noteable works were created, discovered or achieved

Jimi Hendrix and **Handel** both lived at 23 Brook Street. Said Hendrix, 'I didn't even know this was Handel's pad. And, to tell you God's honest truth, I haven't heard much of the fella's stuff.'

EDWARD
D. H. LAWREN
JAMES CLERK MAXW
ELIZABETH BROWNIN
CHARLES DARWIN
SYLVIA PLATH
IAN FLEMING — DADDY
ALEXANDER POPE — CASINO ROYALE
SIR ALFRED HITCHCOCK — THE RAPE OF THE LOCK
SIMON BOLIVAR — REAR WINDOW
AMY JOHNSON — GRAN COLOMBIA
RANDOLPH CALDECOTT — SOLO FLIGHT RECORD, LONDON TO CAPE TOWN
JIMI HENDRIX — THE HOUSE THAT JACK BUILT
VIRGINIA WOOLF — ARE YOU EXPERIENCED?
JOHN SNOW — MRS DALLOWAY
CHARLES DICKENS — CHOLERA MAP
RUDYARD KIPLING — A TALE OF TWO CITIES
EZRA POUND — JUNGLE BOOK
JOHN KEATS — IN A STATION OF THE METRO
ALDOUS HUXLEY — TO AUTUMN
SAMUEL MORSE — BRAVE NEW WORLD
VINCENT van GOGH — MORSE CODE
PERCY SHELLEY — STARRY NIGHT
MAHATMA GANDHI — ADONAIS
BENJAMIN BRITTEN — DANDI SALT MARCH
MICHAEL FARADAY — PETER GRIMES
SIR JOSEPH WILLIAM BAZALGETTE — ELECTROMAGNETIC FIELD
SIR ERNEST SHACKLETON — LONDON'S SEWERS
WOLFGANG A. MOZART — BRITISH ANTARCTIC EXPEDITION
— THE MAGIC FLUTE
JOHN RUSKIN — MODERN PAINTERS
EVELYN WAUGH — VILE BODIES
ROBERT BADEN-POWELL — SCOUTING FOR BOYS
HENRY GRAY — GRAY'S ANATOMY
W. B. YEATS — THE TOWER
ALAN TURING — TURING TEST
LORD BYRON — CHILDE HAROLD'S PILGRAMAGE

80 years old   70   60   50

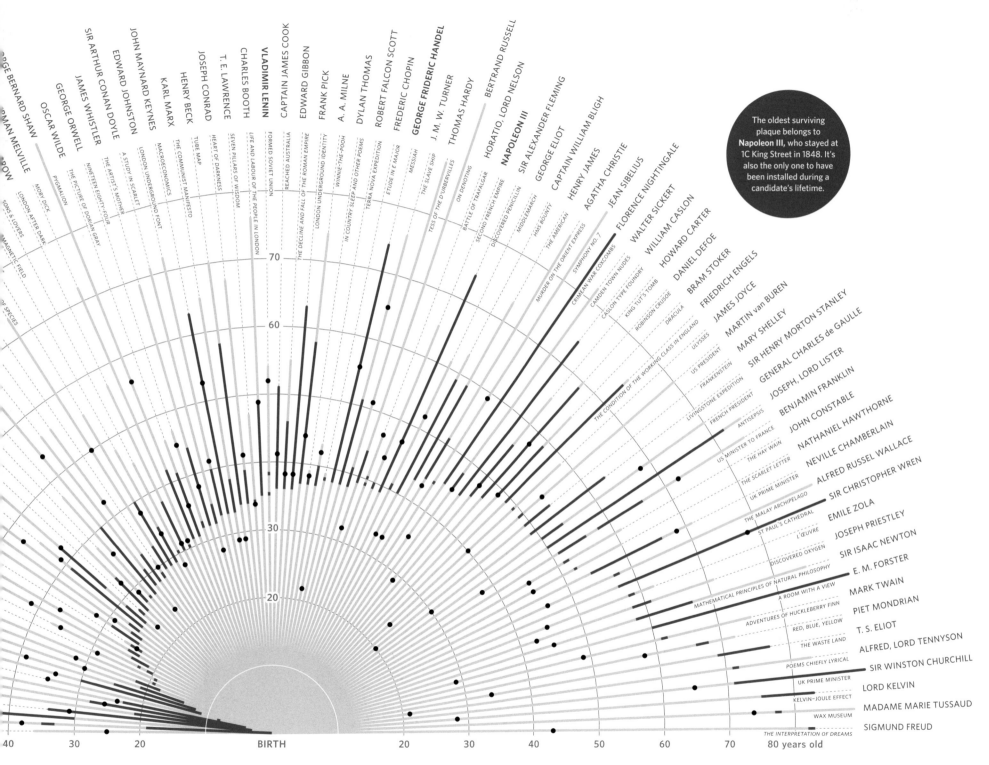

The oldest surviving plaque belongs to **Napoleon III**, who stayed at 1C King Street in 1848. It's also the only one to have been installed during a candidate's lifetime.

GEORGE BERNARD SHAW
HERMAN MELVILLE
BOW

OSCAR WILDE
GEORGE ORWELL
JAMES WHISTLER
SIR ARTHUR CONAN DOYLE
EDWARD JOHNSTON
JOHN MAYNARD KEYNES
KARL MARX
HENRY BECK
JOSEPH CONRAD
T. E. LAWRENCE
CHARLES BOOTH
VLADIMIR LENIN
CAPTAIN JAMES COOK
EDWARD GIBBON
FRANK PICK
A. A. MILNE
DYLAN THOMAS
ROBERT FALCON SCOTT
FREDERIC CHOPIN
GEORGE FRIDERIC HANDEL
J. M. W. TURNER
THOMAS HARDY
BERTRAND RUSSELL
HORATIO, LORD NELSON
NAPOLEON III
SIR ALEXANDER FLEMING
GEORGE ELIOT
CAPTAIN WILLIAM BLIGH
HENRY JAMES
AGATHA CHRISTIE
JEAN SIBELIUS

SONS & LOVERS
LONDON AFTER DARK
MAGNETIC FIELD
OF SPECIES
MOBY DICK
PYGMALION
THE PICTURE OF DORIAN GRAY
NINETEEN EIGHTY-FOUR
THE ARTIST'S MOTHER
A STUDY IN SCARLET
LONDON UNDERGROUND FONT
MACROECONOMICS
THE COMMUNIST MANIFESTO
TUBE MAP
HEART OF DARKNESS
SEVEN PILLARS OF WISDOM
LIFE AND LABOUR OF THE PEOPLE IN LONDON
FORMED SOVIET UNION
THE DECLINE AND FALL OF THE ROMAN EMPIRE
REACHED AUSTRALIA
LONDON UNDERGROUND IDENTITY
WINNIE-THE-POOH
IN COUNTRY SLEEP AND OTHER POEMS
TERRA NOVA EXPEDITION
ETUDE IN E MAJOR
MESSIAH
THE SLAVE SHIP
TESS OF THE D'URBERVILLES
ON DENOTING
BATTLE OF TRAFALGAR
SECOND FRENCH EMPIRE
DISCOVERED PENICILLIN
MIDDLEMARCH
HMS BOUNTY
THE AMERICAN
MURDER ON THE ORIENT EXPRESS
SYMPHONY NO. 7

70
60
30
20
BIRTH

40   30   20   20   30   40   50   60   70   80 years old

FLORENCE NIGHTINGALE
WALTER SICKERT
WILLIAM CASLON
HOWARD CARTER
DANIEL DEFOE
BRAM STOKER
FRIEDRICH ENGELS
JAMES JOYCE
MARTIN van BUREN
MARY SHELLEY
SIR HENRY MORTON STANLEY
GENERAL CHARLES de GAULLE
JOSEPH, LORD LISTER
BENJAMIN FRANKLIN
JOHN CONSTABLE
NATHANIEL HAWTHORNE
NEVILLE CHAMBERLAIN
ALFRED RUSSEL WALLACE
SIR CHRISTOPHER WREN
EMILE ZOLA
JOSEPH PRIESTLEY
SIR ISAAC NEWTON
E. M. FORSTER
MARK TWAIN
PIET MONDRIAN
T. S. ELIOT
ALFRED, LORD TENNYSON
SIR WINSTON CHURCHILL
LORD KELVIN
MADAME MARIE TUSSAUD
SIGMUND FREUD

CRIMEAN WAR COXCOMBS
CAMDEN TOWN NUDES
CASLON TYPE FOUNDRY
KING TUT'S TOMB
ROBINSON CRUSOE
DRACULA
THE CONDITION OF THE WORKING CLASS IN ENGLAND
ULYSSES
US PRESIDENT
FRANKENSTEIN
LIVINGSTONE EXPEDITION
FRENCH PRESIDENT
ANTISEPSIS
US MINISTER TO FRANCE
THE HAY WAIN
THE SCARLET LETTER
UK PRIME MINISTER
THE MALAY ARCHIPELAGO
ST PAUL'S CATHEDRAL
L'ŒUVRE
DISCOVERED OXYGEN
MATHEMATICAL PRINCIPLES OF NATURAL PHILOSOPHY
A ROOM WITH A VIEW
ADVENTURES OF HUCKLEBERRY FINN
RED, BLUE, YELLOW
THE WASTE LAND
POEMS CHIEFLY LYRICAL
UK PRIME MINISTER
KELVIN–JOULE EFFECT
WAX MUSEUM
THE INTERPRETATION OF DREAMS

SOURCES: *LIVED IN LONDON*, EMILY COLE; OPENPLAQUES.ORG; WIKIPEDIA. PHOTO: OLIVER UBERTI

WHERE WE GO

Twitter Trips

Londoners go global.

Tweeting Londoners have become one of the city's truly 21st-century exports. Here we show where 120,000 of them went between September 2012 and November 2013. We defined London tweeters as those who typically send most of their messages from within the Greater London Authority boundary. As they travelled abroad for business or pleasure, they stayed connected to share adventures in 140-character bursts. Each tweet added to the arcs on this map. These globetrotters made it to 3,600 places, including Rome, Dubai, Las Vegas and Disney World.

The tweets shown here are but a sample of the millions posted by Londoners. We omitted spambots and users who only sent a couple of messages. Of the remainder, not all had accurate location information, so these were also removed.

Number of Twitter users
September 2012 – November 2013

——— More than 1,000
——— 101–1,000
——— 11–100
——— 2–10

SOURCES: ALISTAIR LEAK AND MUHAMMAD ADNAN, UNIVERSITY COLLEGE LONDON; TWITTER

NORTH AMERICA

Seattle

New York

Las Vegas

Dallas

Orlando

Honolulu

Mexico City

EQUATOR

PACIFIC

OCEAN

SOUTH AMERICA

Buenos Aires

Glasgow
Belfast
London
Berlin
EUROPE
Milan
Rome
Ibiza
Málaga
Canary
Islands

ASIA

Tokyo
Shanghai
Dubai
Hong Kong
Jeddah
AFRICA

Lagos

Singapore

ATLANTIC

OCEAN

INDIAN

OCEAN

AUSTRALIA

Cape Town

Not all lines go through
London because some
tweeters visited multiple
cities while travelling.

Sydney
Melbourne
Auckland

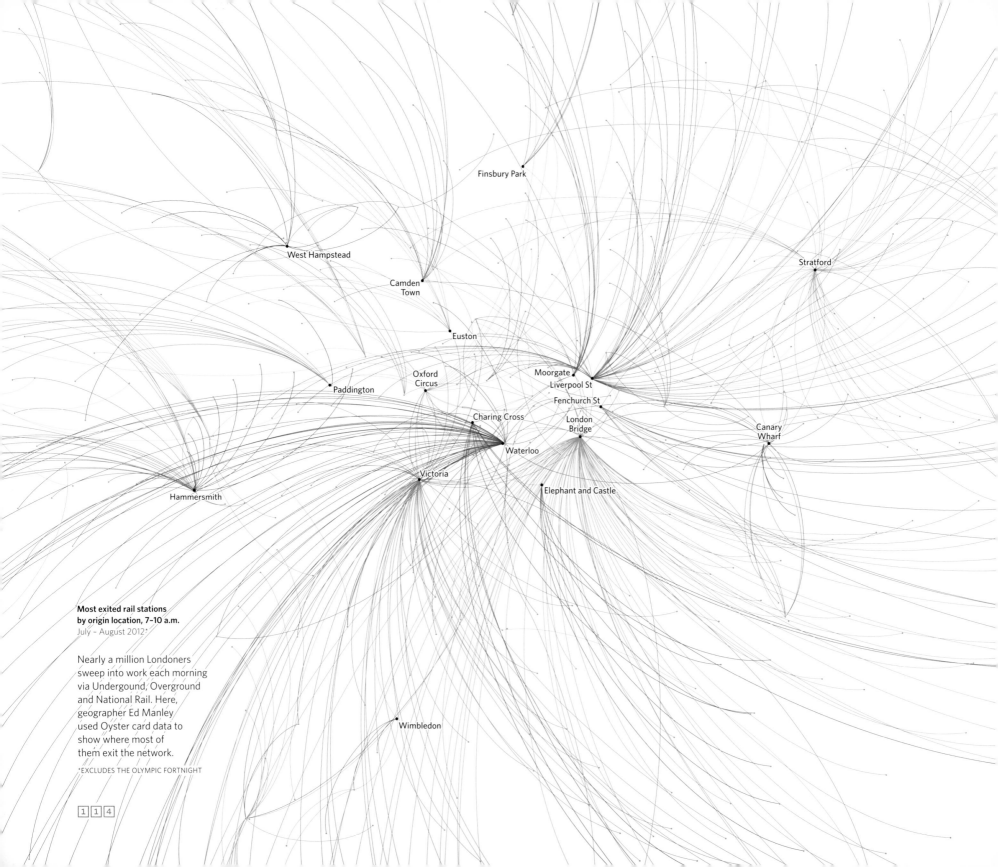

West Hampstead

Stratford

Camden
Town

Finsbury Park

Euston

Oxford
Circus

Moorgate
Liverpool St

Paddington

Fenchurch St

Charing Cross

Canary
Wharf

London
Bridge

Waterloo

Victoria

Elephant and Castle

Hammersmith

**Most exited rail stations
by origin location, 7–10 a.m.**
July – August 2012*

Nearly a million Londoners
sweep into work each morning
via Undergound, Overground
and National Rail. Here,
geographer Ed Manley
used Oyster card data to
show where most of
them exit the network.

*EXCLUDES THE OLYMPIC FORTNIGHT

Wimbledon

There is order and beauty in the chaos of your commute

Barking

Almost every journey taken in London leaves a digital trace in its wake. Flights are tracked, travel cards logged and minicabs monitored. It may be hard to appreciate as you squeeze onto a Tube or bus in the morning, but you are one of millions adding to the beauty of the currents captured in the following pages.

Take this graphic, for example. Geographer Ed Manley at University College London's Centre for Advanced Spatial Analysis used Oyster card data to trace 48.9 million morning commutes. He drew arcs between all of London's Underground, Overground and National Rail stations and their most popular destinations. Giving each destination a colour illustrates interdependencies between regions. For example, most traffic south of the Thames flows into only three stations: Waterloo, Victoria and London Bridge. Meanwhile, in the City's financial district, Liverpool Street and Fenchurch Street stations attract commuters from the eastern suburbs.

Looking at these city-wide flows, the transport system certainly appears

predictable. There's a fixed number of stations, a known number of trains and decent estimates of the likely number of passengers. Zoom into stations, however, and things become much more turbulent. People wrestle through barriers, down escalators, onto platforms and into trains. At this level, individual decisions count. If the same decision is made by thousands of people simultaneously – to bypass a delay on the Central line via the Piccadilly, for example – the entire network can feel the impact. While it may never be possible to predict the next signal failure or bus breakdown, we can explore the data from past service disruptions to anticipate how people will react in the future.

Think of all this commuter data like the River Thames. As it courses through the city, its flow is monitored at control centres around the capital. Transport for London (TfL) alone logs 24 million journeys a day across its network. Their controllers, planners and researchers aren't drowning; they're learning how to swim. For the first time, they can truly immerse themselves and develop ways to make our trains more reliable, our cyclists safer and, ultimately, our commutes faster.

TfL's biggest challenge, however, is keeping pace with demand. Technologies already exist to accommodate a million new commuters; you just need double-decker trains and longer station platforms. The problem is, these things can't be implemented without re-digging the entire Underground network. Crossrail may be the largest construction project in Europe (see pp. 56–7), but it will only increase rail transport capacity by 10%. With London's population growing 12% in ten years (see p. 78), the great hope is that data will allow 21st-century London to work better with what its steam-minded forebears laid down centuries ago.

Untangled On Arrival

The longest queues in London form overhead.

With 1,500 flights from more than 300 destinations arriving each day, aircraft contrails tie a giant bow over the city. Don't let this knotted appearance fool you. At Heathrow Airport, precise choreography guides a plane onto the tarmac every 150 seconds.

As they land, planes give off swirling 'wake turbulence'. Larger planes can handle flying through it, but smaller ones must wait for it to subside. In a perfect world, planes would arrive in order of size, smallest to largest. They don't, so air traffic controllers pace out incoming flights in circular holding patterns above London called 'stacks'. Four of the city's eight – Bovingdon, Lambourne, Ockham and Biggin Hill – service Heathrow exclusively. To see them up close, turn the page.

FI 450
Reykjavik to Heathrow

IRELAND

SHANNON

DL 618
Detroit to Heathrow

Arriving flights
22–23 August 2013

ATLANTIC

OCEAN

VS 64
Havana to Gatwick

Europe
North America
Asia
Africa
South America & the Caribbean
Oceania

0   50 km

Celtic Sea

SOURCE: FLIGHTRADAR24.COM

NEWCASTLE UPON TYNE

BELFAST

UNITED
KINGDOM

North Sea

DUBLIN

MANCHESTER

SHEFFIELD

JL 401
Tokyo
to Heathrow

BA 38
Beijing
to Heathrow

*Irish
Sea*

ENGLAND

NORWICH

AMSTERDAM

WALES

THE HAGUE

NETHERLANDS

BA 2
New York to
London City

Luton   *Stansted*

Heathrow   LONDON

NEWPORT

ANTWERP

BELGIUM

AI 111
Delhi
to Heathrow

Gatwick

AREA ENLARGED

BRUSSELS

English Channel

BA 248
Rio de Janeiro
to Heathrow

PARIS

LX 454
Zurich
to London City

FRANCE

BREST

EZY 2092
Ibiza
to Luton

SA 234
Johannesburg
to Heathrow

FI 450
Reykjavik to
Heathrow

BNN
Bovingdon
Stack

LAM
Lambourne
Stack

AI 111
Delhi to
Heathrow

GREATER LONDON
AUTHORITY
BOUNDARY

BA 2
New York to
London City

BA 38
Beijing
to Heathrow

Heathrow
Airport

London City
Airport

River Thames

DL 618
Detroit to
Heathrow

BIG
Biggin Hill
Stack

OCK
Ockham
Stack

BA 248
Rio de Janeiro
to Heathrow

SA 234
Johannesburg
to Heathrow

EZY 2092
Ibiza to
Luton

VS 64
Havana to
Gatwick

Gatwick
Airport

Luton
Airport

Stansted
Airport

JL 401
Tokyo to Heathrow ✈

Southend
Airport

Thames Estuary

Proposed location for
'London Britannia Airport'

Arriving flights
22–23 August 2013

Europe
North America
Asia
Africa
South America & the Caribbean
Oceania

0   10 km

To keep pace with global demand,
Heathrow hopes to build a third
runway. 'It's not about more
tarmac,' they argue. 'It's about
Britain's place in the world.' The
airport is competing with plans
for a bigger airport in the middle
of the Thames Estuary. Supporters say this would clear the skies
over London; critics fear an envi-
ronmental disaster. Either way,
London needs to decide soon if
it wants to remain a 'Hub for the
World' (see pp. 40-41).

LX 454
Zurich
to London City ✈

English Channel

Thames Gateway

The world converges on the city through its estuary.

Now that skyscrapers tower above the cranes on London's docks and wharves, many have forgotten that the Thames was once a gateway to the world. Perhaps for this reason, in January 2006, the sea gods sent Londoners a reminder of their city's nautical ties in the form of a northern bottlenose whale. Just as thousands of ships do each year, the maverick whale navigated the estuary's treacherous sand banks, past its relics of war and Southend's pleasure pier. It could have veered left up the River Medway and into Kent. Instead, it pressed on into the Yantlet Channel and the Thames proper, overtaking enormous container ships as they slowed to dock at Tilbury. Upstream, the Thames becomes too shallow for these 'supercarriers', so the whale was able to continue on alone. Turn the page to follow its journey.

The Port of London Authority covers 95 miles of the River Thames, overseeing the safe passage of thousands of vessels a year that contribute £3.7 billion to the UK economy. In this graphic we show only 24 hours of the action, which still features 334 tracks from ships registered in 26 different countries from Serbia to Hong Kong, Norway to Saint Vincent and the Grenadines.

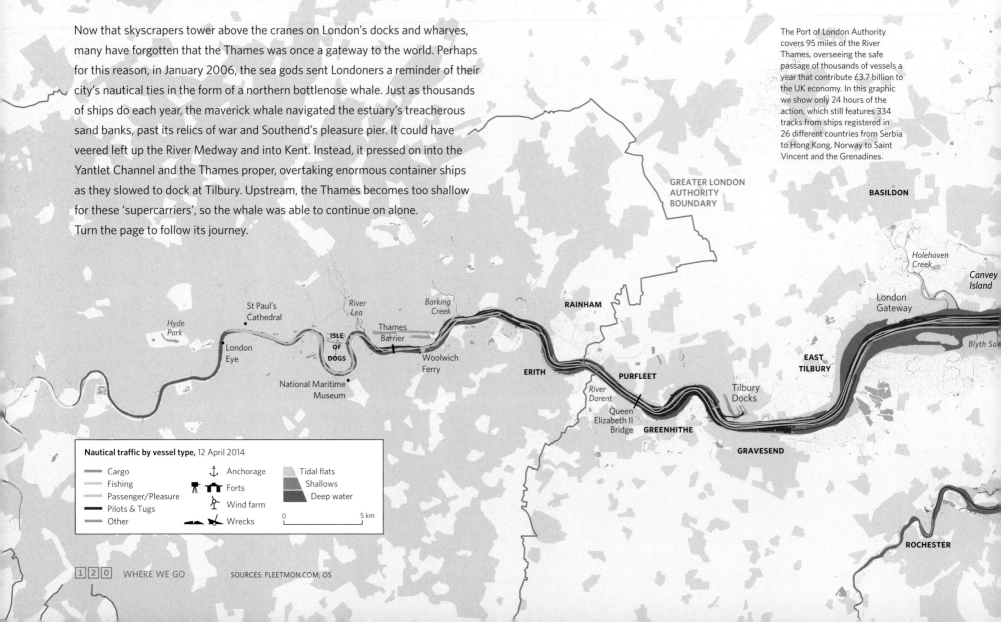

Nautical traffic by vessel type, 12 April 2014

- Cargo
- Fishing
- Passenger/Pleasure
- Pilots & Tugs
- Other

⚓ Anchorage
🏰 Forts
🗼 Wind farm
⛵ Wrecks

Tidal flats
Shallows
Deep water

0 ———— 5 km

SOURCES: FLEETMON.COM; OS

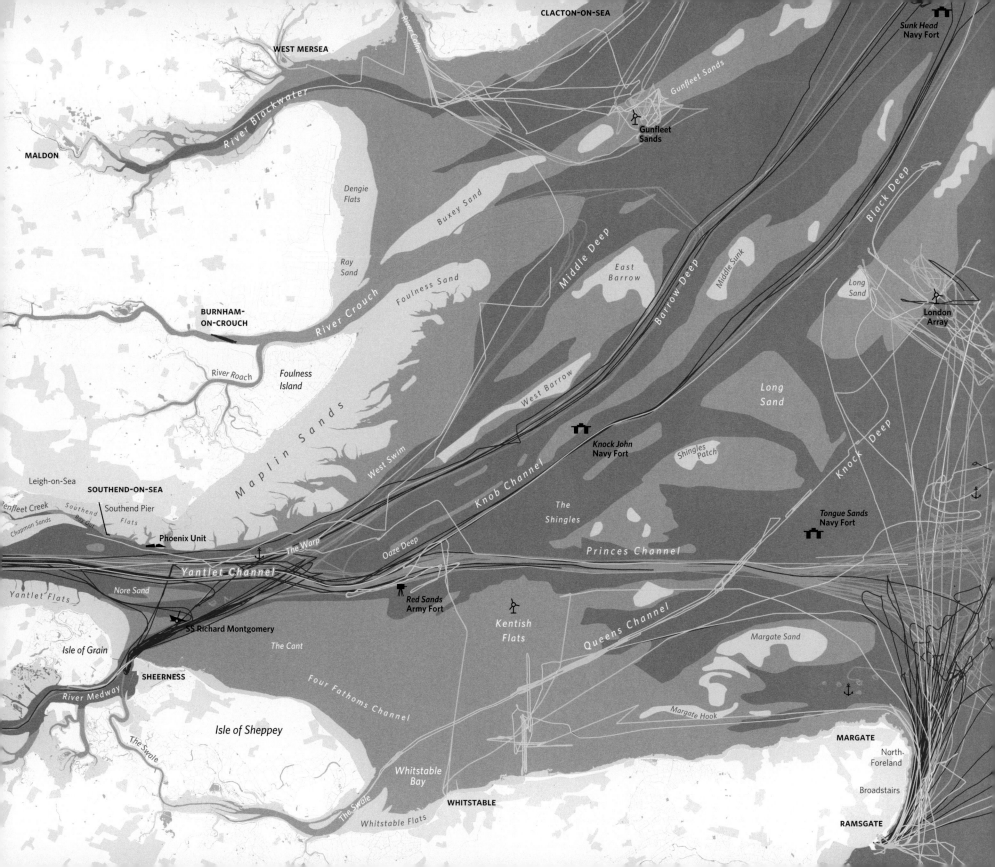

CLACTON-ON-SEA

Sunk Head
Navy Fort

WEST MERSEA

River Colne

Gunfleet Sands

MALDON

River Blackwater

*Dengie
Flats*

Buxey Sand

*Gunfleet
Sands*

Black Deep

Middle Deep

*East
Barrow*

Barrow Deep

Middle Sunk

*Ray
Sand*

Foulness Sand

BURNHAM-
ON-CROUCH

River Crouch

*Long
Sand*

*London
Array*

River Roach

*Foulness
Island*

West Barrow

*Long
Sand*

Maplin Sands

West Swim

Knob Channel

Knock John
Navy Fort

*Shingles
Patch*

Knock Deep

Leigh-on-Sea

SOUTHEND-ON-SEA

The Shingles

Tongue Sands
Navy Fort

Benfleet Creek

*Southend
Bay Gut*

*Southend
Flats*

Southend Pier

Chapman Sands

Phoenix Unit

The Warp

Oaze Deep

Princes Channel

Yantlet Channel

Nore Sand

Yantlet Flats

Red Sands
Army Fort

SS Richard Montgomery

The Cant

*Kentish
Flats*

Queens Channel

Margate Sand

Isle of Grain

SHEERNESS

River Medway

Four Fathoms Channel

Margate Hook

MARGATE

Isle of Sheppey

North-
Foreland

The Swale

*Whitstable
Bay*

Broadstairs

The Swale

WHITSTABLE

Whitstable Flats

RAMSGATE

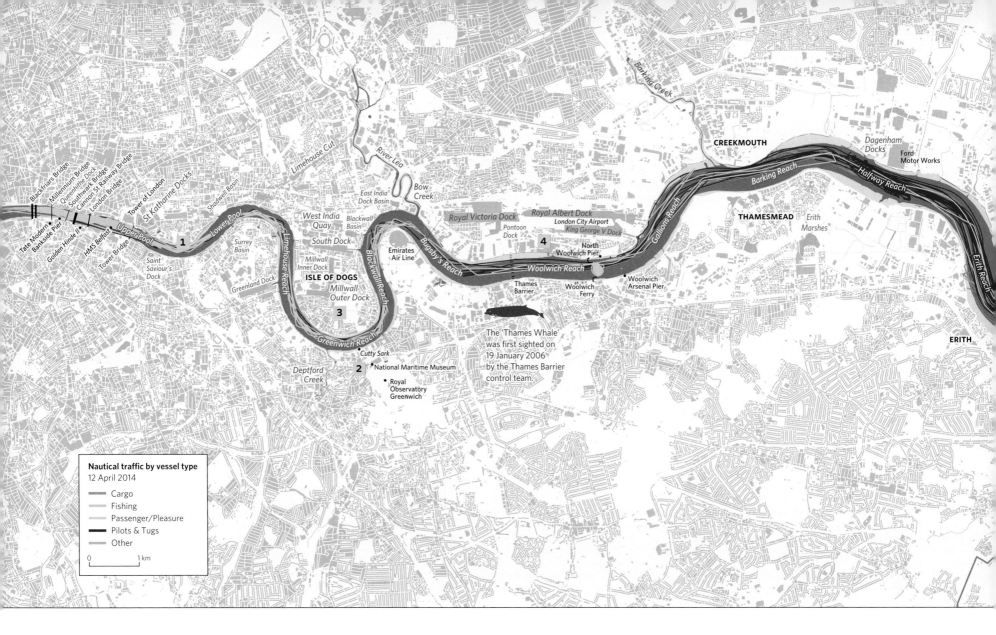

Nautical traffic by vessel type
12 April 2014

— Cargo
— Fishing
— Passenger/Pleasure
— Pilots & Tugs
— Other

0   1 km

The 'Thames Whale'
was first sighted on
19 January 2006
by the Thames Barrier
control team.

As the whale slipped past the Thames Barrier and towards the iconic meander, it swam through what John Burns famously described as 'liquid history'. Whales, or more precisely blubber, kick-started the development of London's first large-scale docks in this area in the 17th century. (Greenland Dock owes its name to the island's whaling seas.) Like the Docklands themselves, attitudes have changed. Thousands lined the river to will the 'Thames Whale' back to sea. Sadly, the whale did not survive, but its bones remain preserved in the Natural History Museum.

1 CRIME AND PUNISHMENT

In 1798 the 'Marine Police Force' was created to deter some 11,000 light-fingered Londoners on London's overcrowded docks. Nearby, the hangman's noose at the infamous 'Execution Dock' was rarely slack. Pirates from all over the world were sent to their deaths here by the British Admiralty. Once killed, they were hung in metal cages called 'gibbets' along the Thames as a warning against piracy.

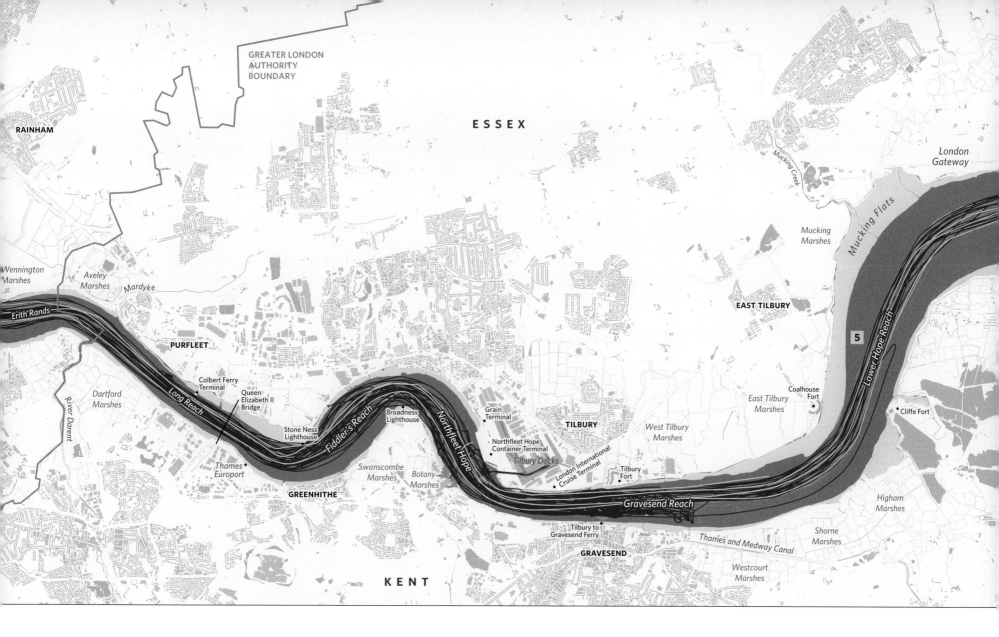

2 GREENWICH

Declared a UNESCO World Heritage site in 1997, London's 'green port' has gone from an invader's encampment to Tudor Palace and then Royal Naval College. Atop a hill in Greenwich Park, the world's east and west hemispheres meet at the Royal Observatory – the source of 'Greenwich Mean Time' and the 'Prime Meridian' – which has been the basis for global navigation systems since 1884.

3 ISLE OF DOGS

Enclosed by the Thames' distinctive meander, this oddly named place is at the heart of the Docklands' transition from boats to banks. Its etymology remains a mystery. Some say it's where Edward III kept his kennels; others cite a corruption of 'Isle of Ducks' or even 'Isle of Hogs' (the Bishop of London kept 5,000 of them there). It might just have been a miserable place to live.

4 TATE AND LYLE

Look closely at a tin of 'Lyle's Golden Syrup' and you will see 'Out of the strong came forth sweetness.' Britain's oldest brand should adapt its biblical motto to 'Out of the Thames came forth sweetness' since the river has been the primary means of importing its ingredients for more than 130 years. Even today, it owns a dock capable of handling 72,000 tons of raw sugar.

5 HOPE REACH

Just as the nomenclature of London's streets can reveal their origins and purpose, so too can the names along the river. This is perhaps most clear from 'Hope Reach', a stretch of the lower Thames where sailors lifted their anchors for the last time before heading out on voyages around the globe.

SOURCE: FLEETMON.COM; OS

MOST USED MODES OF TRANSPORT

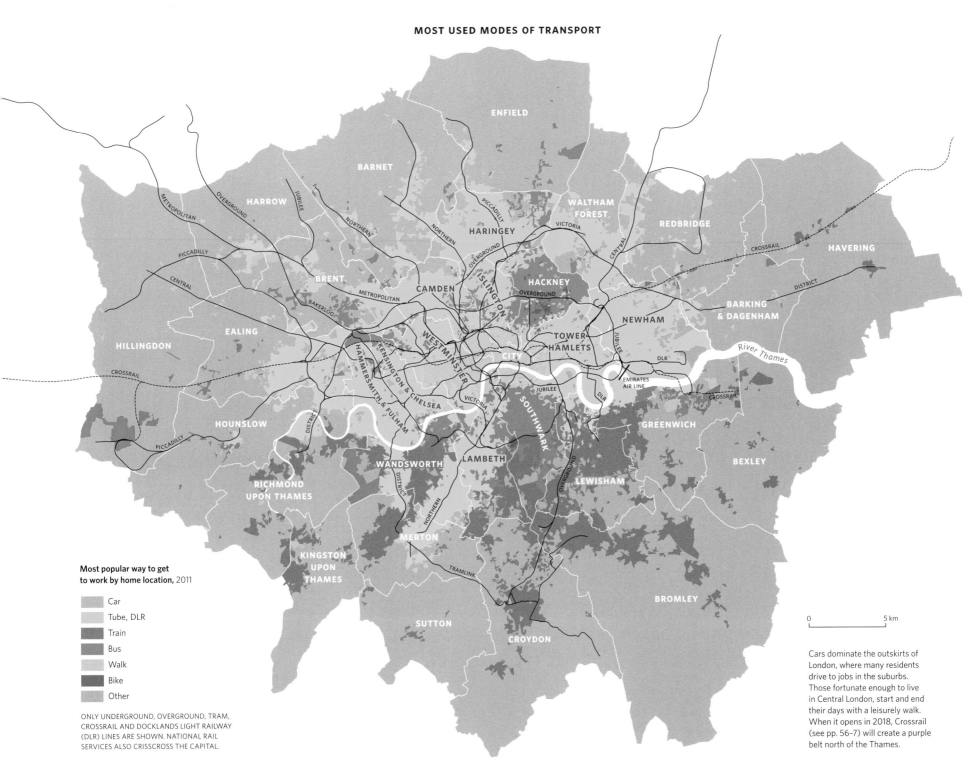

Most popular way to get to work by home location, 2011

- Car
- Tube, DLR
- Train
- Bus
- Walk
- Bike
- Other

ONLY UNDERGROUND, OVERGROUND, TRAM, CROSSRAIL AND DOCKLANDS LIGHT RAILWAY (DLR) LINES ARE SHOWN. NATIONAL RAIL SERVICES ALSO CRISSCROSS THE CAPITAL.

Cars dominate the outskirts of London, where many residents drive to jobs in the suburbs. Those fortunate enough to live in Central London, start and end their days with a leisurely walk. When it opens in 2018, Crossrail (see pp. 56–7) will create a purple belt north of the Thames.

0   5 km

Getting to Work

Where we live colours how we choose to commute.

The Underground may be the best-known way to get around London, but it is not an option for everyone. Few stations exist south of the Thames, where sandy soil made it difficult to dig tunnels. In these areas, most residents say they take cars (blue), trains (purple) and buses (red) to work. Buses are the workhorses of London's transport system. In 2013 alone, riders took 2.4 billion journeys, almost double the number of Tube riders. Price may factor in. Regardless of distance, peak bus fare costs £1.45, half as much as a Tube journey through Central London and a fraction of one through all zones of the network (£5).

SECOND MOST USED

A clear divide emerges when you look at the second most used transport modes. To the north, the Tube is popular while those in the south board trains.

THIRD MOST USED

Buses and bikes speckle the map of London's third most popular transport modes. Some suburbanites leave their keys and Oyster card at home and walk.

SOURCE: 2011 CENSUS, ONS; OLIVER O'BRIEN, UNIVERSITY COLLEGE LONDON (TRANSPORT LINES)

To and Fro, on the Tube

For 150 years, the Underground has helped Londoners connect the dots.

In the 1850s, when Charles Pearson pitched the idea for the world's
first subterranean railway, even he was not so confident as to claim he
was developing a scheme capable of transporting every person in the world,
a sum then estimated at 1.2 billion. Today, this is precisely the number of journeys
taken on the Tube each year. Here we show a sample of 668,000 journeys
by Oyster card users during the first week of November 2009. Thick orange
lines represent the most travelled routes such as King's Cross St Pancras
to London Bridge or Canary Wharf to North Greenwich.

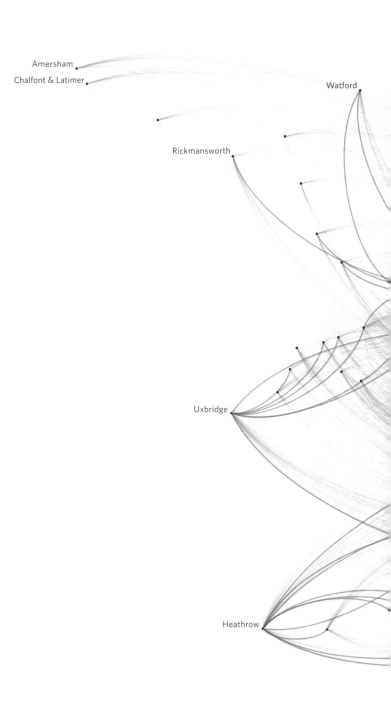

SOURCE: TRANSPORT FOR LONDON

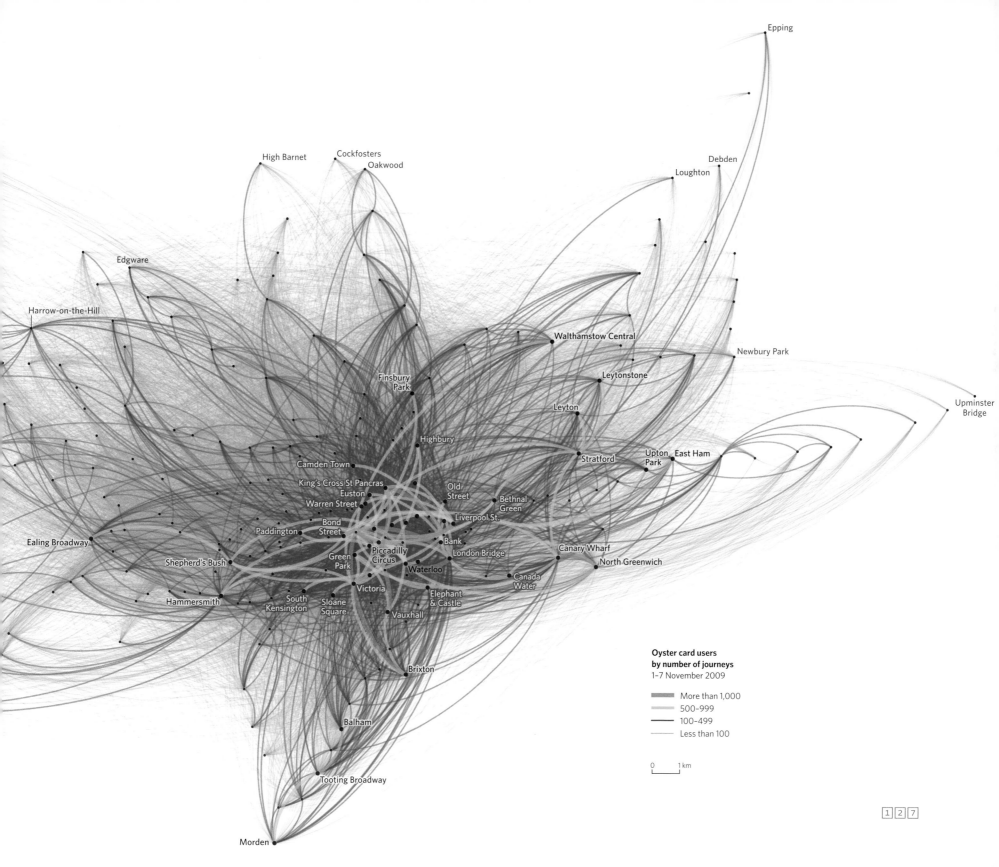

Epping

Cockfosters
High Barnet   Oakwood

Edgware   Loughton
                                                                                    Debden

Harrow-on-the-Hill
                                                                    Walthamstow Central
                                                                                        Newbury Park

                                                Finsbury
                                                Park   Leytonstone
                                                                                            Upminster
                                                                Leyton   Bridge
                                        Highbury

                                Camden Town   Stratford   Upton   East Ham
                                                                                        Park
                        King's Cross St Pancras   Old
                        Euston   Street
                        Warren Street   Bethnal
                                                    Green
                                    Bond   Liverpool St.
Ealing Broadway   Paddington Street   Bank   Canary Wharf
                                                        London Bridge   North Greenwich
            Shepherd's Bush   Green   Piccadilly
                                    Park   Circus
                                            Waterloo   Canada
                                                          Water
        Hammersmith   South   Sloane   Victoria
                            Kensington Square   Elephant
                                            Vauxhall   & Castle

                                                Brixton

Oyster card users
by number of journeys
1–7 November 2009

━━━ More than 1,000
━━━ 500–999
─── 100–499
─── Less than 100

0   1 km
        Balham
├────┤

            Tooting Broadway

Morden

A Week on the Underground

Record-breaking traffic puts the Tube's health to the test.

During the first full week of the 2012 Olympic Games, London Underground broke its all-time ridership record – three times. 4.25 million passengers boarded on Tuesday, followed by 4.3 on Wednesday and 4.4 on Friday. To check the network's vitals, Jon Reades, a geographer at King's College London, administered an electrocardiogram of sorts. The waveforms below represent the number of Oyster card users entering and exiting 258 stations from Sunday 29 July to Saturday 4 August. Stations are grouped and coloured by the lines they serve. His diagnosis? Activity peaked during the morning and evening commutes. Nothing too irregular there other than the volume of people pumping through the system.

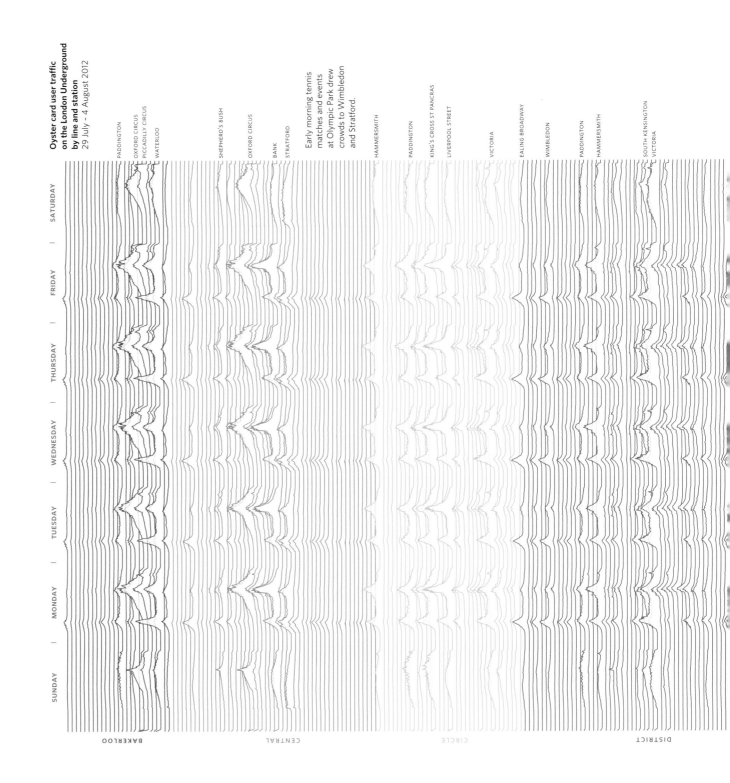

Oyster card user traffic on the London Underground by line and station
29 July – 4 August 2012

SUNDAY | MONDAY | TUESDAY | WEDNESDAY | THURSDAY | FRIDAY | SATURDAY

PADDINGTON
OXFORD CIRCUS
PICCADILLY CIRCUS
WATERLOO

SHEPHERD'S BUSH
OXFORD CIRCUS
BANK
STRATFORD

Early morning tennis matches and events at Olympic Park drew crowds to Wimbledon and Stratford.

HAMMERSMITH
PADDINGTON
KING'S CROSS ST PANCRAS
LIVERPOOL STREET
VICTORIA

EALING BROADWAY
WIMBLEDON
PADDINGTON
HAMMERSMITH
SOUTH KENSINGTON
VICTORIA

BAKERLOO
CENTRAL
CIRCLE
DISTRICT

The Games brought heavy flows into London via railway stations like King's Cross St Pancras, Waterloo and Paddington.

Stations near financial centres like Canary Wharf, Bank and Liverpool Street saw their heartbeats spike on weekdays. By Saturday they slowed to a murmur.

Areas with nightlife such as Piccadilly and Leicester Square experienced a third peak before midnight, especially at the weekend.

PADDINGTON
BAKER STREET
KING'S CROSS ST PANCRAS
LIVERPOOL STREET

BOND STREET
WATERLOO
LONDON BRIDGE
CANARY WHARF
STRATFORD

BAKER STREET
KING'S CROSS ST PANCRAS
LIVERPOOL STREET

WATERLOO
LONDON BRIDGE
BANK
LEICESTER SQUARE
ANGEL
KING'S CROSS ST PANCRAS
CAMDEN TOWN

HAMMERSMITH
SOUTH KENSINGTON
PICCADILLY CIRCUS
LEICESTER SQUARE
HOLBORN
KING'S CROSS ST PANCRAS

KING'S CROSS ST PANCRAS
OXFORD CIRCUS
VICTORIA
WATERLOO

SUNDAY | MONDAY | TUESDAY | WEDNESDAY | THURSDAY | FRIDAY | SATURDAY

HAMMERSMITH & CITY
JUBILEE
METROPOLITAN
NORTHERN
PICCADILLY
VICTORIA
WATERLOO & CITY

SOURCE: TRANSPORT FOR LONDON

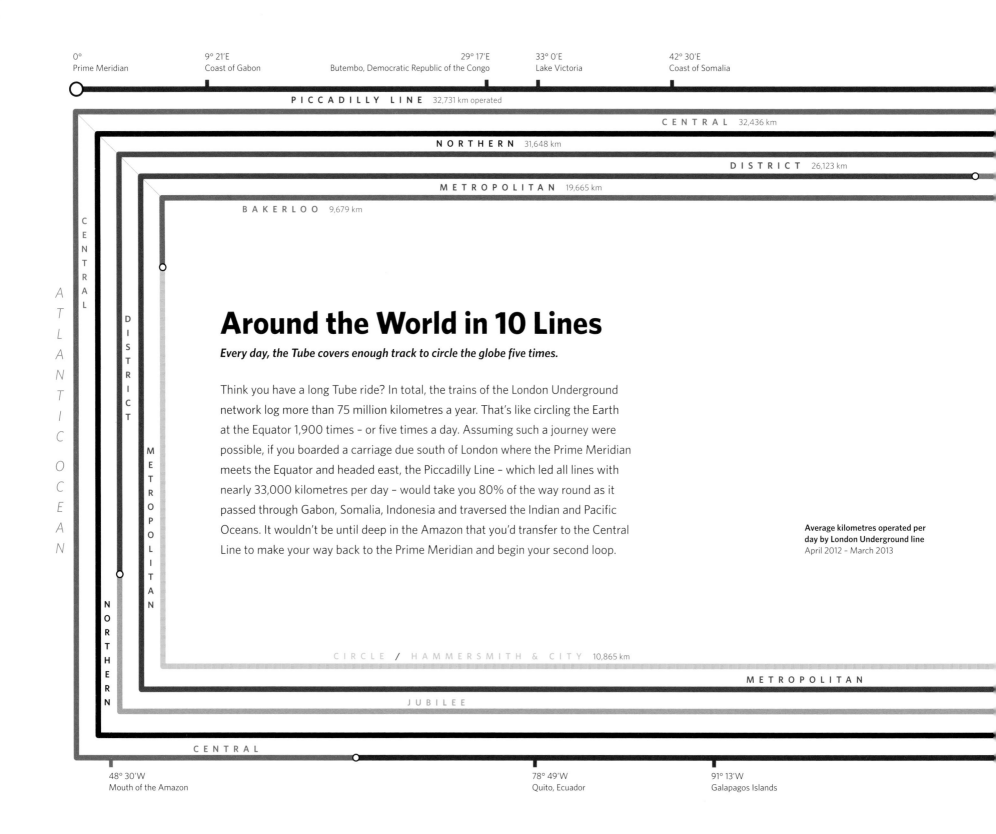

0°
Prime Meridian

9° 21'E
Coast of Gabon

29° 17'E
Butembo, Democratic Republic of the Congo

33° 0'E
Lake Victoria

42° 30'E
Coast of Somalia

PICCADILLY LINE 32,731 km operated

CENTRAL 32,436 km

NORTHERN 31,648 km

DISTRICT 26,123 km

METROPOLITAN 19,665 km

BAKERLOO 9,679 km

A T L A N T I C   O C E A N

C E N T R A L

D I S T R I C T

M E T R O P O L I T A N

N O R T H E R N

Around the World in 10 Lines

Every day, the Tube covers enough track to circle the globe five times.

Think you have a long Tube ride? In total, the trains of the London Underground network log more than 75 million kilometres a year. That's like circling the Earth at the Equator 1,900 times – or five times a day. Assuming such a journey were possible, if you boarded a carriage due south of London where the Prime Meridian meets the Equator and headed east, the Piccadilly Line – which led all lines with nearly 33,000 kilometres per day – would take you 80% of the way round as it passed through Gabon, Somalia, Indonesia and traversed the Indian and Pacific Oceans. It wouldn't be until deep in the Amazon that you'd transfer to the Central Line to make your way back to the Prime Meridian and begin your second loop.

Average kilometres operated per day by London Underground line
April 2012 – March 2013

CIRCLE / HAMMERSMITH & CITY 10,865 km

METROPOLITAN

JUBILEE

CENTRAL

48° 30'W
Mouth of the Amazon

78° 49'W
Quito, Ecuador

91° 13'W
Galapagos Islands

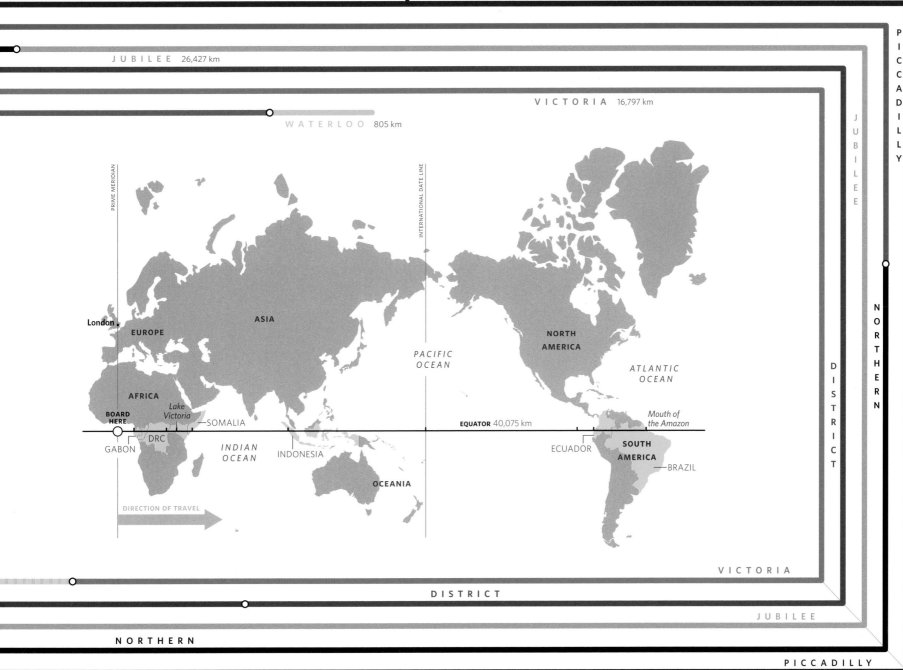

INDIAN OCEAN

98° 12'E
Coast of Indonesia

JUBILEE   26,427 km

VICTORIA   16,797 km

WATERLOO   805 km

PICCADILLY

JUBILEE

PACIFIC OCEAN

NORTHERN

DISTRICT

VICTORIA

JUBILEE

180°
International
Date Line

NORTHERN

DISTRICT

PICCADILLY

PRIME MERIDIAN

INTERNATIONAL DATE LINE

London

EUROPE

ASIA

NORTH
AMERICA

PACIFIC
OCEAN

ATLANTIC
OCEAN

AFRICA

Lake
Victoria

SOMALIA

BOARD
HERE

DRC

GABON

INDIAN
OCEAN

INDONESIA

EQUATOR   40,075 km

ECUADOR

Mouth of
the Amazon

SOUTH
AMERICA

BRAZIL

OCEANIA

DIRECTION OF TRAVEL

PACIFIC OCEAN

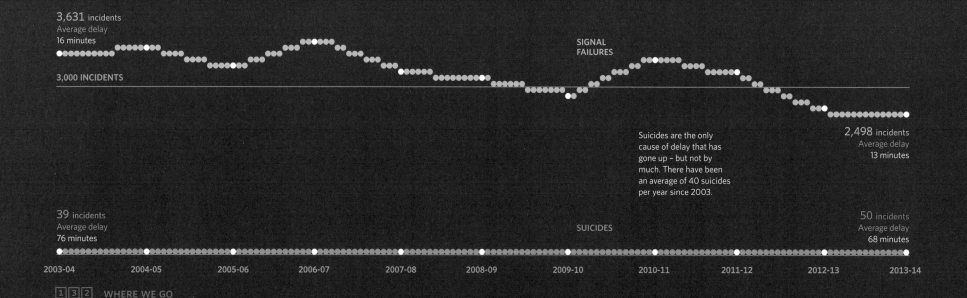

Disrupted

As the Tube improves, Londoners may only have the weather left to complain about.

To commuters, every second counts. Any time shaved off a journey will accumulate to minutes and even hours over the course of a year. The opposite is also true. Delays on the Tube cost passengers 1.86 billion hours in the year ending March 2014. That's actually good news. The figure is less than half of what it was ten years ago. And that's not all. Over the past decade, there have been 600 fewer station closures, 4,600 fewer delays caused by staff or signal failures (see chart) and 2,000 fewer delays lasting longer than fifteen minutes – all of which has dropped the average wait time to one minute from a little over two. Preparations for the Olympics certainly sparked improvement. Since 2011, more than 97% of the scheduled trains have shown up on time. Better still, when things do go bad now, response times are quicker.

12,162 incidents
Average delay
6 minutes

12,000 INCIDENTS

STAFF
DELAYS

9,000

Staff-related delays are down 29% since 2003. This is amazing considering current demand. Victoria Line drivers have just 218 seconds to change over when they reach the end of the line.

8,642 incidents
Average delay
5.5 minutes

6,000 INCIDENTS

3,631 incidents
Average delay
16 minutes

SIGNAL
FAILURES

3,000 INCIDENTS

Suicides are the only cause of delay that has gone up – but not by much. There have been an average of 40 suicides per year since 2003.

2,498 incidents
Average delay
13 minutes

39 incidents
Average delay
76 minutes

SUICIDES

50 incidents
Average delay
68 minutes

2003-04   2004-05   2005-06   2006-07   2007-08   2008-09   2009-10   2010-11   2011-12   2012-13   2013-14

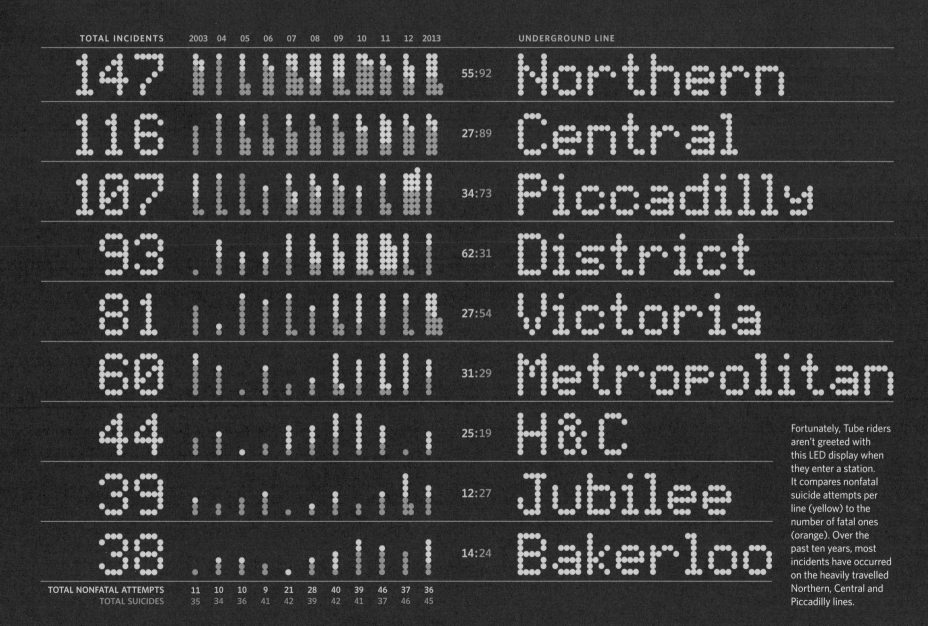

TOTAL INCIDENTS	2003	04	05	06	07	08	09	10	11	12	2013		UNDERGROUND LINE
147												55:92	Northern
116												27:89	Central
107												34:73	Piccadilly
93												62:31	District
81												27:54	Victoria
60												31:29	Metropolitan
44												25:19	H&C
39												12:27	Jubilee
38												14:24	Bakerloo

TOTAL NONFATAL ATTEMPTS	11	10	10	9	21	28	40	39	46	37	36
TOTAL SUICIDES	35	34	36	41	42	39	42	41	37	46	45

Fortunately, Tube riders aren't greeted with this LED display when they enter a station. It compares nonfatal suicide attempts per line (yellow) to the number of fatal ones (orange). Over the past ten years, most incidents have occurred on the heavily travelled Northern, Central and Piccadilly lines.

SOURCE: TRANSPORT FOR LONDON

The Tube Challenge

Here's how to visit all 270 tube stations in one day.

If, while waiting for a train at Chesham station one morning, you glance over to see a few super-excited joggers holding a stopwatch, video camera and a dozen energy bars, think nothing of it – unless you happen to see them again sixteen hours later exiting a train at Heathrow's Terminal 5. In that case, offer to sign their logbook. You could be a witness to history.

The *Guinness Book of Records* credits R. J. Lewis and D. R. Longley with completing the first Tube Challenge on 13 June 1959. Since then, the game has evolved with the Tube map. Yet the essential rule remains: visit every station. To do so requires meticulous planning; endurance helps too for running between stations. Given the effort involved, Tube Challengers are understandably secretive about their routes. Andi James and Steve Wilson only released their record-setting route from 2009 (adapted here) after setting a new record – 16 hours, 29 minutes and 13 seconds – on 27 May 2011. The mark stood for two years. Then Geoff Marshall and Anthony Smith beat it by eight minutes and forty-six seconds on 16 August 2013.

To commemorate the Tube's 150th anniversary in 2013, Art on the Underground invited artist Mark Wallinger to create 270 original works, one for each station. He made labyrinths. Each one is unique and numbered in order of the stations visited on the route to the right.

THE BASICS

1 You don't have to cover every stretch of track or step on every platform, but you must arrive at or depart from every Underground station by train. (Overground, National Rail and Docklands Light Railway stations not included).

2 You may take buses or run between stations.

3 You must keep a log.

4 An independent witness must start and stop a master stopwatch at the beginning and end of the attempt.

For a full list of rules, go to *www.tubeforum.co.uk/rules*

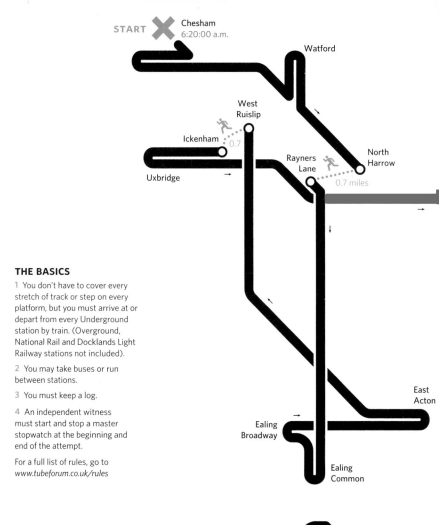

START ✕ Chesham 6:20:00 a.m.

Watford

West Ruislip

Ickenham 0.7

Uxbridge

Rayners Lane 0.7 miles

North Harrow

East Acton

Ealing Broadway

Ealing Common

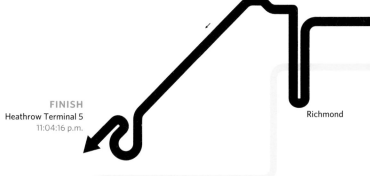

FINISH
Heathrow Terminal 5
11:04:16 p.m.

Richmond

SOURCE: ART ON THE UNDERGROUND, TRANSPORT FOR LONDON. PHOTO: OLIVER UBERTI

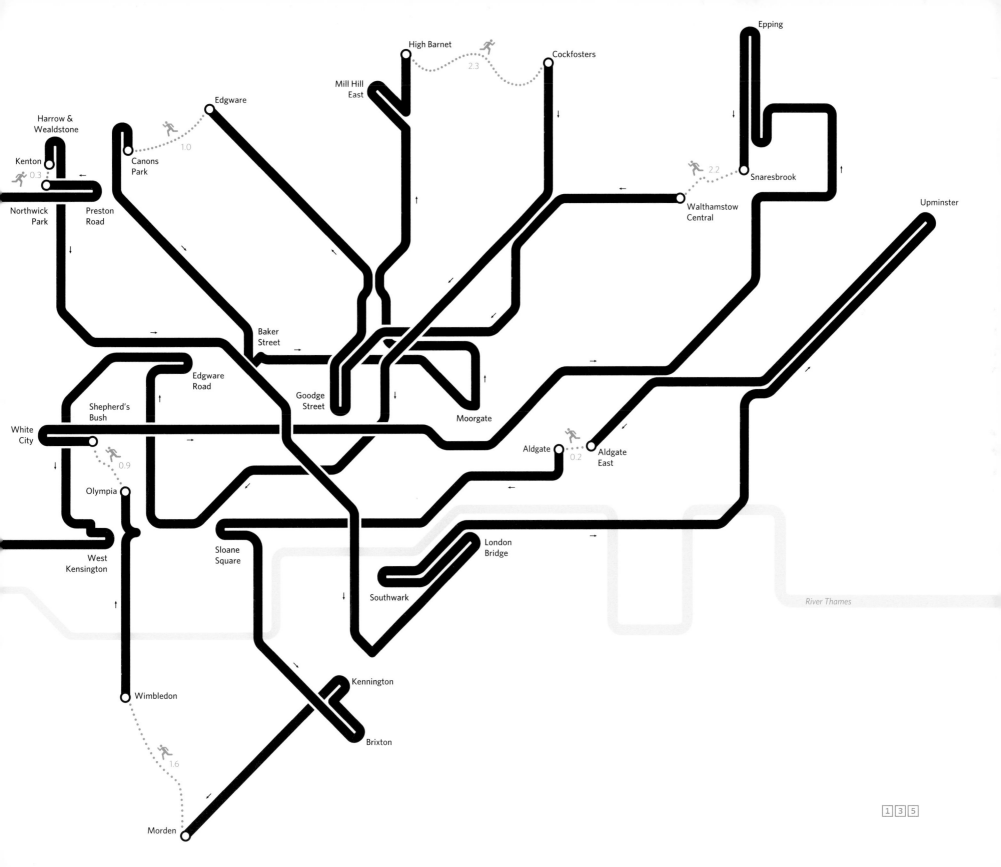

Epping

High Barnet
🏃 2.3

Cockfosters

Mill Hill
East

Edgware

Harrow &
Wealdstone
🏃 1.0

Canons
Park

Kenton
🏃 0.3

Northwick
Park

Preston
Road

Snaresbrook
🏃 2.2

Walthamstow
Central

Upminster

Baker
Street

Edgware
Road

Goodge
Street

Shepherd's
Bush

Moorgate

White
City

Aldgate
🏃 0.2

Aldgate
East

Olympia
🏃 0.9

Sloane
Square

London
Bridge

West
Kensington

Southwark

River Thames

Wimbledon

Kennington

Brixton

Morden
🏃 1.6

1 3 5

Route Masters

The next bus is closer than you think.

Londoners often say, 'I waited ages for a bus and then they all turned up at once.' If all the scheduled buses actually did arrive at the same time, you would be stuck in a long, red traffic jam. Transport researcher Joan Serras used these schedules to determine how many buses pass each of London's 22,565 bus stops each day. He then mapped the routes buses would take between them. Roads with more buses running along them appear wider and redder; those with fewer buses are narrower and paler. Roads with no buses have been excluded. In total, his map shows 114,000 daily trips. Next time you can't find a bus, try Waterloo Bridge. There, one crosses the Thames every sixteen seconds.

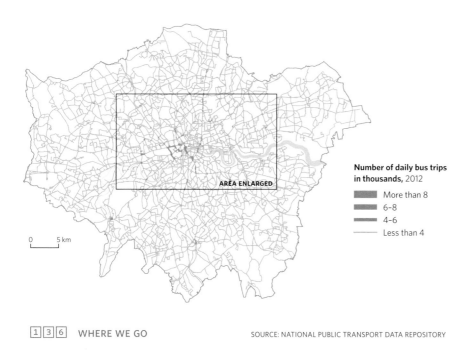

AREA ENLARGED

0   5 km

Number of daily bus trips in thousands, 2012

More than 8
6–8
4–6
Less than 4

SOURCE: NATIONAL PUBLIC TRANSPORT DATA REPOSITORY

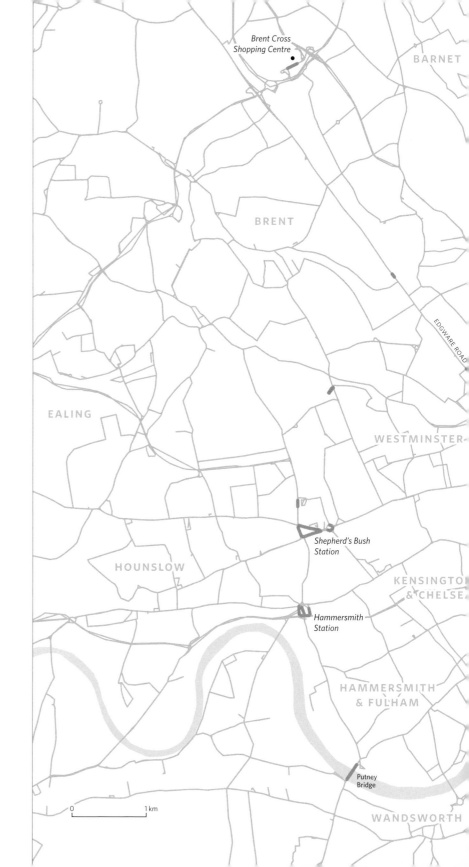

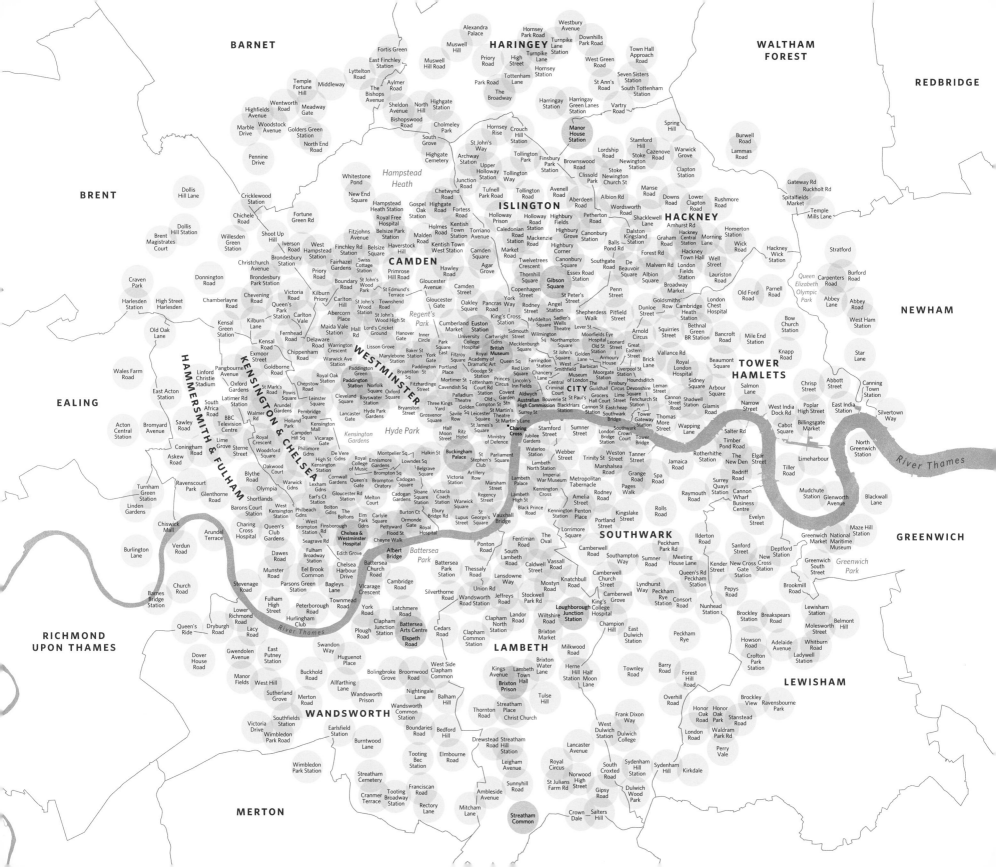

Mental Maps

To become a London cabbie, memorize the map on the left.

They call it 'The Knowledge' – 320 taxi routes within a six-mile radius that extends from Charing Cross east to the Lea Valley, west to Chiswick, up to Alexandra Palace and down to Crystal Palace. Learn these 'runs' and you're barely halfway there. Then you just need to know the names and locations of all the streets, businesses and landmarks within a quarter-mile radius of each end (yellow circles).

'We call it the Dumbbell Effect,' says Malcolm Linskey, managing director of Knowledge Point School in Islington. Examiners never ask trainees to recite the exact runs in his books, such as No. 1: Manor House Station to Gibson Square (right). Instead, 'they'll say take me from John Scott Health Centre to the Almeida Theatre,' says Linskey, 'which is effectively the same route, but they got to know how to link up onto the route and how to come off at the other end.'

With 60,000 streets and more than 100,000 'points of interest' within those yellow circles, it takes most trainees two to four years to acquire The Knowledge. So why do it? With that Black Cab and green badge come certain perks: good pay, flexible hours, local pride, even a larger hippocampus (the area of the brain that governs spatial awareness and memory). As Linskey says, 'Once a cabbie's done it, he don't need a map anymore.'

Featured run

0   1 km

Unlike minicab drivers who often rely on satellite navigation, London cabbies drive by memory. Frequently, they use side streets to get from A to B on the straightest line possible. To see how more Knowledge routes compare with Google Maps, turn the page.

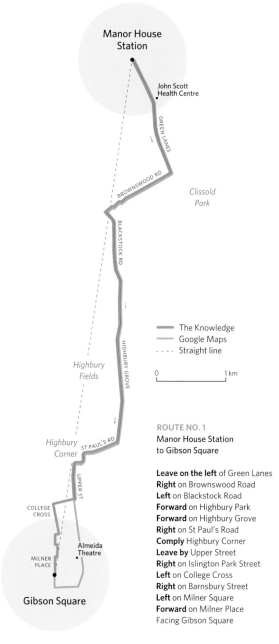

The Knowledge
Google Maps
Straight line

0   1 km

ROUTE NO. 1
Manor House Station to Gibson Square

Leave on the left of Green Lanes
Right on Brownswood Road
Left on Blackstock Road
Forward on Highbury Park
Forward on Highbury Grove
Right on St Paul's Road
Comply Highbury Corner
Leave by Upper Street
Right on Islington Park Street
Left on College Cross
Right on Barnsbury Street
Left on Milner Square
Forward on Milner Place
Facing Gibson Square

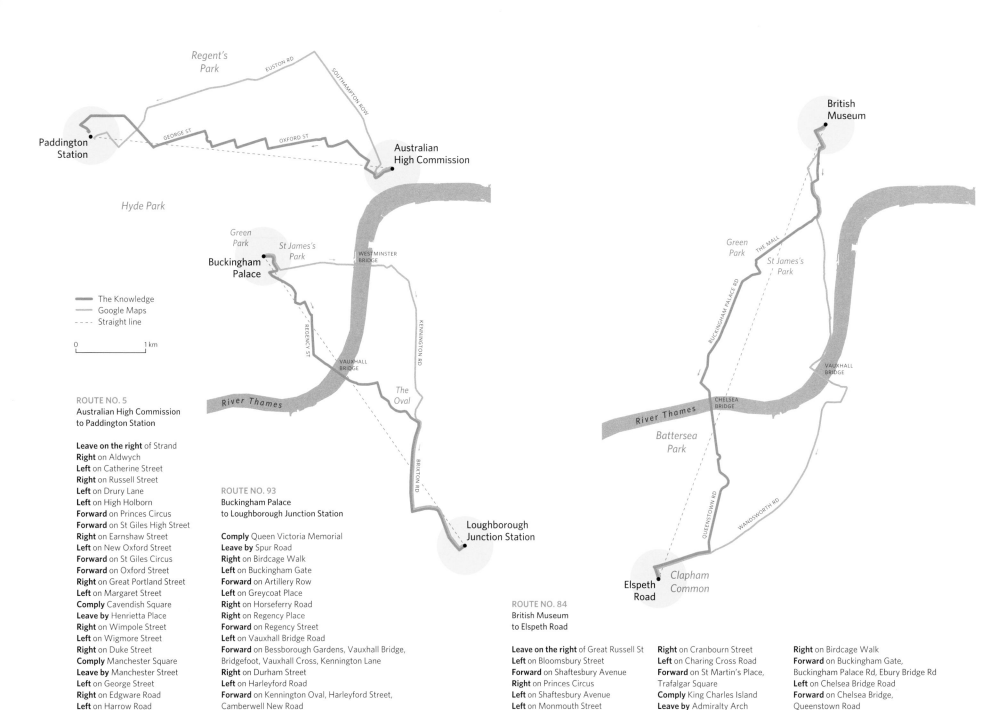

ROUTE NO. 5

Australian High Commission
to Paddington Station

Leave on the right of Strand
Right on Aldwych
Left on Catherine Street
Right on Russell Street
Left on Drury Lane
Left on High Holborn
Forward on Princes Circus
Forward on St Giles High Street
Right on Earnshaw Street
Left on New Oxford Street
Forward on St Giles Circus
Forward on Oxford Street
Right on Great Portland Street
Left on Margaret Street
Comply Cavendish Square
Leave by Henrietta Place
Right on Wimpole Street
Left on Wigmore Street
Right on Duke Street
Comply Manchester Square
Leave by Manchester Street
Left on George Street
Right on Edgware Road
Left on Harrow Road
Comply Bishop's Bridge Roundabout
Leave by Bishop's Bridge Road
Left on Paddington Taxi Road

ROUTE NO. 93

Buckingham Palace
to Loughborough Junction Station

Comply Queen Victoria Memorial
Leave by Spur Road
Right on Birdcage Walk
Left on Buckingham Gate
Forward on Artillery Row
Left on Greycoat Place
Right on Horseferry Road
Right on Regency Place
Forward on Regency Street
Left on Vauxhall Bridge Road
Forward on Bessborough Gardens, Vauxhall Bridge,
Bridgefoot, Vauxhall Cross, Kennington Lane
Right on Durham Street
Left on Harleyford Road
Forward on Kennington Oval, Harleyford Street,
Camberwell New Road
Right on Brixton Road
Left on Loughborough Road
Left on Coldharbour Lane

ROUTE NO. 84

British Museum
to Elspeth Road

Leave on the right of Great Russell St
Left on Bloomsbury Street
Forward on Shaftesbury Avenue
Right on Princes Circus
Left on Shaftesbury Avenue
Left on Monmouth Street
Comply Seven Dials
Leave by Monmouth Street
Forward on Upper St Martins Lane

Right on Cranbourn Street
Left on Charing Cross Road
Forward on St Martin's Place,
Trafalgar Square
Comply King Charles Island
Leave by Admiralty Arch
Forward on The Mall
Comply Queen Victoria Memorial
Leave by Spur Road

Right on Birdcage Walk
Forward on Buckingham Gate,
Buckingham Palace Rd, Ebury Bridge Rd
Left on Chelsea Bridge Road
Forward on Chelsea Bridge,
Queenstown Road
Comply Queen's Circus
Leave by Queenstown Road
Right on Lavender Hill

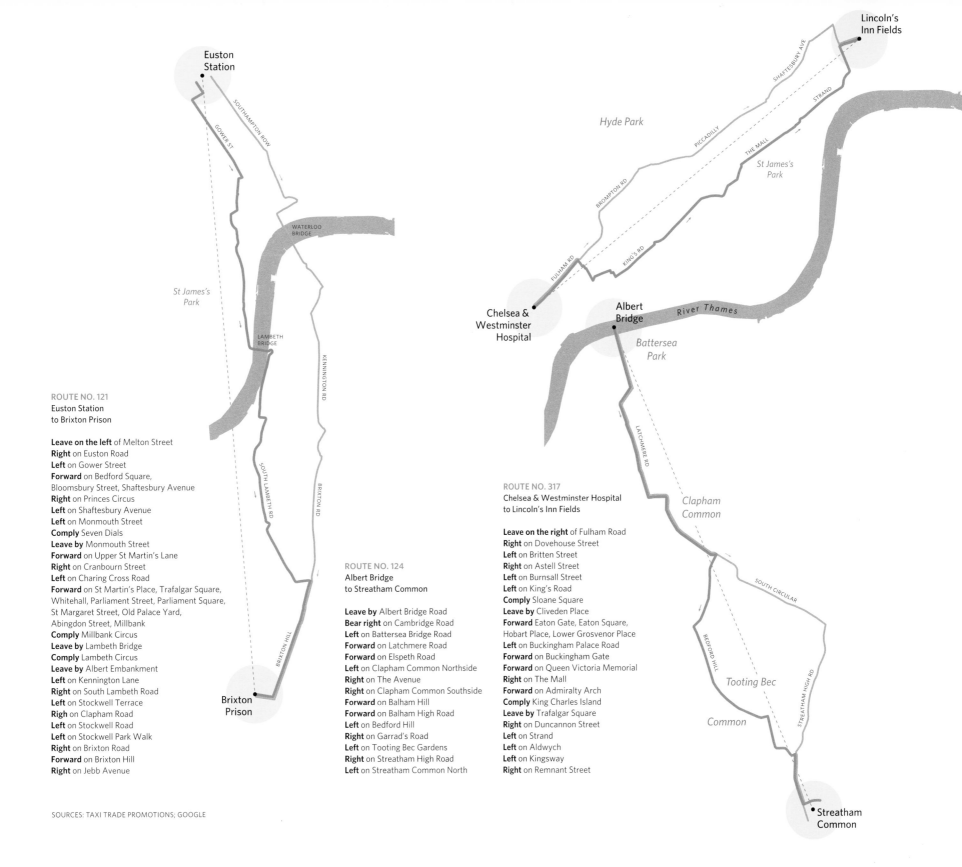

Euston
Station

Lincoln's
Inn Fields

SOUTHAMPTON ROW

GOWER ST

SHAFTESBURY AVE

PICCADILLY

STRAND

THE MALL

Hyde Park

St James's
Park

BROMPTON RD

KING'S RD

FULHAM RD

Chelsea &
Westminster
Hospital

Albert
Bridge

River Thames

Battersea
Park

WATERLOO
BRIDGE

St James's
Park

LAMBETH
BRIDGE

KENNINGTON RD

SOUTH LAMBETH RD

BRIXTON RD

BRIXTON HILL

LATCHMERE RD

Clapham
Common

SOUTH CIRCULAR

BEDFORD HILL

STREATHAM HIGH RD

Tooting Bec

Common

ROUTE NO. 121
Euston Station
to Brixton Prison

Leave on the left of Melton Street
Right on Euston Road
Left on Gower Street
Forward on Bedford Square,
Bloomsbury Street, Shaftesbury Avenue
Right on Princes Circus
Left on Shaftesbury Avenue
Left on Monmouth Street
Comply Seven Dials
Leave by Monmouth Street
Forward on Upper St Martin's Lane
Right on Cranbourn Street
Left on Charing Cross Road
Forward on St Martin's Place, Trafalgar Square,
Whitehall, Parliament Street, Parliament Square,
St Margaret Street, Old Palace Yard,
Abingdon Street, Millbank
Comply Millbank Circus
Leave by Lambeth Bridge
Comply Lambeth Circus
Leave by Albert Embankment
Left on Kennington Lane
Right on South Lambeth Road
Left on Stockwell Terrace
Righ on Clapham Road
Left on Stockwell Road
Left on Stockwell Park Walk
Right on Brixton Road
Forward on Brixton Hill
Right on Jebb Avenue

Brixton
Prison

ROUTE NO. 124
Albert Bridge
to Streatham Common

Leave by Albert Bridge Road
Bear right on Cambridge Road
Left on Battersea Bridge Road
Forward on Latchmere Road
Forward on Elspeth Road
Left on Clapham Common Northside
Right on The Avenue
Right on Clapham Common Southside
Forward on Balham Hill
Forward on Balham High Road
Left on Bedford Hill
Right on Garrad's Road
Left on Tooting Bec Gardens
Right on Streatham High Road
Left on Streatham Common North

ROUTE NO. 317
Chelsea & Westminster Hospital
to Lincoln's Inn Fields

Leave on the right of Fulham Road
Right on Dovehouse Street
Left on Britten Street
Right on Astell Street
Left on Burnsall Street
Left on King's Road
Comply Sloane Square
Leave by Cliveden Place
Forward Eaton Gate, Eaton Square,
Hobart Place, Lower Grosvenor Place
Left on Buckingham Palace Road
Forward on Buckingham Gate
Forward on Queen Victoria Memorial
Right on The Mall
Forward on Admiralty Arch
Comply King Charles Island
Leave by Trafalgar Square
Right on Duncannon Street
Left on Strand
Left on Aldwych
Left on Kingsway
Right on Remnant Street

Streatham
Common

SOURCES: TAXI TRADE PROMOTIONS; GOOGLE

Minicab Corridors

The paths of minicab drivers redraw the map of London's motorways.

With their knowledge of side streets and shortcuts, London's iconic black cabs have the run of the city. Their unmetered rivals, the city's 67,000 minicabs, travel further afield on pre-arranged prices, often ushering passengers to destinations outside The Knowledge's six-mile radius (see pp. 138–141). With dispatchers tracking their efficiency via GPS, minicab drivers tend to stick to the routes recommended by their trusty SatNavs.

Using three months' worth of these GPS points, Ed Manley at University College London's Centre for Advanced Spatial Analysis wove the web of driver behaviour you see here. Every time a minicab passed between two junctions on the road network, he drew a line. More lines meant stronger connections. The stronger the connection, the more likely a driver was to use those roads together.

To distinguish these regional clusters, Manley added colour. For example, the reds of the M4 signal journeys to and from Heathrow Airport, while the many hues of the M25 and North Circular suggest, as Manley puts it, 'Drivers don't get on and travel around. They travel for a bit and then get off again.'

Minicab journeys
December 2010 – February 2011

Whilst major arteries can be discerned, this map does not trace roads. It depicts straight lines between junctions passed through by the minicabs. On the outskirts, coloured clusters appear larger and sparser because there are fewer junctions.

SOURCE: ADDISON LEE

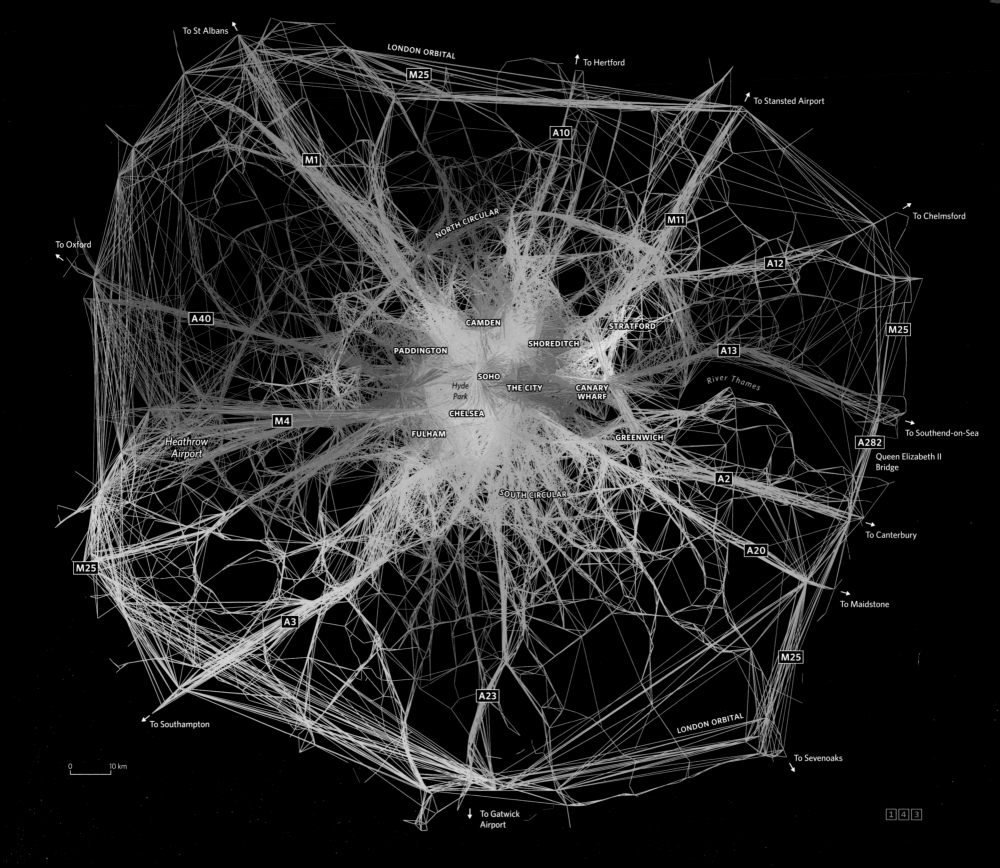

To St Albans

LONDON ORBITAL

M25

To Hertford

To Stansted Airport

A10

M1

M11

To Chelmsford

A12

To Oxford

NORTH CIRCULAR

A40

CAMDEN

STRATFORD

M25

PADDINGTON

SHOREDITCH

A13

River Thames

SOHO

Hyde
Park

THE CITY

CANARY
WHARF

To Southend-on-Sea

Heathrow
Airport

M4

CHELSEA

A282

Queen Elizabeth II
Bridge

FULHAM

GREENWICH

A2

SOUTH CIRCULAR

To Canterbury

A20

M25

To Maidstone

A3

M25

A23

To Southampton

LONDON ORBITAL

To Sevenoaks

0   10 km

To Gatwick
Airport

Lost & Found

Heathrow logs all that we leave behind.

Visitors to London leave more than digital traces on the city. They leave physical traces too – tens of thousands of them. In 2013 alone, the lost property office at Heathrow Airport logged 34,000 items (shown to the right), including violins, rings, stuffed animals, cars, a kayak, a Rottweiler and a phonograph.

Think that's a lot? Transport for London's Lost Property Office stockpiles more than 240,000 items a year found on the city's trains, buses and black cabs. Like Heathrow, they hold everything for three months. During the high travel season from July to September 2013, roughly one in five items were reclaimed at a rate of about 160 per day. While most retrievals occur at their office on Baker Street, TfL posts 50 or so items a month overseas.

In the chaos of travel, arriving home without a phone, sunglasses or jewellery appears to be a common enough mistake. Although you have to wonder how 100 travellers got far without their walking sticks.

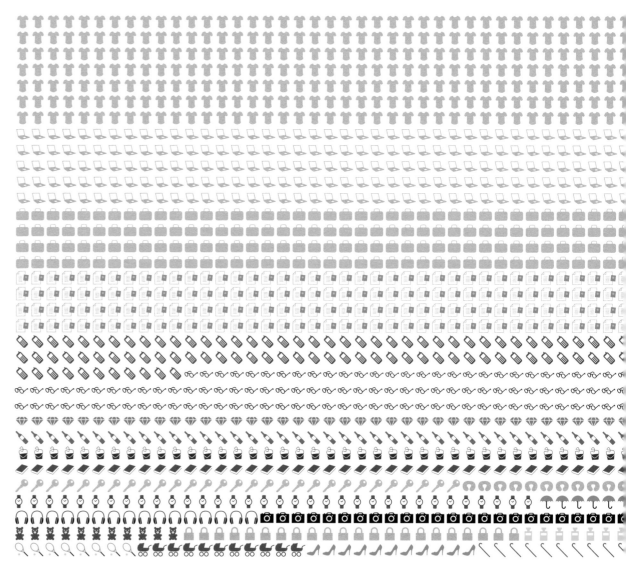

Items lost at Heathrow Airport, 2013   EACH ICON = 10 ITEMS

Clothes 6,570
Computers, tablets and electronics 5,090
Luggage 4,160
Passports, IDs and security documents 3,710
Mobile phones 2,580
Glasses and sunglasses 2,380

Jewellery 1,250
Duty-free items and food 1,110
Purses and wallets 1,060
Books and magazines 730
Keys 650
Neck pillows, blankets and mats 540

Watches 510
Umbrellas 430
Headphones 390
Photo and video equipment 390
Art 330
Toys and games 230

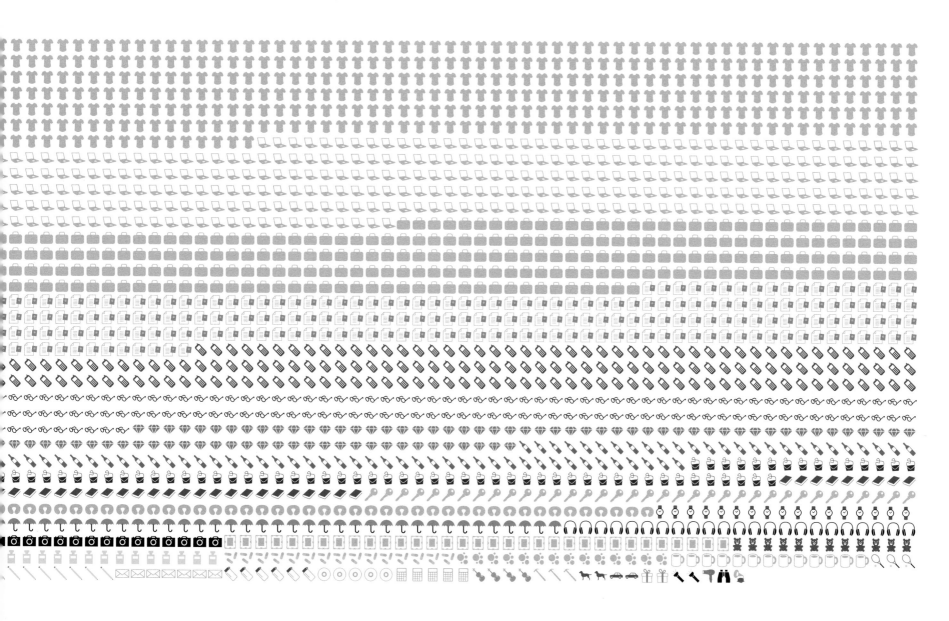

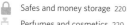 Safes and money storage 220

Perfumes and cosmetics 220

Medicine 150

Coins 140

Various souvenirs 130

Sports and outdoor gear 110

Baby supplies 110

Shoes 110

Walking sticks 100

Writing utensils 80

Post and packing supplies 70

Bottles, flasks and crockery 60

CDs and DVDs 50

Office supplies 50

Musical instruments 40

Tools 30

Pet supplies 20

Cars and automotive parts 20

Gifts 20

Torches 20

Hair dryers 10

Binoculars 10

Antiques 10

SOURCE: MISSINGX.COM

Hampstead
Heath

Queen
Elizabeth
Olympic
Park

Stratford

Regent's
Park

King's Cross
St Pancras

St Paul's
Cathedral

Trafalgar
Square

Canary
Wharf

Hyde
Park

London
Eye

The
Shard

Greenwich
Park

Battersea
Park

Richmond
Park

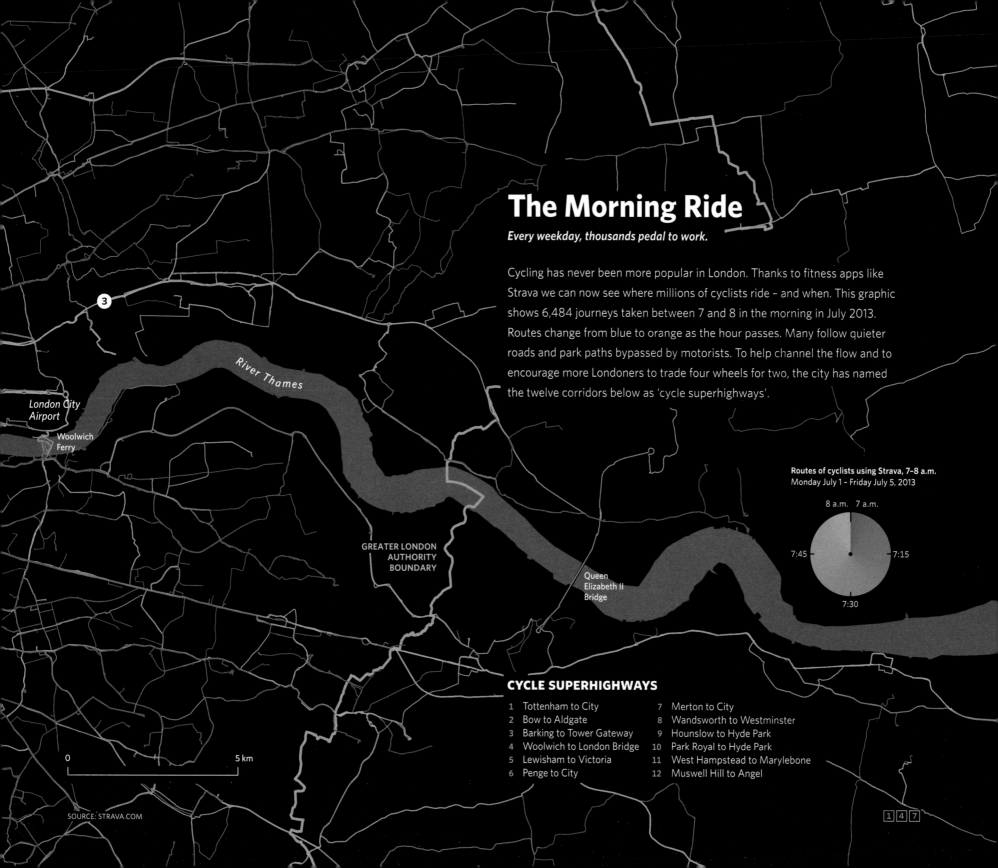

The Morning Ride

Every weekday, thousands pedal to work.

Cycling has never been more popular in London. Thanks to fitness apps like Strava we can now see where millions of cyclists ride – and when. This graphic shows 6,484 journeys taken between 7 and 8 in the morning in July 2013. Routes change from blue to orange as the hour passes. Many follow quieter roads and park paths bypassed by motorists. To help channel the flow and to encourage more Londoners to trade four wheels for two, the city has named the twelve corridors below as 'cycle superhighways'.

River Thames

London City Airport

Woolwich Ferry

GREATER LONDON AUTHORITY BOUNDARY

Queen Elizabeth II Bridge

Routes of cyclists using Strava, 7–8 a.m.
Monday July 1 – Friday July 5, 2013

8 a.m.   7 a.m.

7:45   7:15

7:30

0   5 km

CYCLE SUPERHIGHWAYS

1	Tottenham to City	7	Merton to City
2	Bow to Aldgate	8	Wandsworth to Westminster
3	Barking to Tower Gateway	9	Hounslow to Hyde Park
4	Woolwich to London Bridge	10	Park Royal to Hyde Park
5	Lewisham to Victoria	11	West Hampstead to Marylebone
6	Penge to City	12	Muswell Hill to Angel

Boris's Best Bikers

Making this list requires hundreds of hours in the saddle.

London's cycle hire scheme offers nearly 10,000 bikes for users to ride and then return to any of the 700 or so 'docking stations' in the heart of town. 'Boris Bikes' – named after mayor Boris Johnson who launched the scheme – offer a cheap and healthy way of getting around. Most riders take a few trips a year. On this page, we honour twenty-five of the scheme's 'super users' who logged more than 900 journeys in 2012. Some were regular commuters who pedalled to the same stations near work, home or the tube many times over; others toured the city in a series of one-way trips. Wherever they went, each left a unique digital signature behind.

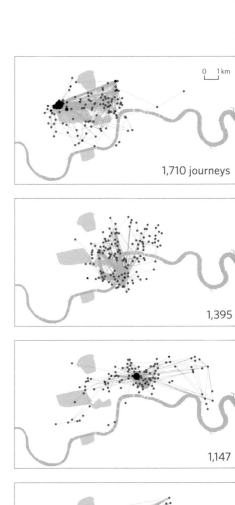

1,710 journeys

1,395

1,147

1,081

970

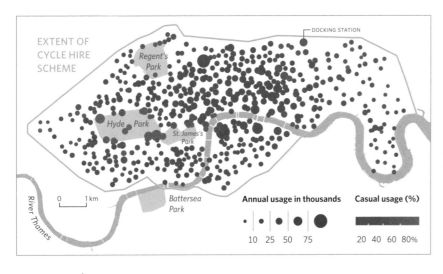

EXTENT OF CYCLE HIRE SCHEME

Regent's Park

Hyde Park

St. James's Park

Battersea Park

River Thames

DOCKING STATION

0   1 km

Annual usage in thousands

10   25   50   75

Casual usage (%)

20   40   60   80%

Regular 'Boris Bikers' apply for a key to avoid entering payment details every time they hire a bicycle. 'Casual' users don't bother with this because they are visitors or only cycle occasionally. The map to the left shows regulars picking up bikes near train stations and the City versus casual cyclists who stick to the larger parks.

Top 25 Boris Bikers by number of journeys, 2012

One-way journeys

Over 300

200

100

50

< 5

• Docking station

Round trips

10   20   30

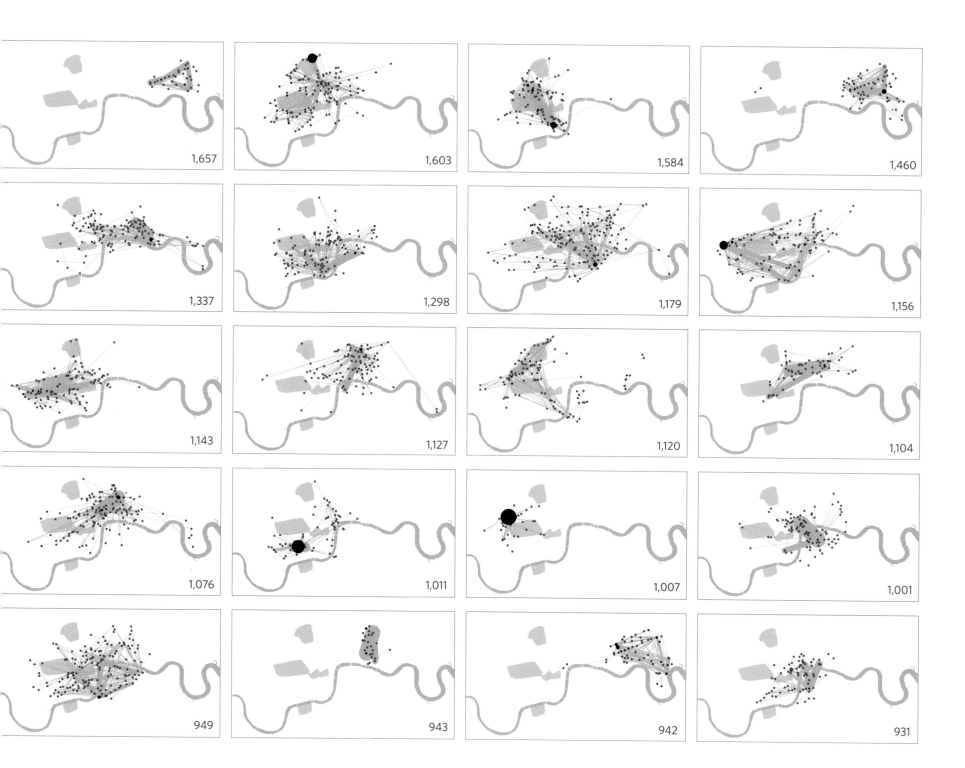

1,657

1,603

1,584

1,460

1,337

1,298

1,179

1,156

1,143

1,127

1,120

1,104

1,076

1,011

1,007

1,001

949

943

942

931

London Zoo

Regent's Park

CAMDEN

ISLINGTON

*King's Cross
St Pancras
Station*

SHOREDITCH

CLERKENWELL

BLOOMSBURY

PADDINGTON

British
Museum

*Liverpool St
Station*

*Paddington
Station*

MARYLEBONE

Oxford
Circus

SOHO

St Paul's
Cathedral

CITY

Covent
Garden

*Kensington
Gardens*

Hyde Park

MAYFAIR

Trafalgar
Square

Waterloo
Bridge

Blackfriars
Bridge

Southwark
Bridge

London
Bridge

Tower
of London

*Green
Park*

*St. James's
Park*

London
Eye

SOUTH BANK

*London Bridge
Station*

Tower
Bridge

KENSINGTON

Buckingham
Palace

*Waterloo
Station*

The Shard

Science
Museum

Westminster
Bridge

*Victoria
Station*

Lambeth
Bridge

Elephant
and Castle

Vauxhall
Bridge

VAUXHALL

CHELSEA

We don't know the exact
routes taken by Boris Bikers,
so we have taken our best
guess using the shortest,
most cycle-friendly routes
between the start and end
points of their journeys.

Exhausting Rides

Biking is healthy unless you're pedalling through smog.

This map shows the air pollution facing London's bike share users as they coursed through the city in 2012. Many endured diesel-choked tailbacks at junctions and traffic lights, especially when crossing the Thames. Those seeking fresher rides were wise to head for parks and back streets.

Over the past century, the 'Big Smoke' has become a big haze as engines belch particulates into the air. The European Union says concentrations should not exceed 20 parts per million (ppm). Orange roads on this map exceed 25. Their impact depends on how much time you spend inhaling them, but by any measure London can do better. Air pollution is believed to contribute to more than 3,300 deaths a year.

BOW

STEPNEY

Canary Wharf

River Thames

ISLE OF DOGS

Cutty Sark

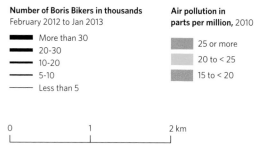

Number of Boris Bikers in thousands
February 2012 to Jan 2013

━━━ More than 30
━━ 20-30
── 10-20
── 5-10
── Less than 5

Air pollution in parts per million, 2010

25 or more
20 to < 25
15 to < 20

0   1   2 km

SOURCES: OLIVER O'BRIEN, UNIVERSITY COLLEGE LONDON; TRANSPORT FOR LONDON; LONDON ATMOSPHERIC EMISSIONS INVENTORY; OSM

Cable Car to Nowhere

Hardly anyone is riding the Emirates Air Line.

Like a piñata dangling from a string, London's cable car has taken a bashing from critics. They loathe its location (see map) and complain that their taxes went to waste on a tourist attraction rather than a viable transport option. Passenger figures certainly back them up. The hexagons to the right show the number of passengers per hour during one week in October 2012 (blue) and the same week in 2013 (orange). With a ten-person cabin passing through each of its two stations every 30 seconds, the system would max out at 2,400 passengers per hour. On weekends after the 2012 Olympics, it came close. Since then, interest has fallen. Even on the busiest hour of our sample week in 2013, more than half of its gondolas were ferrying ghosts.

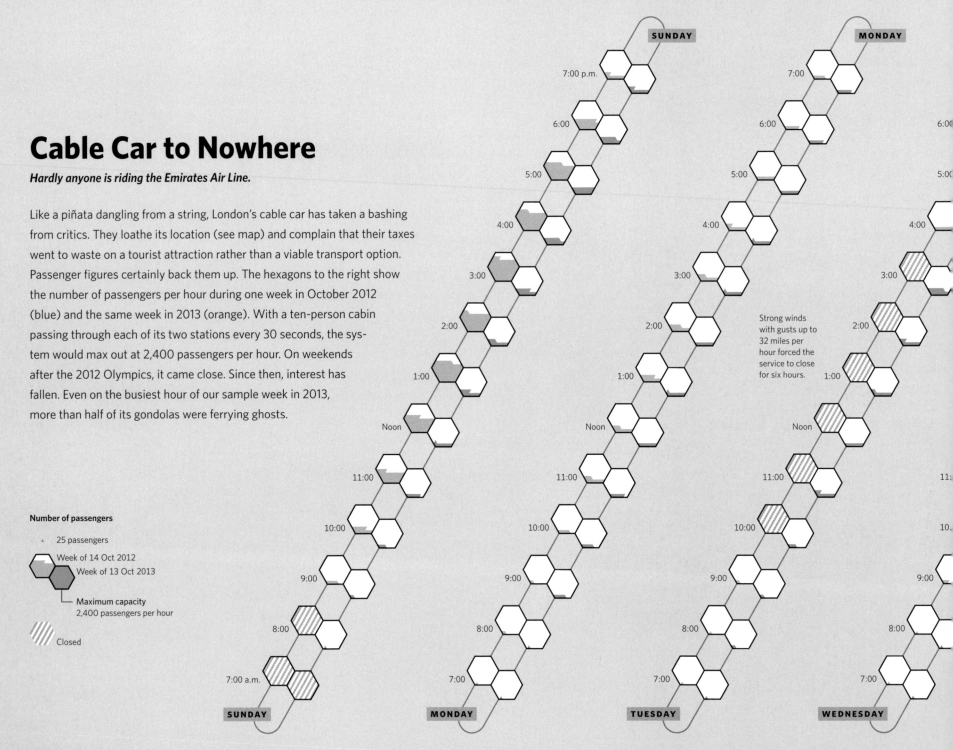

Strong winds with gusts up to 32 miles per hour forced the service to close for six hours.

Number of passengers

- ▲ 25 passengers

Week of 14 Oct 2012
Week of 13 Oct 2013

Maximum capacity
2,400 passengers per hour

Closed

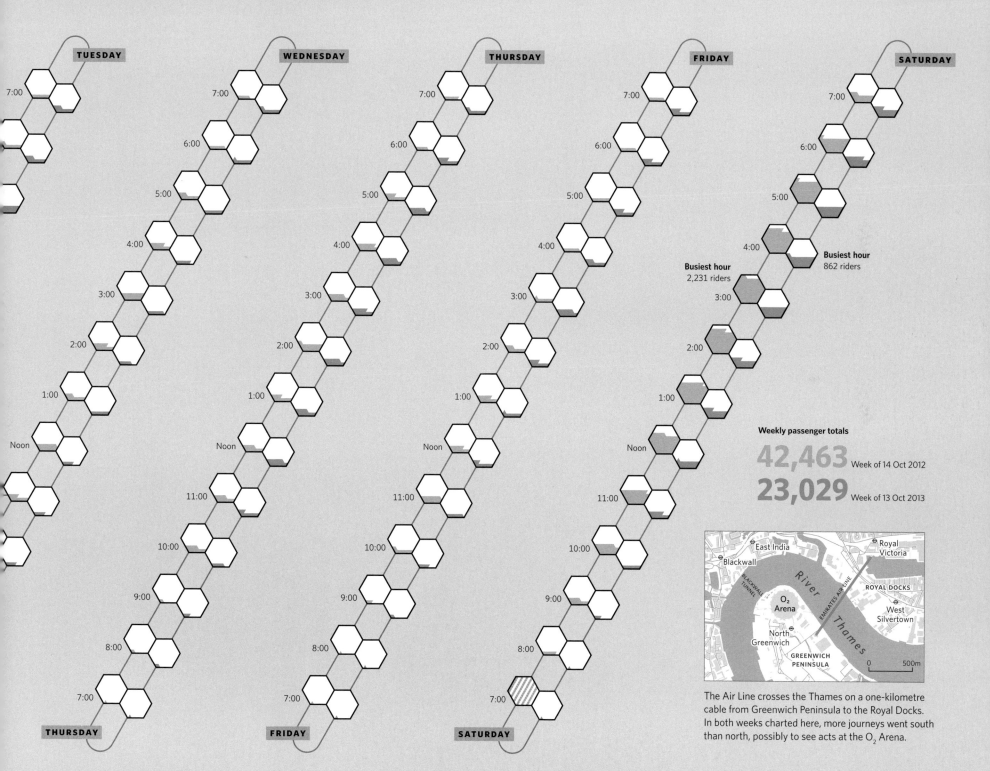

TUESDAY
7:00
6:00
5:00
4:00
3:00
2:00
1:00
Noon
11:00
10:00
9:00
8:00
7:00
THURSDAY

WEDNESDAY
7:00
6:00
5:00
4:00
3:00
2:00
1:00
Noon
11:00
10:00
9:00
8:00
7:00
FRIDAY

THURSDAY
7:00
6:00
5:00
4:00
3:00
2:00
1:00
Noon
11:00
10:00
9:00
8:00
7:00
SATURDAY

FRIDAY
7:00
6:00
5:00
4:00
3:00
2:00
1:00
Noon
11:00
10:00
9:00
8:00

Busiest hour
2,231 riders

SATURDAY
7:00
6:00
5:00
4:00
3:00
2:00

Busiest hour
862 riders

Weekly passenger totals

42,463 Week of 14 Oct 2012

23,029 Week of 13 Oct 2013

East India
Blackwall
BLACKWALL TUNNEL
River Thames
O₂ Arena
EMIRATES AIR LINE
North Greenwich
GREENWICH PENINSULA
Royal Victoria
ROYAL DOCKS
West Silvertown
0   500m

The Air Line crosses the Thames on a one-kilometre cable from Greenwich Peninsula to the Royal Docks. In both weeks charted here, more journeys went south than north, possibly to see acts at the O₂ Arena.

SOURCE: TRANSPORT FOR LONDON

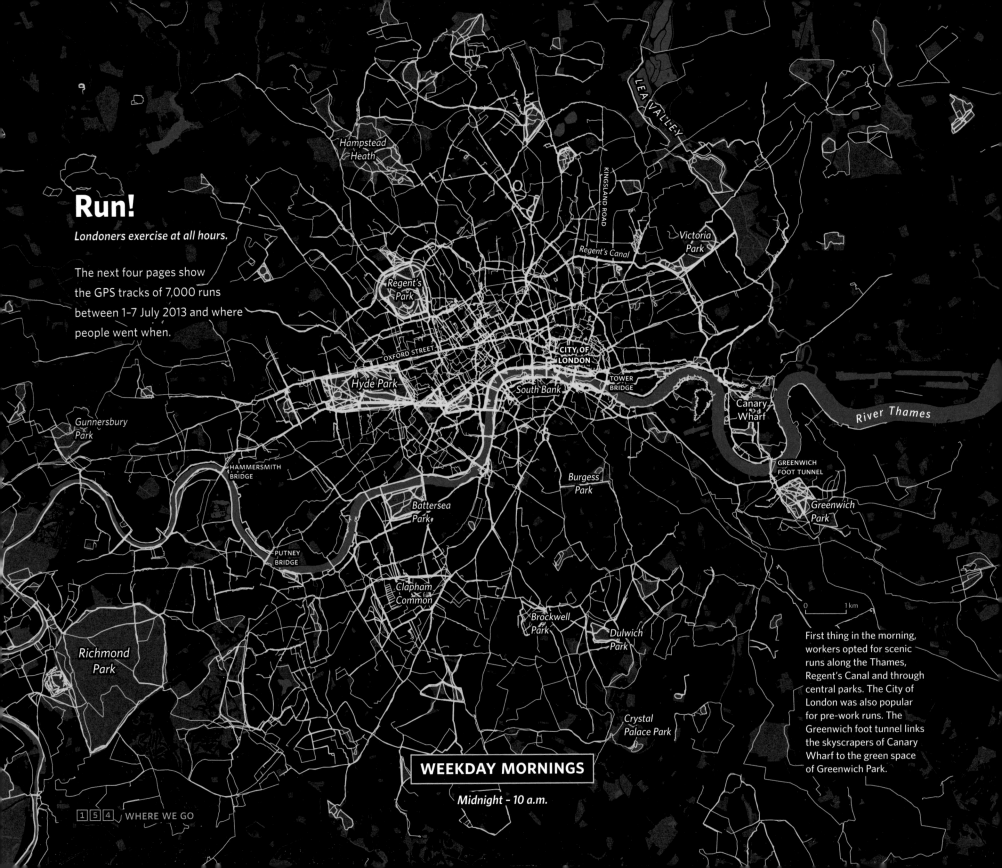

Run!

Londoners exercise at all hours.

The next four pages show the GPS tracks of 7,000 runs between 1–7 July 2013 and where people went when.

LEA VALLEY

Hampstead Heath

KINGSLAND ROAD

Victoria Park

Regent's Canal

Regent's Park

OXFORD STREET

CITY OF LONDON

Hyde Park

TOWER BRIDGE

South Bank

Canary Wharf

River Thames

Gunnersbury Park

HAMMERSMITH BRIDGE

GREENWICH FOOT TUNNEL

Burgess Park

Greenwich Park

Battersea Park

PUTNEY BRIDGE

Clapham Common

Richmond Park

Brockwell Park

Dulwich Park

Crystal Palace Park

WEEKDAY MORNINGS

Midnight – 10 a.m.

First thing in the morning, workers opted for scenic runs along the Thames, Regent's Canal and through central parks. The City of London was also popular for pre-work runs. The Greenwich foot tunnel links the skyscrapers of Canary Wharf to the green space of Greenwich Park.

LEA VALLEY

Hampstead
Heath

KINGSLAND ROAD

Victoria
Park

Regent's
Park

Regent's Canal

OXFORD STREET

CITY OF
LONDON

Hyde Park

South Bank

TOWER
BRIDGE

Canary
Wharf

River Thames

Gunnersbury
Park

HAMMERSMITH
BRIDGE

GREENWICH
FOOT TUNNEL

Burgess
Park

Greenwich
Park

Battersea
Park

PUTNEY
BRIDGE

0   1 km

Clapham
Common

Richmond
Park

Brockwell
Park

Dulwich
Park

During weekday lunch hours
and afternoon breaks, loops
were popular around parks
or along the north and
south banks of the Thames.
Runners from the City and
Canary Wharf also streamed
north to the Regent's Canal.
Outer parks were less busy.

Crystal
Palace Park

WEEKDAY AFTERNOONS

10 a.m. – 5 p.m.

LEA VALLEY

Hampstead
Heath

KINGSLAND ROAD

Victoria
Park

Regent's Canal

Regent's
Park

OXFORD STREET

CITY OF
LONDON

Hyde Park

TOWER
BRIDGE

South Bank

Canary
Wharf

River Thames

Gunnersbury
Park

GREENWICH
FOOT TUNNEL

HAMMERSMITH
BRIDGE

Burgess
Park

Greenwich
Park

Battersea
Park

PUTNEY
BRIDGE

Clapham
Common

Richmond
Park

Brockwell
Park

Dulwich
Park

0   1 km

Many favoured a post-work
run into the evening. All
parks were popular with
running clubs encouraging
their use. Putney Bridge
to Hammersmith Bridge
was an especially popular
Thames side circuit.

Crystal
Palace Park

WEEKDAY EVENINGS

5 p.m. – Midnight

LEA VALLEY

Hampstead
Heath

KINGSLAND ROAD

Regent's Canal

Victoria
Park

Regent's
Park

OXFORD STREET

CITY OF
LONDON

Hyde Park

South Bank

TOWER
BRIDGE

River Thames

Canary
Wharf

Gunnersbury
Park

HAMMERSMITH
BRIDGE

GREENWICH
FOOT TUNNEL

Burgess
Park

Battersea
Park

Greenwich
Park

PUTNEY
BRIDGE

Midnight – 10 a.m.
10 a.m. – 5 p.m.
5 p.m. – Midnight

Clapham
Common

0   1 km

Brockwell
Park

Dulwich
Park

The weekend saw a shift
away from pre-work routes
to suburban circuits in some
of the outer parks, notably
Hampstead Heath and
Richmond Park. A thread
of runners passed through
the Lea Valley.

Richmond
Park

Crystal
Palace Park

WEEKEND

Midnight – Midnight

SOURCE: STRAVA

Why Not Walk It?

To truly know London, walk the lines.

It took writer Mark Mason 912,384 footsteps to hike the length of every Tube line. You don't have to go quite that far to share his passion for London's streets. As Mason says, the joy of walking through London is 'about claiming the city's greatness, or at least some small part of it, for yourself.' Central London is very walkable. In many cases, it is quicker to do so than take the Tube or a bus.

When Henry Beck designed his now iconic map of the Tube network in 1931, his aim was clarity, not geographic accuracy. He expanded Central London on his map in order to accommodate its many stations and their labels. Therefore it doesn't show the distance between stops to scale. Still, his map remains so effective that it seems to make sense to take the Tube at every opportunity. Look at our map and you'll think otherwise. Charing Cross to Embankment, Leicester Square to Piccadilly Circus and Farringdon to Barbican are all short strolls. If you're still not convinced, just look at how close Lancaster Gate is to Paddington: 9 minutes on foot or 18 minutes via the Central then District lines.

**Estimated walking times
in minutes at an average pace
of 2 metres per second**
ALL TIMES ROUNDED UP TO THE NEAREST MINUTE

Station   5 min   Station

The routes shown here are designed to follow the lines themselves. If you want real gains, try shortcuts between them. Take in the university district between Goodge Street and Russell Square or admire the City between Barbican and St Paul's.

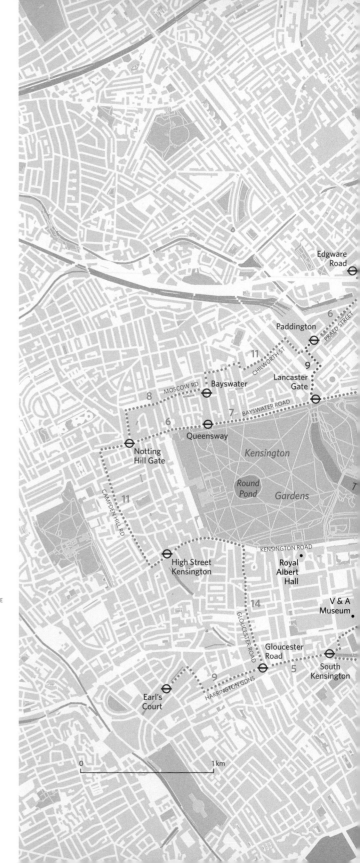

SOURCE: OSM

4 HOW WE'RE DOING

Islington Has Issues

New research seeks to improve well-being by identifying who's hurting.

Since 2011, the Office for National Statistics (ONS) has asked UK residents to rate their feelings of life satisfaction, purpose, happiness and anxiety on a scale of zero to ten. In the faces to the right, we have linked each of those four questions to a different facial attribute. For example, Kensington and Chelsea shines with high life satisfaction, whereas the rest of Inner London seems lost in a mental fog.

This is not to say Londoners are *completely* miserable. Borough averages did range between six and eight for life satisfaction, purpose and happiness and between a low two and four for anxiety. Still, it's hard to ignore the average scores for the rest of the UK, where bright-eyed, smiling visages makes most Londoners seem rather tired of life by comparison. Whilst the reasons behind these differences are not yet fully understood, follow-up studies have revealed that people's perceptions of their own health, employment status and relationships mirror their sense of well-being. In other words, if you see yourself as unfit, unqualified and unlovable, there's a good chance you're unhappy.

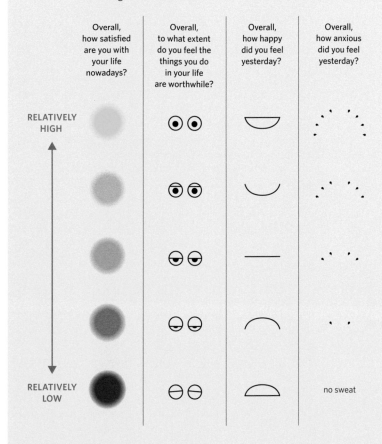

Average personal well-being by borough
April 2012 – March 2013

Responses to the following questions ranged from 0 to 10 where 0 is 'not at all' and 10 is 'completely'. We didn't use that scale here. Instead, we rescaled London's borough averages relative to each other.

| Overall, how satisfied are you with your life nowadays? | Overall, to what extent do you feel the things you do in your life are worthwhile? | Overall, how happy did you feel yesterday? | Overall, how anxious did you feel yesterday? |

RELATIVELY HIGH

RELATIVELY LOW

no sweat

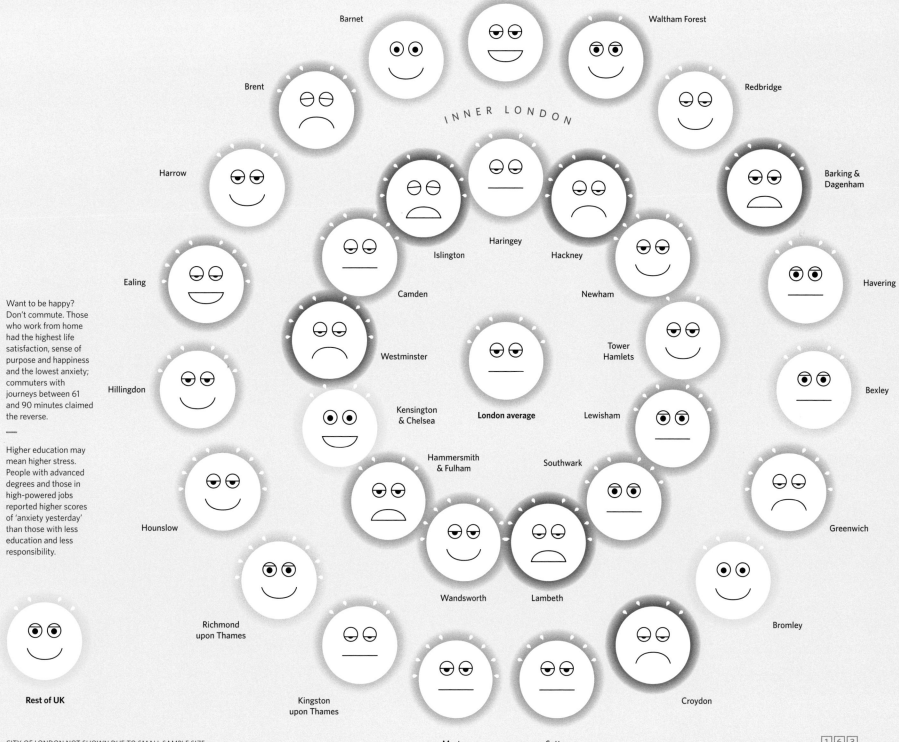

OUTER LONDON

INNER LONDON

Enfield

Barnet

Waltham Forest

Brent

Redbridge

Harrow

Islington   Haringey   Hackney   Barking & Dagenham

Ealing

Camden   Newham   Havering

Westminster   Tower Hamlets   Bexley

Hillingdon

London average   Lewisham

Kensington & Chelsea

Hammersmith & Fulham   Southwark

Hounslow

Wandsworth   Lambeth   Greenwich

Richmond upon Thames

Bromley

Rest of UK

Kingston upon Thames

Croydon

Merton   Sutton

Want to be happy? Don't commute. Those who work from home had the highest life satisfaction, sense of purpose and happiness and the lowest anxiety; commuters with journeys between 61 and 90 minutes claimed the reverse.

—

Higher education may mean higher stress. People with advanced degrees and those in high-powered jobs reported higher scores of 'anxiety yesterday' than those with less education and less responsibility.

CITY OF LONDON NOT SHOWN DUE TO SMALL SAMPLE SIZE.
SOURCE: ONS

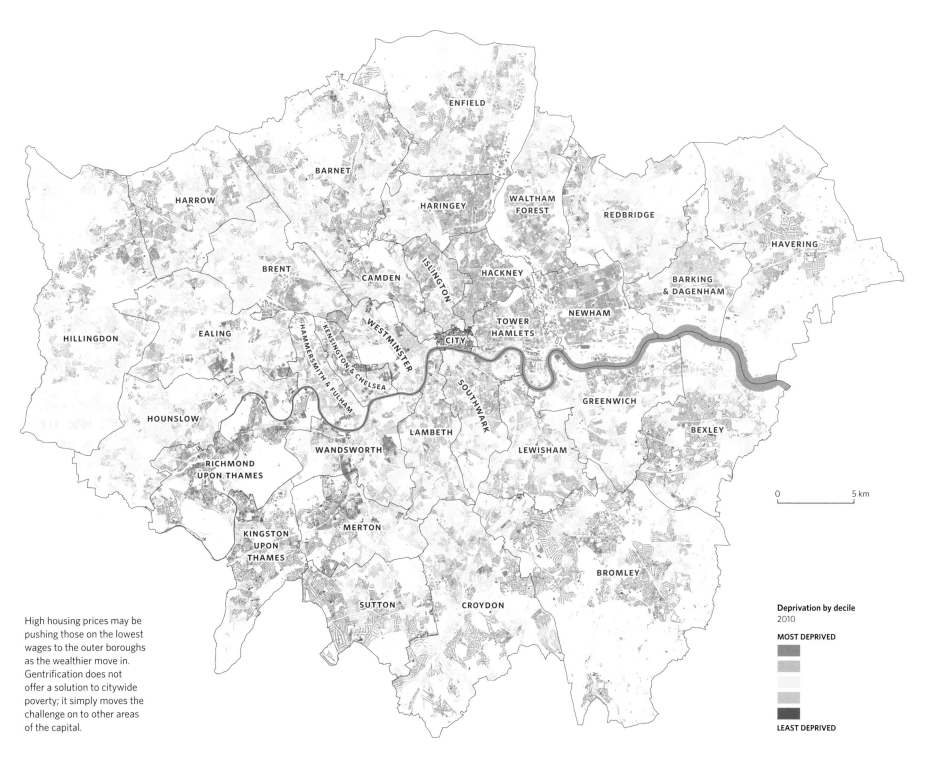

ENFIELD

BARNET

HARROW

HARINGEY

WALTHAM FOREST

REDBRIDGE

HAVERING

BRENT

CAMDEN

ISLINGTON

HACKNEY

BARKING & DAGENHAM

HILLINGDON

EALING

HAMMERSMITH & FULHAM

KENSINGTON & CHELSEA

WESTMINSTER

CITY

TOWER HAMLETS

NEWHAM

HOUNSLOW

SOUTHWARK

GREENWICH

BEXLEY

LAMBETH

WANDSWORTH

LEWISHAM

RICHMOND UPON THAMES

KINGSTON UPON THAMES

MERTON

SUTTON

CROYDON

BROMLEY

High housing prices may be pushing those on the lowest wages to the outer boroughs as the wealthier move in. Gentrification does not offer a solution to citywide poverty; it simply moves the challenge on to other areas of the capital.

0   5 km

Deprivation by decile
2010

MOST DEPRIVED

LEAST DEPRIVED

'It was the best of times, it was the worst of times...'

In 1854, five years before Charles Dickens wrote the first line of *A Tale of Two Cities,* the physician John Snow made a map. With cholera inexplicably ravaging West London, Snow set out to find its source. By plotting the locations of its victims, he noticed that many clustered near a particular water pump on Broad Street in Soho.

'The result of the inquiry,' he wrote, 'is that there has been no particular outbreak or prevalence of cholera in this part of London except among the persons who were in the habit of drinking the water of the above-mentioned pump well.' Not only did his map save lives, it kick-started the science of epidemiology and the notion that maps and graphics can be agents for the greater good.

In the light of such advances, it is surprising that it took thirty years before someone applied these techniques to the very poverty Dickens wrote about. That someone was Charles Booth. Having made a fortune in shipping, Booth invested it on the most comprehensive social survey of London ever undertaken. He then visualized his findings in a series of detailed 'poverty maps' published in 1889 (see p. 25). Given their simplicity – strips of colour drawn over an off-the-shelf map of the city – it is easy to overlook that each one required a visit from Booth or his colleagues to assess a street's 'social condition'. This painstaking work illustrated London's class spectrum from wealth through to destitution and offered the first definitive map of where Londoners were most in need.

Times have changed, but London's poverty remains largely concentrated in the East End. The persistent have/have-not divide casts a shadow over many of the graphics in this chapter. On the left, we show a contemporary measure of poverty called the Index of Multiple Deprivation. It depicts the most (red) and least deprived (green) areas of London based on their inhabitants' education, income, employment, health, experience of crime, housing accessibility and living environment. For many in the reddest areas, daily life demands a series of fundamental decisions about sourcing your next meal, your next rent payment, your child's school uniform. The Index is widely used by those seeking to rid Londoners of this centuries-old reality, but in comparison to its Victorian predecessor, it offers little in the way of visual innovation.

So if Booth were alive today, what would he do? We'd like to think he'd get data scientists, computer programmers, designers, policy makers and other volunteers together to mine any number of datasets posted online by charities and the government. Who knows what life-saving maps they might generate? Better still, he might offer training to those without the Internet (see pp. 194–5), empowering them to access the same open health and crime data we've visualized in this chapter. Data literally offer strength in numbers. The more of us who can use them, the stronger we will be.

Lives on the Line

'Mind the Gap' in life expectancy.

To see inequalities across London in the twenty-first century, look no further than the Jubilee Line. For every two stops east between Westminster and Canning Town, the London Health Observatory estimates that life expectancy of local residents drops one year. The Tube therefore acts as a new measuring tool for the city. Pick any two stations that matter to you and see how values fluctuate between them. For example, the life expectancy of those living in Vauxhall is nine years less than that of those living near Victoria Station just two stops to the north.

91 Knightsbridge
90
89
88
87 — Life expectancy at birth +/- 3 years
86   2006-2010 (rolling average)
85
84
83 — Female Citywide Average
82
81
80
79 — Male Citywide Average
78
77
76
75 Lewisham

Underground
--- Overground
···· Docklands Light Rail

◯ No data

SOURCE: LONDON HEALTH PROGRAMMES

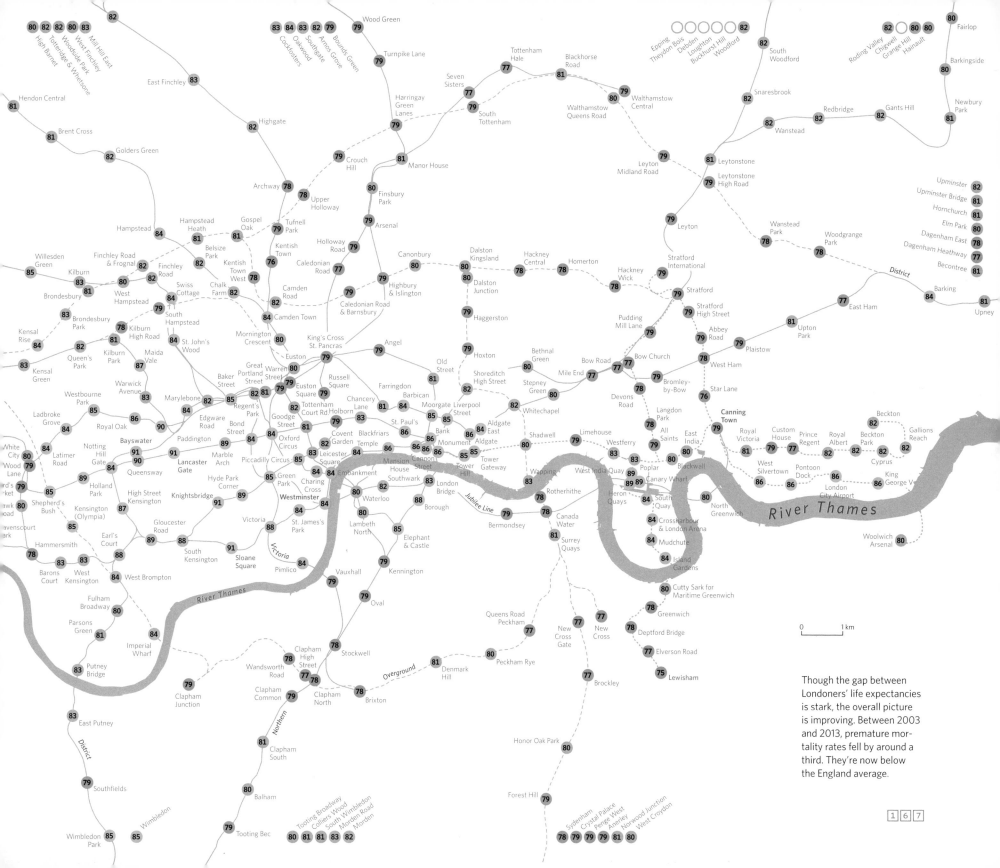

Though the gap between Londoners' life expectancies is stark, the overall picture is improving. Between 2003 and 2013, premature mortality rates fell by around a third. They're now below the England average.

What's to Eat?

Your options depend on where you live.

The Food Standards Agency database contains the name and address of every food outlet in London (with the exception of Greenwich). We overlaid these on our poverty map (see p. 164) to see the most frequently used words in the names of 1,680 restaurants, canteens, takeaways and sandwich shops from the richest and poorest parts of London. As we show here, you would struggle to find fried chicken on your plate in Mayfair or haute French cuisine in Poplar, but fish and pizza are universally enjoyed whatever your means.

Top 150 words used in café or restaurant names in London's most (top 10%) and least (bottom 10%) deprived areas, 2014

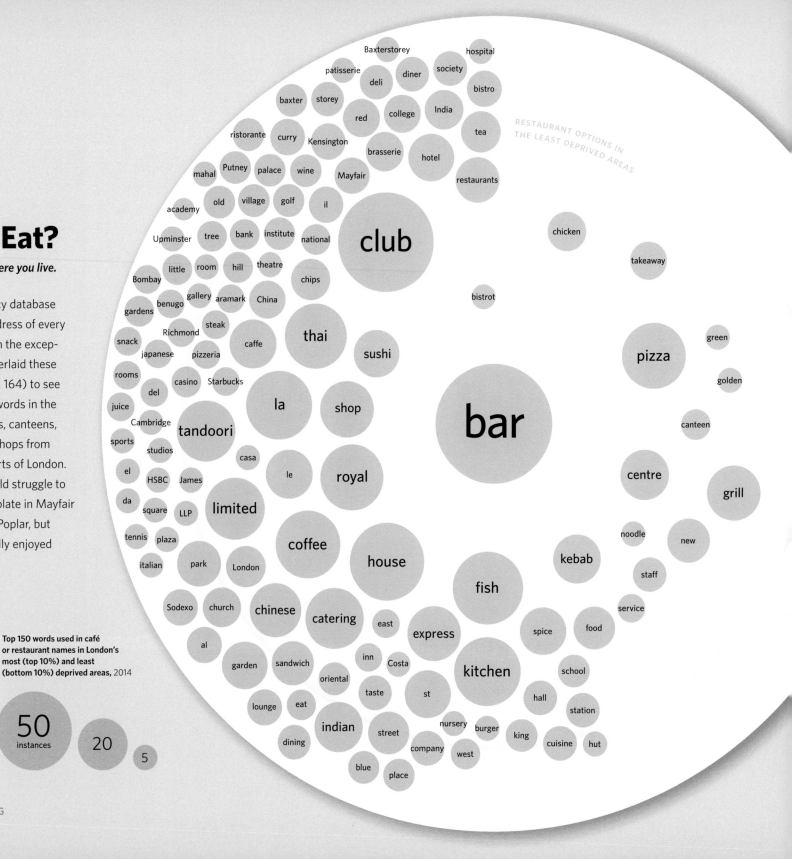

RESTAURANT OPTIONS IN THE LEAST DEPRIVED AREAS

239 instances
restaurant

café
227 instances

50 instances 20 5

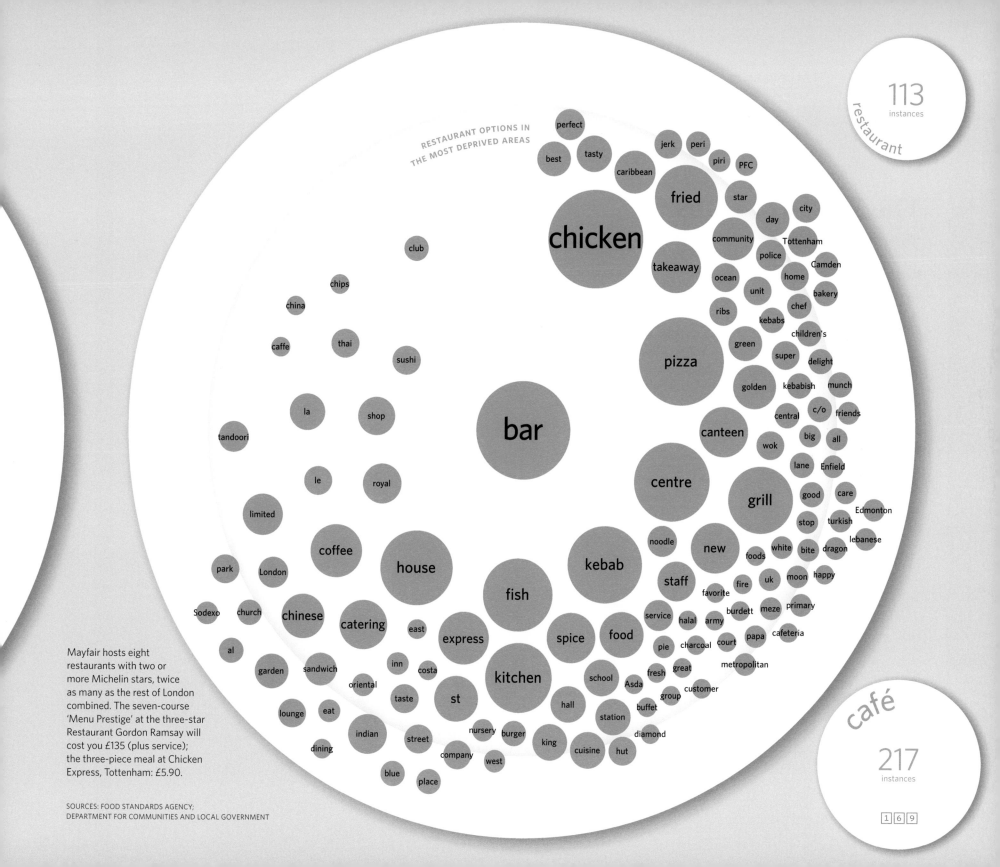

RESTAURANT OPTIONS IN
THE MOST DEPRIVED AREAS

perfect · best · tasty · jerk · peri · piri · PFC · caribbean · fried · star · city · day · community · Tottenham · takeaway · police · Camden · ocean · home · unit · bakery · ribs · chef · kebabs · children's · green · super · delight · pizza · golden · kebabish · munch · central · c/o · friends · canteen · big · all · wok · lane · Enfield · centre · good · care · grill · stop · turkish · Edmonton · noodle · new · white · bite · dragon · lebanese · foods · staff · fire · uk · moon · happy · kebab · favorite · service · halal · army · burdett · meze · primary · pie · charcoal · court · papa · cafeteria · spice · food · fresh · great · metropolitan · kitchen · school · Asda · group · customer · hall · buffet · station · diamond · king · cuisine · hut

club · chips · china · thai · sushi · caffe · la · shop · tandoori · bar · le · royal · limited · coffee · house · fish · park · London · church · chinese · catering · east · express · Sodexo · al · inn · costa · sandwich · garden · oriental · st · taste · lounge · eat · indian · street · dining · blue · place · company · west · nursery · burger

Mayfair hosts eight
restaurants with two or
more Michelin stars, twice
as many as the rest of London
combined. The seven-course
'Menu Prestige' at the three-star
Restaurant Gordon Ramsay will
cost you £135 (plus service);
the three-piece meal at Chicken
Express, Tottenham: £5.90.

SOURCES: FOOD STANDARDS AGENCY;
DEPARTMENT FOR COMMUNITIES AND LOCAL GOVERNMENT

113 instances
restaurant

café
217 instances

The Shape of Obesity

Where wallets contract, waistlines expand.

Some of the heaviest children in England live in London. In order to show where, we expanded or contracted each borough to reflect the extent to which children living there are more or less obese than the English average (18.9%). The geography may be distorted, but the inequalities are not. In more deprived areas like Newham and Tower Hamlets – where the obesity rate stretches above 25% – the bulge threatens to burst the buckle off the Thames. Compare this to wealthier boroughs like Richmond and Kingston upon Thames, where rates below 15% shrink their boundaries to thin lines.

Percentage of 10–11-year-olds classified obese, 2012-13

■ More than 25%
▨ 20-25
English average — □ Less than 20%
18.9%

Body Mass Index (BMI) is the measure used to determine a healthy weight. It divides a person's weight in kilograms by the square of their height in metres. In population statistics, children whose BMI is at or above the 95th percentile are classified as obese.

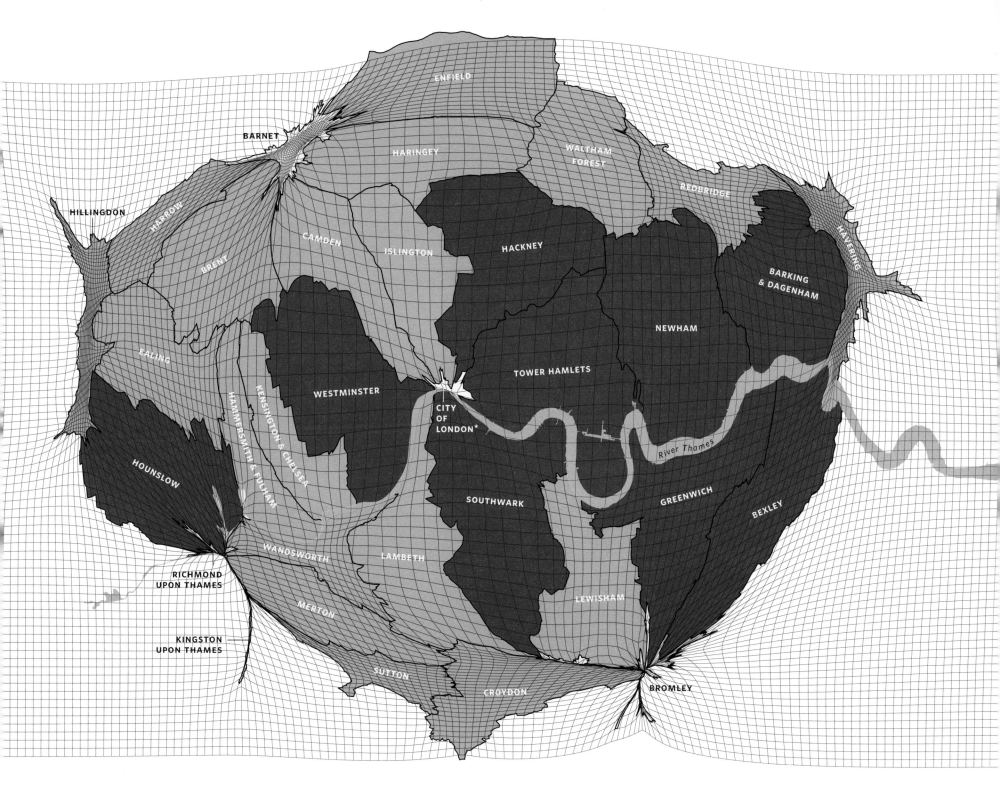

ENFIELD

BARNET

HARINGEY

WALTHAM FOREST

HILLINGDON

HARROW

REDBRIDGE

HAVERING

CAMDEN

ISLINGTON

HACKNEY

BRENT

BARKING & DAGENHAM

EALING

NEWHAM

KENSINGTON & CHELSEA

HAMMERSMITH & FULHAM

WESTMINSTER

TOWER HAMLETS

CITY OF LONDON*

River Thames

HOUNSLOW

SOUTHWARK

GREENWICH

BEXLEY

RICHMOND UPON THAMES

WANDSWORTH

LAMBETH

LEWISHAM

MERTON

KINGSTON UPON THAMES

SUTTON

CROYDON

BROMLEY

*CITY OF LONDON DATA NOT SHOWN DUE TO SMALL SAMPLE SIZE
SOURCE: THE HEALTH AND SOCIAL CARE INFORMATION CENTRE

Causes of Death

We're not dying like we used to.

Three and a half centuries ago, a haberdasher-turned-demographer named John Graunt began to wonder how we die. For thirty years, he tallied the causes of death in London before publishing them in his *Bills of Mortality* in 1662. His 'Table of Casualties' inspired ours, but it looked far different from the one you see to the right. For one, in 1650, the top cause of death was 'Consumption, and Cough'. Today, heart disease leads the list – and no one dies from 'Teeth and Worms', 'Itch' or 'Wolf'.

By adding gender and borough data to the table, we can now see patterns Graunt would have envied. Note how, in most boroughs, the death rates for their ten leading causes have gone down apart from dementia and Alzheimer's, which have climbed into the top ten for women in more boroughs than men. Men, however, are more likely to die from liver disease. In case you were wondering, that's how Graunt died.

To aid your exploration, we've highlighted the boroughs with the top three death rates for each cause. Boroughs and causes were ordered by total death rate in 2012.

Age-standardized rates per 100,000 people for each gender's ten leading causes of death, 2001–2012

- Top 3 boroughs per cause
- Higher than 2001
- No change
- Lower than 2001
- No rate calculated

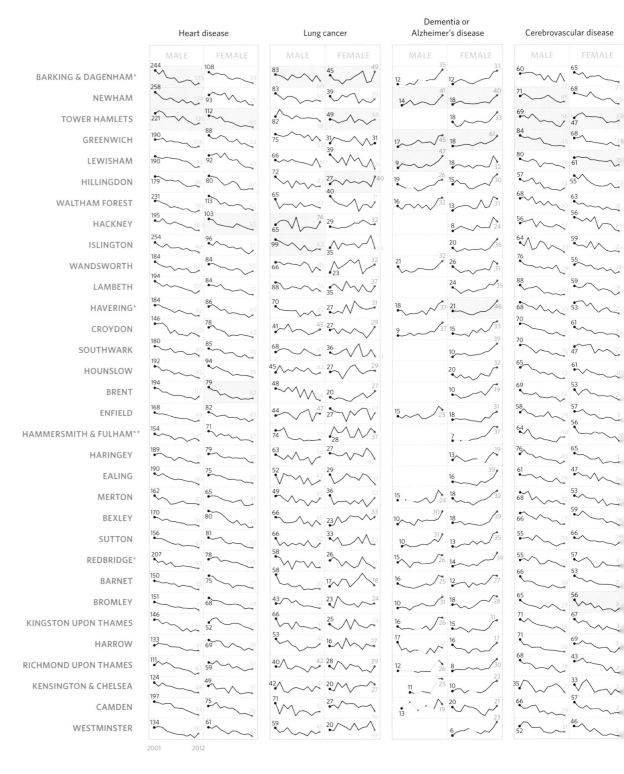

Chronic lower respiratory diseases · Influenza or pneumonia · Colon cancer · Heart failure and ill-defined heart disease · Lymphoma or Leukemia · Breast cancer · Prostate cancer · Liver disease · Urinary system diseases · Suicide

*ONLY 19 CAUSES SHOWN. TOP MALE CAUSES INCLUDE AORTIC ANEURYSM (BARKING & DAGENHAM, HAVERING) AND URINARY SYSTEM DISEASES (REDBRIDGE).
**21 CAUSES SHOWN BECAUSE OF A TIE. URINARY SYSTEM DISEASES AND LYMPHOMA CAUSED THE SAME TOTAL NUMBER OF DEATHS IN FEMALES.

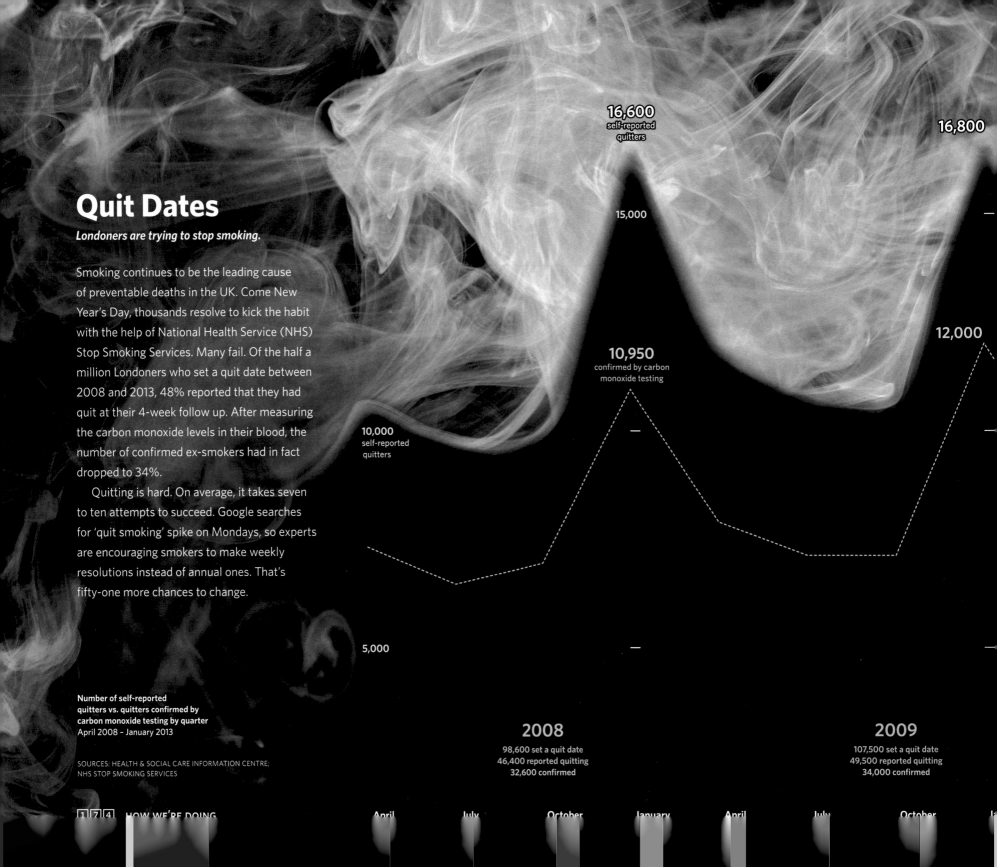

Quit Dates

Londoners are trying to stop smoking.

Smoking continues to be the leading cause of preventable deaths in the UK. Come New Year's Day, thousands resolve to kick the habit with the help of National Health Service (NHS) Stop Smoking Services. Many fail. Of the half a million Londoners who set a quit date between 2008 and 2013, 48% reported that they had quit at their 4-week follow up. After measuring the carbon monoxide levels in their blood, the number of confirmed ex-smokers had in fact dropped to 34%.

    Quitting is hard. On average, it takes seven to ten attempts to succeed. Google searches for 'quit smoking' spike on Mondays, so experts are encouraging smokers to make weekly resolutions instead of annual ones. That's fifty-one more chances to change.

Number of self-reported quitters vs. quitters confirmed by carbon monoxide testing by quarter
April 2008 – January 2013

SOURCES: HEALTH & SOCIAL CARE INFORMATION CENTRE;
NHS STOP SMOKING SERVICES

16,600
self-reported
quitters

16,800

15,000

10,950
confirmed by carbon
monoxide testing

12,000

10,000
self-reported
quitters

5,000

2008
98,600 set a quit date
46,400 reported quitting
32,600 confirmed

2009
107,500 set a quit date
49,500 reported quitting
34,000 confirmed

April   July   October   January   April   July   October

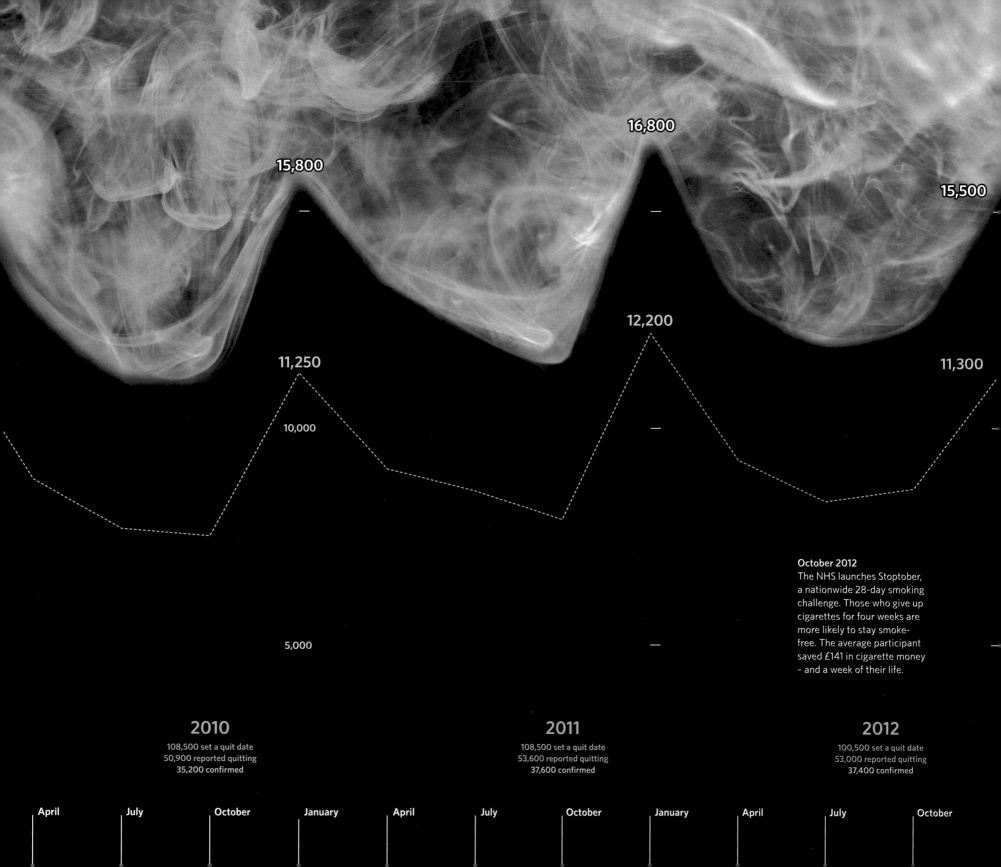

16,800

15,800

15,500

12,200

11,300

11,250

10,000

5,000

October 2012
The NHS launches Stoptober,
a nationwide 28-day smoking
challenge. Those who give up
cigarettes for four weeks are
more likely to stay smoke-
free. The average participant
saved £141 in cigarette money
– and a week of their life.

2010
108,500 set a quit date
50,900 reported quitting
35,200 confirmed

2011
108,500 set a quit date
53,600 reported quitting
37,600 confirmed

2012
100,500 set a quit date
53,000 reported quitting
37,400 confirmed

April | July | October | January | April | July | October | January | April | July | October

Pill Boxes

London's prescriptions indicate its health concerns.

Over the course of a year, National Health Service general practitioners prescribe more than a billion items in England. Doctors in London contribute 116 million to this total. The graphic on the right shows the 120 most-prescribed drugs in the capital, sized by number of prescriptions and grouped by general purpose. (Several drugs have multiple uses.) Heart disease, hypertension and cholesterol are the most frequently treated conditions.

   Darker shades of green indicate higher prices. Branded drugs such as Atorvastatin are often more expensive than generic varieties, so they tend to be prescribed far less. For £1.40, Simvastatin offers a much cheaper means of reducing cholesterol and the risks of heart attack and stroke. In fact, for every ailment listed, there's an option for ten pounds or less.

120 most prescribed drugs by amount, purpose and item cost
March 2013 – February 2014

AVERAGE COST (£)

- 0–10
- 10–20
- 20–30
- 30–40
- 40–50
- 50–60

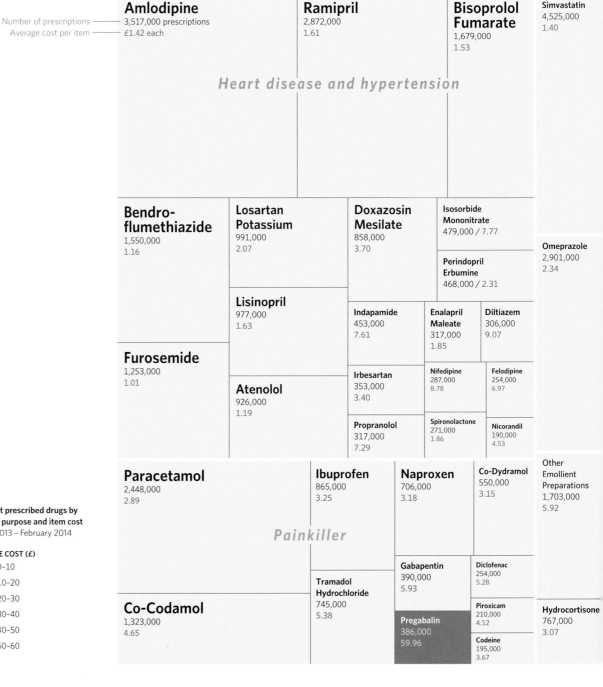

Number of prescriptions ⟶ Amlodipine 3,517,000 prescriptions
Average cost per item ⟶ £1.42 each

Amlodipine
3,517,000 prescriptions
£1.42 each

Ramipril
2,872,000
1.61

Bisoprolol Fumarate
1,679,000
1.53

Simvastatin
4,525,000
1.40

Heart disease and hypertension

Bendro-flumethiazide
1,550,000
1.16

Losartan Potassium
991,000
2.07

Lisinopril
977,000
1.63

Doxazosin Mesilate
858,000
3.70

Isosorbide Mononitrate
479,000 / 7.77

Perindopril Erbumine
468,000 / 2.31

Omeprazole
2,901,000
2.34

Indapamide
453,000
7.61

Enalapril Maleate
317,000
1.85

Diltiazem
306,000
9.07

Furosemide
1,253,000
1.01

Atenolol
926,000
1.19

Irbesartan
353,000
3.40

Nifedipine
287,000
8.78

Felodipine
254,000
6.97

Propranolol
317,000
7.29

Spironolactone
271,000
1.86

Nicorandil
190,000
4.53

Paracetamol
2,448,000
2.89

Ibuprofen
865,000
3.25

Naproxen
706,000
3.18

Co-Dydramol
550,000
3.15

Other Emollient Preparations
1,703,000
5.92

Painkiller

Gabapentin
390,000
5.93

Diclofenac
254,000
5.28

Tramadol Hydrochloride
745,000
5.38

Piroxicam
210,000
4.12

Hydrocortisone
767,000
3.07

Co-Codamol
1,323,000
4.65

Pregabalin
386,000
59.96

Codeine
195,000
3.67

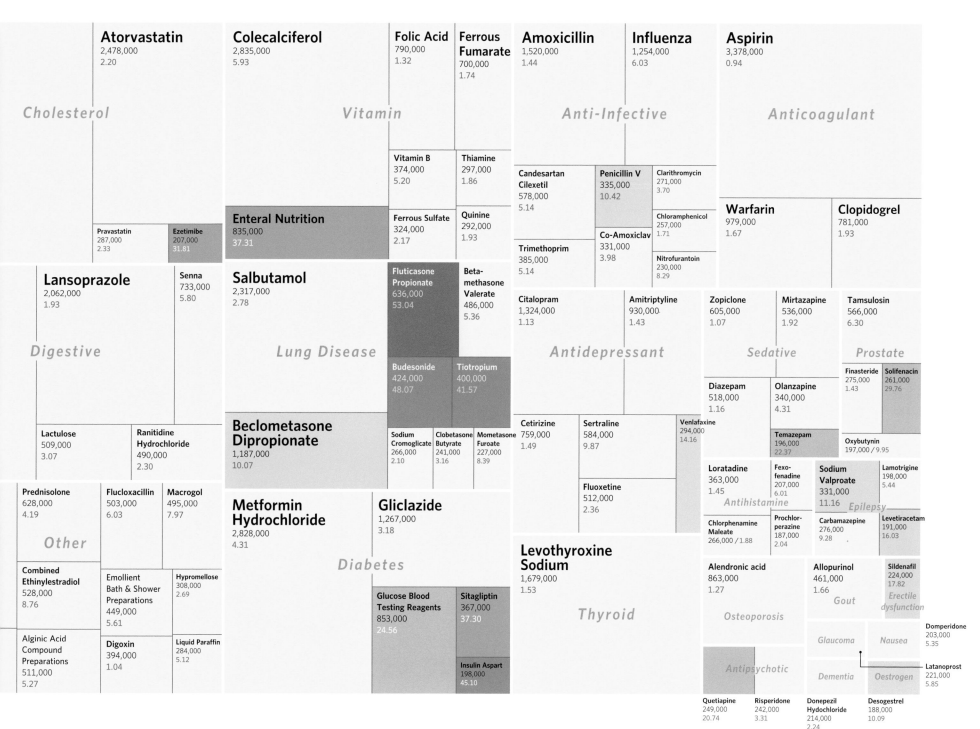

Atorvastatin
2,478,000
2.20

Cholesterol

Pravastatin
287,000
2.33

Ezetimibe
207,000
31.81

Colecalciferol
2,835,000
5.93

Vitamin

Vitamin B
374,000
5.20

Thiamine
297,000
1.86

Enteral Nutrition
835,000
37.31

Ferrous Sulfate
324,000
2.17

Quinine
292,000
1.93

Folic Acid
790,000
1.32

Ferrous Fumarate
700,000
1.74

Amoxicillin
1,520,000
1.44

Influenza
1,254,000
6.03

Anti-Infective

Candesartan Cilexetil
578,000
5.14

Penicillin V
335,000
10.42

Clarithromycin
271,000
3.70

Trimethoprim
385,000
5.14

Co-Amoxiclav
331,000
3.98

Chloramphenicol
257,000
1.71

Nitrofurantoin
230,000
8.29

Aspirin
3,378,000
0.94

Anticoagulant

Warfarin
979,000
1.67

Clopidogrel
781,000
1.93

Lansoprazole
2,062,000
1.93

Senna
733,000
5.80

Digestive

Lactulose
509,000
3.07

Ranitidine Hydrochloride
490,000
2.30

Salbutamol
2,317,000
2.78

Lung Disease

Fluticasone Propionate
636,000
53.04

Beta-methasone Valerate
486,000
5.36

Budesonide
424,000
48.07

Tiotropium
400,000
41.57

Beclometasone Dipropionate
1,187,000
10.07

Sodium Cromoglicate
266,000
2.10

Clobetasone Butyrate
241,000
3.16

Mometasone Furoate
227,000
8.39

Citalopram
1,324,000
1.13

Amitriptyline
930,000
1.43

Antidepressant

Cetirizine
759,000
1.49

Sertraline
584,000
9.87

Venlafaxine
294,000
14.16

Fluoxetine
512,000
2.36

Zopiclone
605,000
1.07

Mirtazapine
536,000
1.92

Tamsulosin
566,000
6.30

Sedative

Prostate

Diazepam
518,000
1.16

Olanzapine
340,000
4.31

Finasteride
275,000
1.43

Solifenacin
261,000
29.76

Temazepam
196,000
22.37

Oxybutynin
197,000 / 9.95

Prednisolone
628,000
4.19

Flucloxacillin
503,000
6.03

Macrogol
495,000
7.97

Other

Combined Ethinylestradiol
528,000
8.76

Emollient Bath & Shower Preparations
449,000
5.61

Hypromellose
308,000
2.69

Alginic Acid Compound Preparations
511,000
5.27

Digoxin
394,000
1.04

Liquid Paraffin
284,000
5.12

Metformin Hydrochloride
2,828,000
4.31

Gliclazide
1,267,000
3.18

Diabetes

Glucose Blood Testing Reagents
853,000
24.56

Sitagliptin
367,000
37.30

Insulin Aspart
198,000
45.10

Levothyroxine Sodium
1,679,000
1.53

Thyroid

Loratadine
363,000
1.45

Fexo-fenadine
207,000
6.01

Sodium Valproate
331,000
11.16

Lamotrigine
198,000
5.44

Antihistamine

Epilepsy

Chlorphenamine Maleate
266,000 / 1.88

Prochlor-perazine
187,000
2.04

Carbamazepine
276,000
9.28

Levetiracetam
191,000
16.03

Alendronic acid
863,000
1.27

Allopurinol
461,000
1.66

Sildenafil
224,000
17.82

Osteoporosis

Gout

Erectile dysfunction

Antipsychotic

Glaucoma

Nausea

Domperidone
203,000
5.35

Dementia

Oestrogen

Latanoprost
221,000
5.85

Quetiapine
249,000
20.74

Risperidone
242,000
3.31

Donepezil Hydochloride
214,000
2.24

Desogestrel
188,000
10.09

SOURCES: HEALTH AND SOCIAL CARE INFORMATION CENTRE; LETTY DORMANDY

Call 999

Drunks are an emergency the city could do without.

9-9-9, the world's first emergency phone service went live in London on 1 July 1937. It was an instant success. In the first week, dispatchers handled 1,300 calls. They'd be pleased to know that seventy-six years later, in 2013, the service responded to 1.1 million calls. They might not be so keen to learn that 32,500 of them were for incapacitated binge-drinkers (see chart).

Alcohol-related hospital admissions cost the National Health Service £3.5 billion a year. To relieve accident and emergency departments, London Ambulance Service began running 'booze buses' in 2005. These specially outfitted ambulances can transport five patients at a time to alcohol recovery centres in Central London. There, patients receive water, a bed and advice on how to drink responsibly.

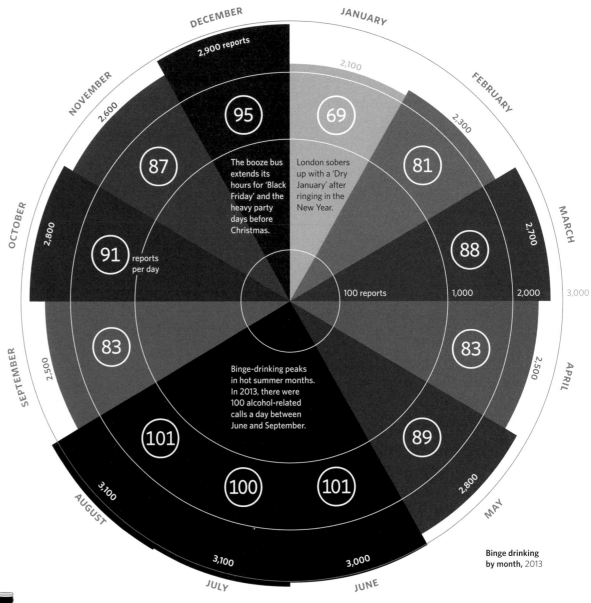

The booze bus extends its hours for 'Black Friday' and the heavy party days before Christmas.

London sobers up with a 'Dry January' after ringing in the New Year.

Binge-drinking peaks in hot summer months. In 2013, there were 100 alcohol-related calls a day between June and September.

reports per day

100 reports

Binge drinking by month, 2013

Boroughs with the most binge-drinking incidents, 2013

 = 300 reports

With its many pubs, clubs and restaurants, Westminster reports the highest number of binge-drinking incidents, more than double the next drunkest boroughs, Camden and Lambeth.

Borough average

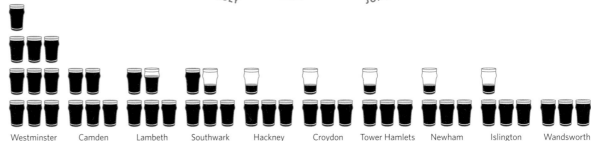

Westminster · Camden · Lambeth · Southwark · Hackney · Croydon · Tower Hamlets · Newham · Islington · Wandsworth

By comparison, this chart shows a much smaller number of 999 reports. In 2013, paramedics attended 1,429 call-outs involving injuries caused by knives (orange); 431 caused by large animals, many of which were dogs (yellow line); and 214 caused by guns (black). Of course, not all victims call 999. By the police's count, there were twice as many: 3,200 crimes involving knife injuries, 830 dog bites and 312 crimes where a gun was fired.

Notice how the overall shape of the injury wedges matches the wedges for binge-drinking. All increased during the hot summer months and in March, October and December. For more correlations between alcohol and violence, turn the page.

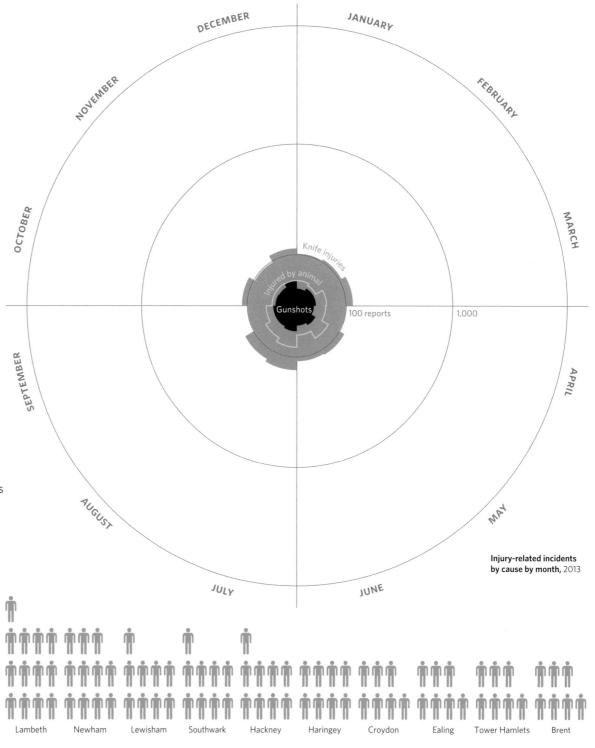

Injury-related incidents by cause by month, 2013

Boroughs with the most incidents involving guns or knives, 2013

 = 10 reports

Ambulances travelled to Lambeth for 112 knife injuries and 17 gun wounds in 2013, more than any other borough. Five of the other boroughs with more than seventy victims were also in Inner London.

Borough average

Lambeth · Newham · Lewisham · Southwark · Hackney · Haringey · Croydon · Ealing · Tower Hamlets · Brent

Flashpoints

Where intoxication increases, violent crime flares up.

The website *police.uk* maps every reported crime down to street level. Using these data, researcher Matt Ashby from University College London's Department of Security and Crime Science identified the violent crime hotspots you see on the right. Between April 2012 and March 2013, nearly 80% of London's streets experienced no such crimes (grey). Those that did, he coloured from more (red) to less (yellow).

As Ashby puts it on his blog, *lesscrime.info*, 'Central London is in a class of its own.' More than 2,000 violent crimes – which include murder, assault, harassment, kidnapping as well as all sex offences – were recorded around Soho and Leicester Square. Shoreditch, Brixton, Camden Town and Whitechapel round out the top five. This is to be expected, although no less acceptable, given the number of people passing through these areas at night, fuelled on alcohol from the many clubs and bars (see pp. 178–9). Further out, violent crime gathers along arterial roads and around suburban town centres. Some of these, such as Romford and Croydon, have given the rest of their borough a bad name, which, as Ashby says, 'must be galling if you live in ultra-leafy Hornchurch or Shirley'.

DODGY AREAS

Over the course of a year, more than 750 violent crimes were reported within a one-kilometre radius of these twenty areas. Seven of the top ten are in Central London.

1. Soho and Leicester Square
2. Shoreditch
3. Brixton
4. Camden Town
5. Whitechapel
6. Hackney
7. Ladbroke Grove and Kensal Town
8. Elephant and Castle
9. Peckham
10. Croydon
11. Archway
12. Stratford
13. Shepherd's Bush
14. King's Cross and Angel
15. Dalston
16. Edgware Road and Marble Arch
17. Poplar
18. Woolwich
19. Kingston
20. Wood Green

Violent crimes
April 2012 – March 2013

MORE CRIME

LESS CRIME

0 ————— 5 km

SOURCES: POLICE.UK; MATT ASHBY, UNIVERSITY COLLEGE LONDON; OS

Top Crimes

Watch your wallet in Westminster.

Tourists take note. Things have a habit of disappearing in London, especially amidst the many shops, pubs and attractions in the centre. In 2012–13, the Metropolitan police (MPS) responded to 37,000 thefts in Westminster alone, three times as many as the next borough. While theft was prevalent in all boroughs, when we focused on the most common crimes in 200 metre by 200 metre areas, new patterns emerged (see right). Pockets of violent and vehicle crime (yellow, orange) appeared, transitioning to a ring of burglaries (purple) in more residential areas. We excluded the 341,000 anti-social behaviour reports, which included 'crimes' like loitering, littering, spitting, begging, door-slamming, loud music, abusive language, fare evasion, fireworks and barking dogs. If we hadn't, they would have covered the whole map!

CRIME'S DECLINE

Though crime rates have dropped in every borough, fear has not. According to an MPS survey, 54% of Newham residents said they were worried about crime, compared to 15% in Kingston. Both experience fewer crimes than London's top three.

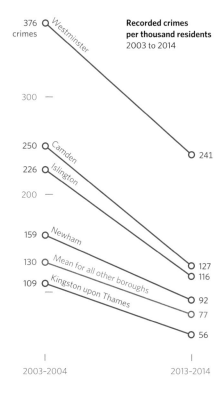

Recorded crimes per thousand residents
2003 to 2014

2003–2004	2013–2014
376 crimes – Westminster	241
250 – Camden	127
226 – Islington	116
159 – Newham	92
130 – Mean for all other boroughs	77
109 – Kingston upon Thames	56
300	
200	

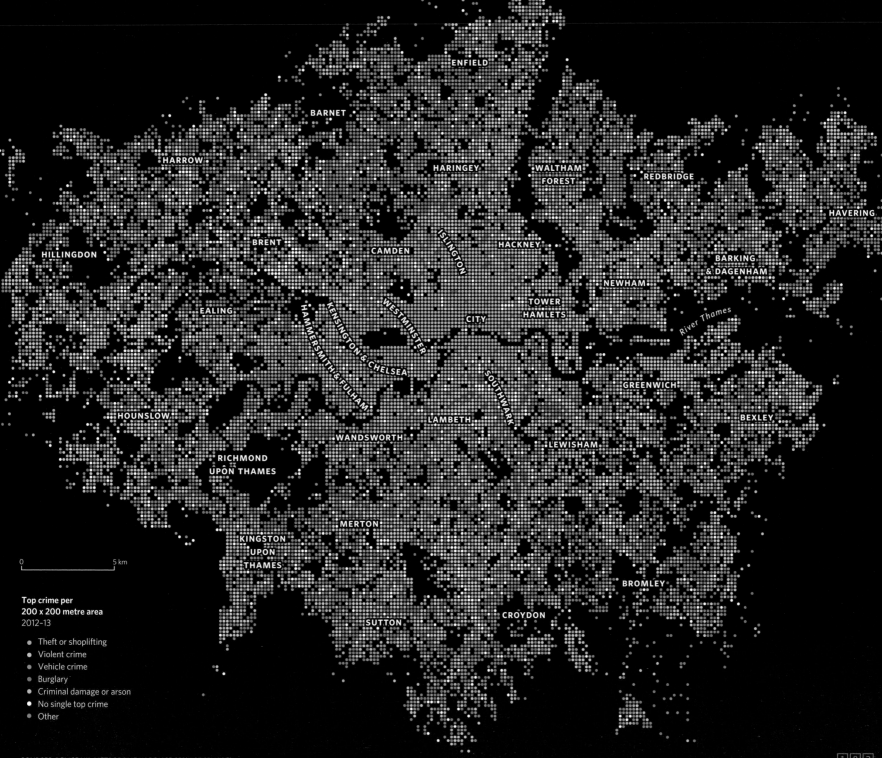

ENFIELD

BARNET

HARROW

HARINGEY

WALTHAM FOREST

REDBRIDGE

HILLINGDON

BRENT

CAMDEN

ISLINGTON

HACKNEY

HAVERING

BARKING & DAGENHAM

EALING

HAMMERSMITH & FULHAM

KENSINGTON & CHELSEA

WESTMINSTER

CITY

TOWER HAMLETS

NEWHAM

River Thames

GREENWICH

HOUNSLOW

LAMBETH

SOUTHWARK

BEXLEY

WANDSWORTH

LEWISHAM

RICHMOND UPON THAMES

MERTON

KINGSTON UPON THAMES

BROMLEY

Top crime per 200 x 200 metre area
2012–13

- Theft or shoplifting
- Violent crime
- Vehicle crime
- Burglary
- Criminal damage or arson
- No single top crime
- Other

SUTTON

CROYDON

0 ____ 5 km

SOURCES: POLICE.UK; METROPOLITAN POLICE SERVICE (CHART)

You Can't Hide

Day or night, police helicopters find suspects on the run.

Altitude isn't their only advantage. The airborne officers can see in the dark. What may seem like great camouflage to a suspect in a garden at 2 a.m. is clearer than day to the helicopter's thermal-imaging sensor, where a warm body contrasts like black ink on a white page. The crew then uses radios and a 30-million candle-power spotlight to guide ground units to the suspect.

The Air Support Unit averages 275 flight hours a month between its three choppers: India 99, 98 and 97. Crews change shifts twice a day: once in the evening and again before criminals wake up. Here, we plotted every mission flown in July 2013, coloured by purpose. The silhouettes indicate when they successfully detained a suspect or located a missing person. When not conducting searches, you may see the helicopter hovering above concerts, demonstrations and sporting events. Its 360-degree video camera provides a vital aerial feed to crowd control officers on the scene. The unit's 100,000 Twitter followers know @MPSinthesky best for another purpose: spectacular photos of the city.

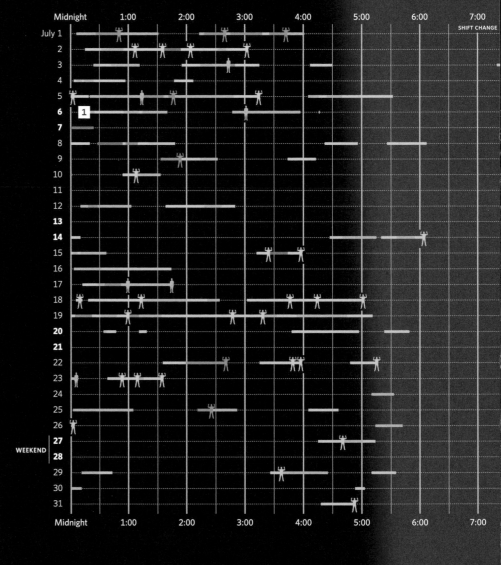

Choppers can fly from their base in Lippitts Hill to West-minster Bridge in six minutes. They don't always start so far away. By conducting routine patrols across the city, the helicopters put themselves in position to respond to incidents in any borough.

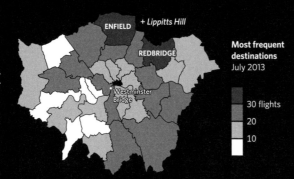

ENFIELD + Lippitts Hill
REDBRIDGE
Westminster Bridge

Most frequent destinations
July 2013

30 flights
20
10

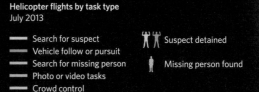

Helicopter flights by task type
July 2013

— Search for suspect
— Vehicle follow or pursuit
— Search for missing person
— Photo or video tasks
— Crowd control
— Tactical support
— Other

Suspect detained

Missing person found

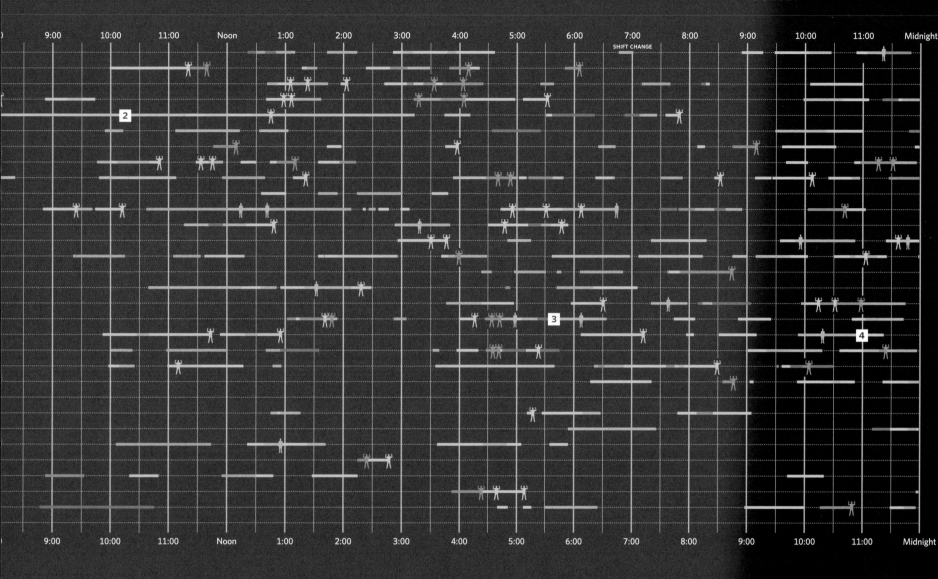

9:00 10:00 11:00 Noon 1:00 2:00 3:00 4:00 5:00 6:00 7:00 8:00 9:00 10:00 11:00 Midnight

SHIFT CHANGE

9:00 10:00 11:00 Noon 1:00 2:00 3:00 4:00 5:00 6:00 7:00 8:00 9:00 10:00 11:00 Midnight

1 **6 JULY**
At midnight, @MPSinthesky tweeted a thermal image of a concert at Wembley Stadium. Later, they posted one of Battersea Power Station 'all lit up'. Such images keep a strong Twitter following, which the crew sometimes enlists to help locate missing persons.

2 **5 JULY**
The unit's longest day of the month kept them airborne for sixteen hours. After a series of late-night searches, the day crew lifted at 7:30 a.m. for a long stretch of crowd control above the first day of the British Summer Time festival in Hyde Park.

3 **18 JULY**
Often when one task ends, another begins. Between 4 and 6:30 p.m., the helicopter located a suspect in Westminster; made vehicle stops in Hackney; found missing persons in Haringey and Bexley; and gave tactical support for a coach fire on the M25.

4 **19 JULY**
Thirty-seven flights – including car chases, roof searches, lost persons, photos of Lord's Cricket Ground and support for firefighters battling a heat-wave-induced grass fire – are all in a day's work for London's chopper coppers.

We obtained these data through a Freedom of Information request (see pp. 22–3). Not all flight records were shared because to do so would 'allow interested parties to gain an upper hand and awareness of policing decisions used to safeguard national security'.

SOURCE: METROPOLITAN POLICE SERVICE

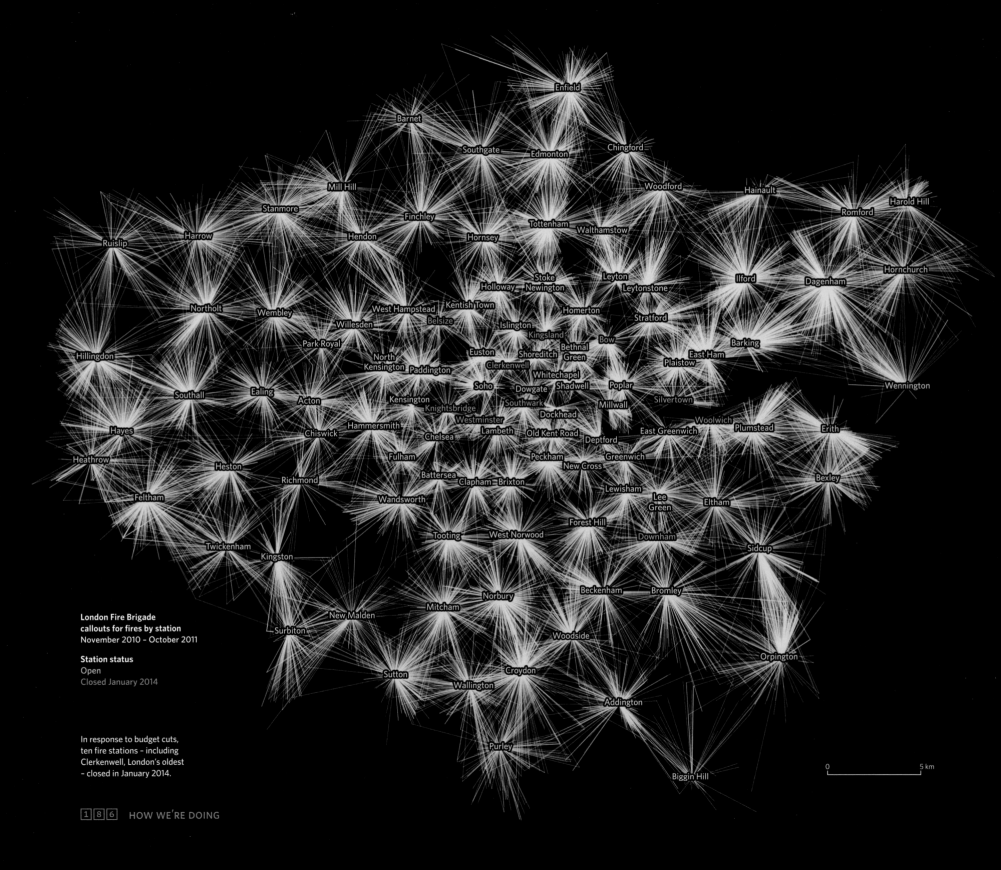

London Fire Brigade
callouts for fires by station
November 2010 – October 2011

Station status
Open
Closed January 2014

In response to budget cuts,
ten fire stations – including
Clerkenwell, London's oldest
– closed in January 2014.

Enfield
Barnet
Southgate Edmonton Chingford
Mill Hill Woodford Hainault
Stanmore Finchley Romford Harold Hill
Harrow Hendon Tottenham Walthamstow
Ruislip Hornsey Ilford Dagenham Hornchurch
Northolt Wembley West Hampstead Kentish Town Stoke Newington Leyton Leytonstone Stratford Barking
Willesden Belsize Islington Homerton East Ham
Hillingdon Park Royal Kingsland Bow
North Kensington Euston Shoreditch Bethnal Green Plaistow
Paddington Clerkenwell Whitechapel
Southall Ealing Soho Dowgate Shadwell Poplar Silvertown Wennington
Acton Kensington Millwall
Knightsbridge Southwark Woolwich Plumstead Erith
Hayes Hammersmith Westminster Dockhead East Greenwich
Chiswick Chelsea Lambeth Old Kent Road Deptford Bexley
Heathrow Heston Fulham Peckham Greenwich
Richmond Battersea New Cross
Clapham Brixton Lewisham Lee Green Eltham
Feltham Wandsworth
Forest Hill Downham
Tooting West Norwood Sidcup
Twickenham Kingston
Norbury Beckenham Bromley
New Malden Mitcham Woodside
Surbiton Sutton Croydon Orpington
Wallington Addington
Purley
Biggin Hill

0   5 km

Sound the Alarm!

Life is never quiet for the London Fire Brigade.

Lighting up the city like an array of fireworks, each of the 30,354 lines to the left connects a fire station to a blaze between November 2010 and October 2011. These bursts form only part of the year's display, however, since only 22% of the total call outs went to actual fires (see below). False alarms triggered by automatic systems at office blocks, hospitals, universities and airports accounted for much of the rest. Additionally, firefighters were often called to provide 'special services', such as freeing people from lifts (9,482 incidents), rescuing animals (698) or assisting the increasing number of people 'stuck or trapped in objects' like handcuffs or toilet seats (416). These often avoidable situations – each costing taxpayers £290 on average – can steal crews away from genuine emergencies. In 2013, the Brigade took to Twitter using the #fiftyshadesofred hashtag to highlight some of the most ridiculous incidents they have ever attended (see right). To avoid being featured, heed their advice: 'If you use handcuffs, always keep the keys handy.'

#FIFTYSHADESOFRED

The Brigade attended more than 1,300 'removal of object' incidents between 2010 and 2013, including:

491 rings stuck on fingers

379 people trapped in or under machinery

79 trapped in handcuffs

36 impaled on objects

18 children with heads stuck in potties

17 children with fingers stuck in toys

9 hands caught in shredders or blenders

9 rings stuck on penises

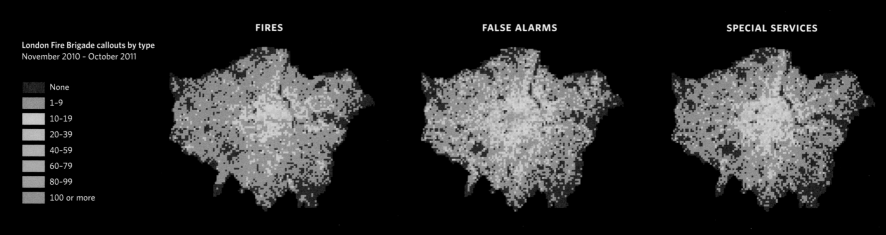

FIRES   **FALSE ALARMS**   **SPECIAL SERVICES**

London Fire Brigade callouts by type
November 2010 - October 2011

None
1-9
10-19
20-39
40-59
60-79
80-99
100 or more

Safer Drivers

London's motorists are heading in the right direction.

Over the past decade, there has been a steady decline in the number of people killed or seriously injured in their cars. Road safety campaigns have helped, but Londoners are also driving less. Between 2001 and 2010, car journeys dropped 13% as drivers opted for other ways to get around the city (see pp. 124-5). Cycling, in contrast, increased 66% over the same period. The surge in ridership led to a surge in accidents such that for the first time, the number of serious cyclist injuries surpassed that of drivers in the summers of 2011 and 2012.

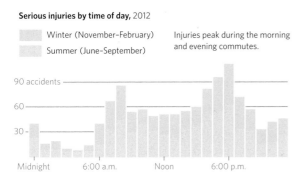

Serious injuries by time of day, 2012

Winter (November–February)

Summer (June–September)

Injuries peak during the morning and evening commutes.

90 accidents

60

30

Midnight   6:00 a.m.   Noon   6:00 p.m.

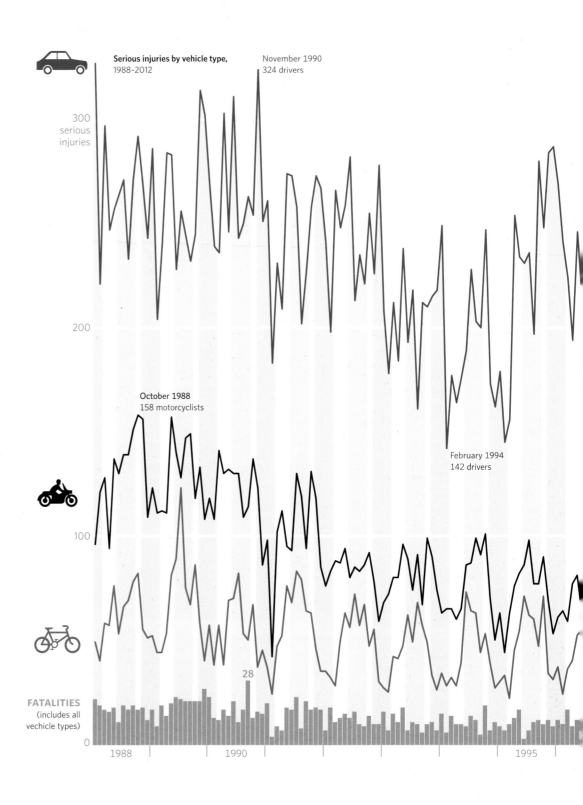

Serious injuries by vehicle type, 1988-2012

November 1990
324 drivers

300 serious injuries

200

October 1988
158 motorcyclists

February 1994
142 drivers

100

28

FATALITIES
(includes all vechicle types)

0

1988   1990   1995

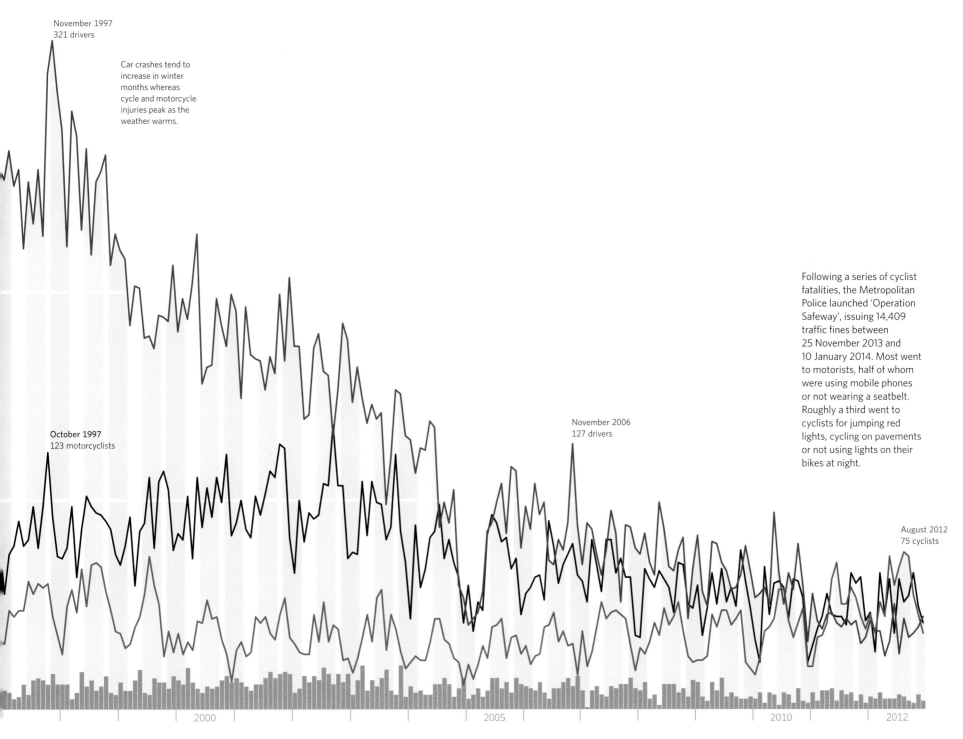

November 1997
321 drivers

Car crashes tend to
increase in winter
months whereas
cycle and motorcycle
injuries peak as the
weather warms.

October 1997
123 motorcyclists

Following a series of cyclist
fatalities, the Metropolitan
Police launched 'Operation
Safeway', issuing 14,409
traffic fines between
25 November 2013 and
10 January 2014. Most went
to motorists, half of whom
were using mobile phones
or not wearing a seatbelt.
Roughly a third went to
cyclists for jumping red
lights, cycling on pavements
or not using lights on their
bikes at night.

November 2006
127 drivers

August 2012
75 cyclists

2000

2005

2010

2012

SOURCE: STATS19

How Cyclists Get Hit

Cars may cause the most accidents but lorries are most lethal.

Cycle superhighways (see pp. 146–7) won't be enough to protect the growing number of Londoners who choose to get around on two wheels. Drivers and cyclists alike must learn to share the road. In the most recent report of its kind, Transport for London (TfL) studied the nature of 466 collisions resulting in serious or fatal injuries to pedal cyclists in 2010. Of the twenty-six manoeuvres tallied, turning left with a lorry proved deadliest. As a result, TfL began awareness training for lorry drivers. In January 2014, they mandated freight companies to install extra mirrors as well as sideguards and encouraged the use of sensors and external audio alerts that announce, 'Caution, vehicle turning left.' Still, deaths by lorry persist. Many in the cycling community want further controls – and they may get them. In 2013, Mayor of London Boris Johnson launched *Safe Streets for London*, a plan that outlines fifty-two key measures for cycle safety including possibly restricting lorries during peak times.

Collisions resulting in serious injury or fatality to a pedal cyclist by manoeuvre, 2010

Cyclist

Vehicle

Pedestrian

× Cyclist fatality

Junction control ignored

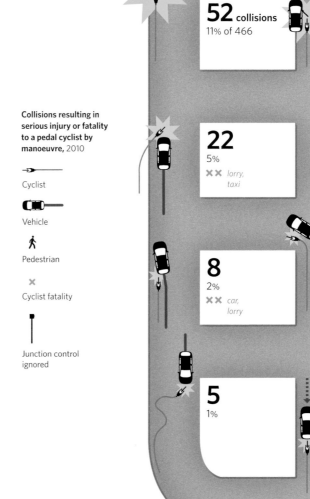

52 collisions
11% of 466

49
11%
× car

22
5%
×× lorry, taxi

16
3%
× car

8
2%
×× car, lorry

6
1%
×× lorries

5
1%

4
1%

THE CASE AGAINST LORRIES

Despite accounting for only 5% of traffic, lorries were involved in nearly half of cyclist deaths between 2010 and 2013. In 2010, one in five collisions with lorries killed the cyclist, the highest rate of any vehicle type.

Collisions resulting in serious injury or fatality to a pedal cyclist by vehicle type, 2010

4	12	18	20	21	50	310
		×	×	××××		××××

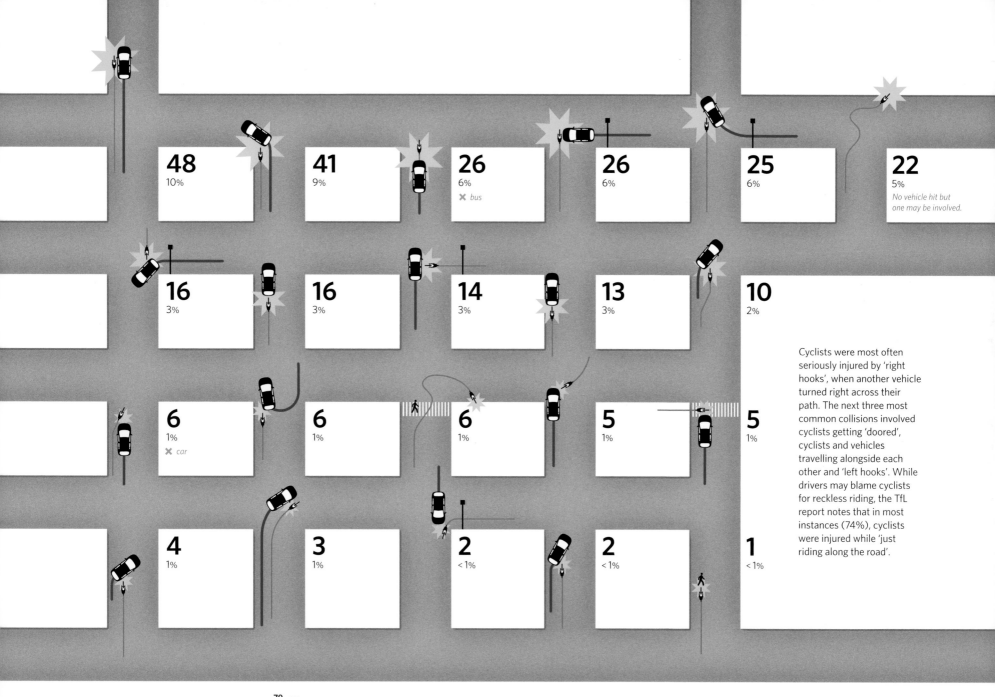

48 10%

41 9%

26 6% ✕ bus

26 6%

25 6%

22 5% *No vehicle hit but one may be involved.*

16 3%

16 3%

14 3%

13 3%

10 2%

6 1% ✕ car

6 1%

6 1%

5 1%

5 1%

4 1%

3 1%

2 <1%

2 <1%

1 <1%

Cyclists were most often seriously injured by 'right hooks', when another vehicle turned right across their path. The next three most common collisions involved cyclists getting 'doored', cyclists and vehicles travelling alongside each other and 'left hooks'. While drivers may blame cyclists for reckless riding, the TfL report notes that in most instances (74%), cyclists were injured while 'just riding along the road'.

Collisions resulting in serious injury or fatality to a pedal cyclist by age-band and gender, 2010

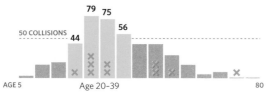

50 COLLISIONS

79 75 56 44

AGE 5   Age 20–39   80

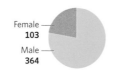

Female **103**

Male **364**

Most of the 466 collisions above involved cyclists in their twenties and thirties. Although more than three-quarters were male, female cyclists remain at greater risk. Between 2005 and 2013, 21 women were killed by lorries versus 15 men, despite women only accounting for an estimated 30% of all riders.

SOURCE: TRANSPORT FOR LONDON

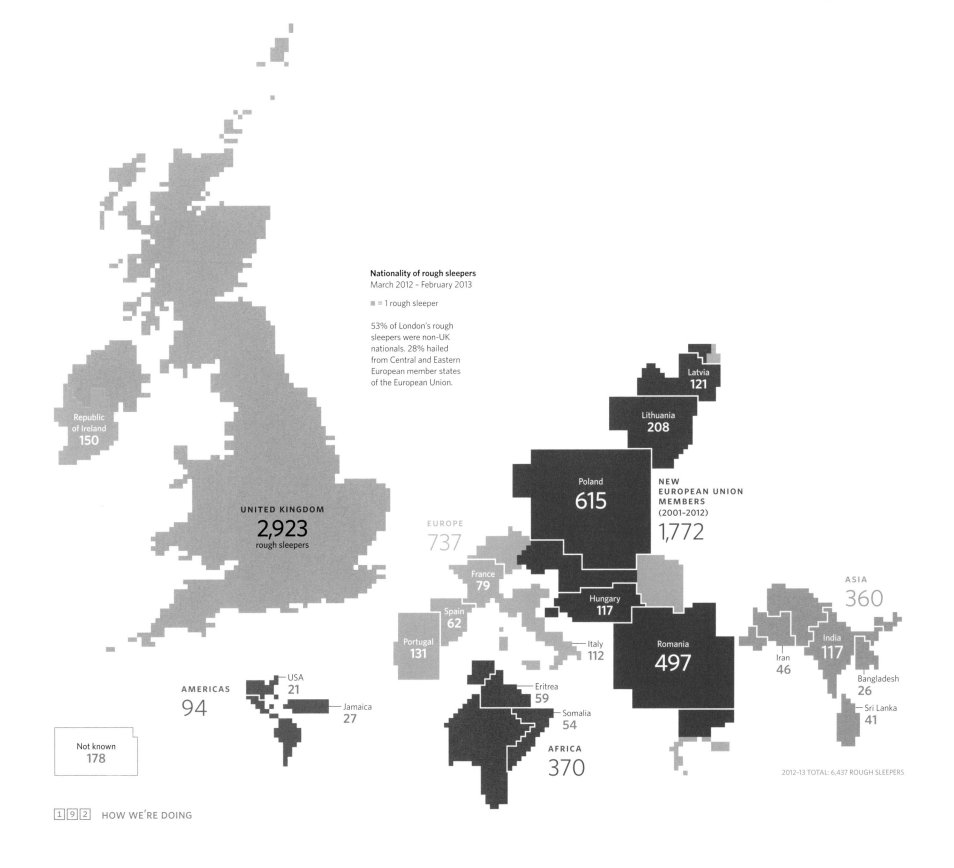

Nationality of rough sleepers
March 2012 – February 2013

■ = 1 rough sleeper

53% of London's rough sleepers were non-UK nationals. 28% hailed from Central and Eastern European member states of the European Union.

Republic of Ireland
150

UNITED KINGDOM
2,923
rough sleepers

EUROPE
737

France
79

Spain
62

Portugal
131

Italy
112

Latvia
121

Lithuania
208

Poland
615

NEW EUROPEAN UNION MEMBERS (2001-2012)
1,772

Hungary
117

Romania
497

ASIA
360

India
117

Iran
46

Bangladesh
26

Sri Lanka
41

AMERICAS
94

USA
21

Jamaica
27

Eritrea
59

Somalia
54

AFRICA
370

Not known
178

2012-13 TOTAL: 6,437 ROUGH SLEEPERS

Street Views

Charities collect data to help London's homeless off the streets for good.

Between March 2012 and February 2013, outreach teams spotted 6,437 'rough sleepers' on London's streets, 68% of whom were spending their first night out. As part of the city's 'No Second Night Out' programme, teams then helped new arrivals to assessment centres where trained staff assessed their needs and began arranging for housing or reconnections. That year, three-quarters of those new rough sleepers spent only one night out.

For 800 of London's more habitual rough sleepers, another plan exists. Private investors have contributed £5 million to a three-year 'social-impact bond'. The deal is simple: charities get the time necessary to focus on individuals with complex health needs (see right); the city saves by reducing reliance on its services; and investors get reimbursed if the charities meet targets such as the number of new homes and jobs sustained or fewer hospital visits. The rough sleepers? They receive personalized care and proof that their lives are worthwhile.

Support needs, 2012–13

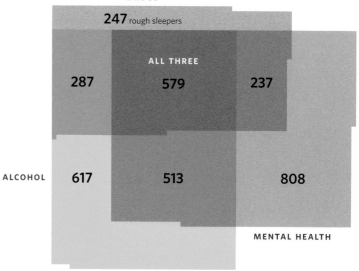

DRUGS

247 rough sleepers

ALL THREE

| 287 | 579 | 237 |

ALCOHOL

| 617 | 513 | 808 |

MENTAL HEALTH

1,492 None   4,874 TOTAL (1,563 NOT KNOWN OR NOT ASSESSED)

Rough sleeping history, 2012–13

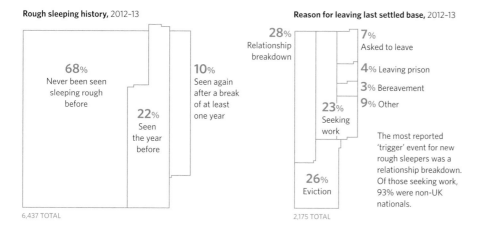

68% Never been seen sleeping rough before

22% Seen the year before

10% Seen again after a break of at least one year

6,437 TOTAL

Reason for leaving last settled base, 2012–13

28% Relationship breakdown

7% Asked to leave

4% Leaving prison

3% Bereavement

9% Other

23% Seeking work

26% Eviction

The most reported 'trigger' event for new rough sleepers was a relationship breakdown. Of those seeking work, 93% were non-UK nationals.

2,175 TOTAL

Drug, alcohol and mental health problems often overlap. Of the 4,874 rough sleepers assessed, 69% suffered from drug or alcohol abuse; 44% had mental health needs; 12% struggled with all three.

If you see someone sleeping rough, you can help them off the street by calling No Second Night Out on 0870 383 3333 twenty-four hours a day.

The Unconnected

Who remains offline?

According to the 2013 Labour Force Survey, an estimated 655,000 Londoners aged 16 and older have never used the Net. As we show to the right, very few live in Camden or Richmond upon Thames (dark blue); many more live in deprived boroughs such as Hounslow, Havering and Barking & Dagenham (orange). They span all ethnicities and both sexes. 59,000 earn less than £200 a week, and nearly a third have no educational qualifications. What unites them most is their age. 87% were born before 1963. The times they are a-changin'.

Percentage of residents aged 16 and older who have used the Internet by borough, 2013

 95–100%

 90–94.9

 85–89.9

 80–84.9

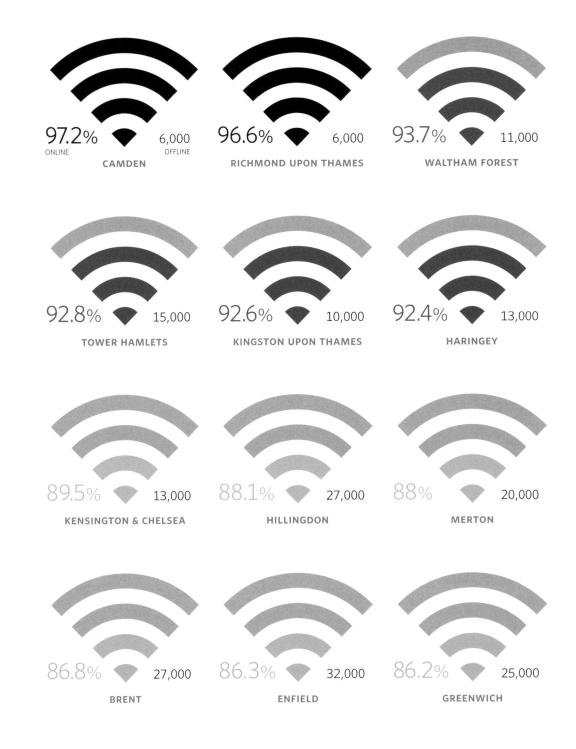

97.2% ONLINE — 6,000 OFFLINE
CAMDEN

96.6% — 6,000
RICHMOND UPON THAMES

93.7% — 11,000
WALTHAM FOREST

92.8% — 15,000
TOWER HAMLETS

92.6% — 10,000
KINGSTON UPON THAMES

92.4% — 13,000
HARINGEY

89.5% — 13,000
KENSINGTON & CHELSEA

88.1% — 27,000
HILLINGDON

88% — 20,000
MERTON

86.8% — 27,000
BRENT

86.3% — 32,000
ENFIELD

86.2% — 25,000
GREENWICH

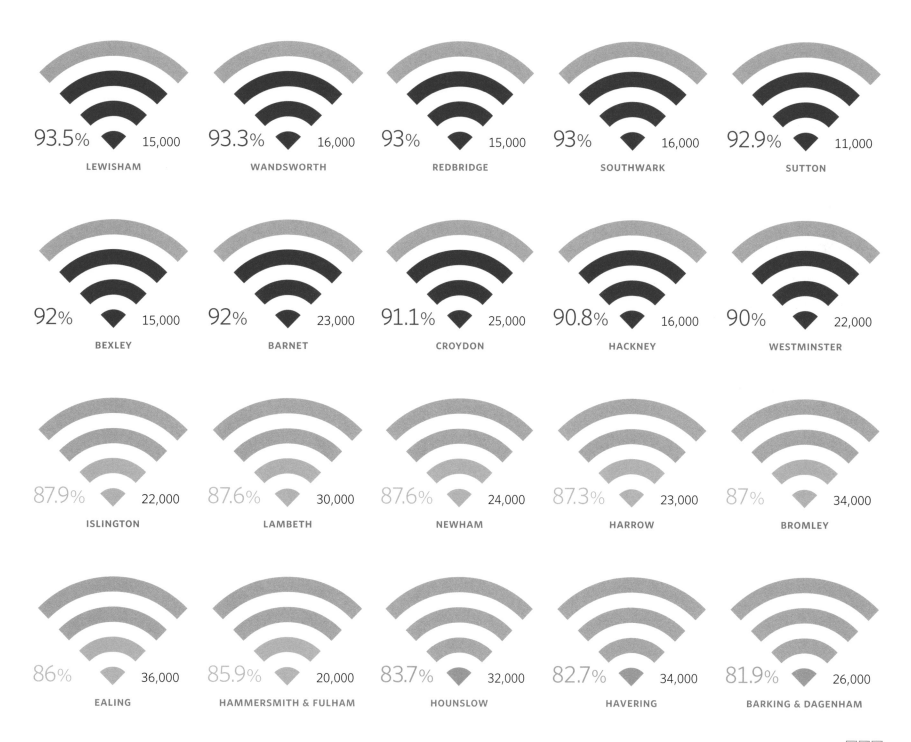

93.5% 15,000 **LEWISHAM**

93.3% 16,000 **WANDSWORTH**

93% 15,000 **REDBRIDGE**

93% 16,000 **SOUTHWARK**

92.9% 11,000 **SUTTON**

92% 15,000 **BEXLEY**

92% 23,000 **BARNET**

91.1% 25,000 **CROYDON**

90.8% 16,000 **HACKNEY**

90% 22,000 **WESTMINSTER**

87.9% 22,000 **ISLINGTON**

87.6% 30,000 **LAMBETH**

87.6% 24,000 **NEWHAM**

87.3% 23,000 **HARROW**

87% 34,000 **BROMLEY**

86% 36,000 **EALING**

85.9% 20,000 **HAMMERSMITH & FULHAM**

83.7% 32,000 **HOUNSLOW**

82.7% 34,000 **HAVERING**

81.9% 26,000 **BARKING & DAGENHAM**

SOURCE: ONS

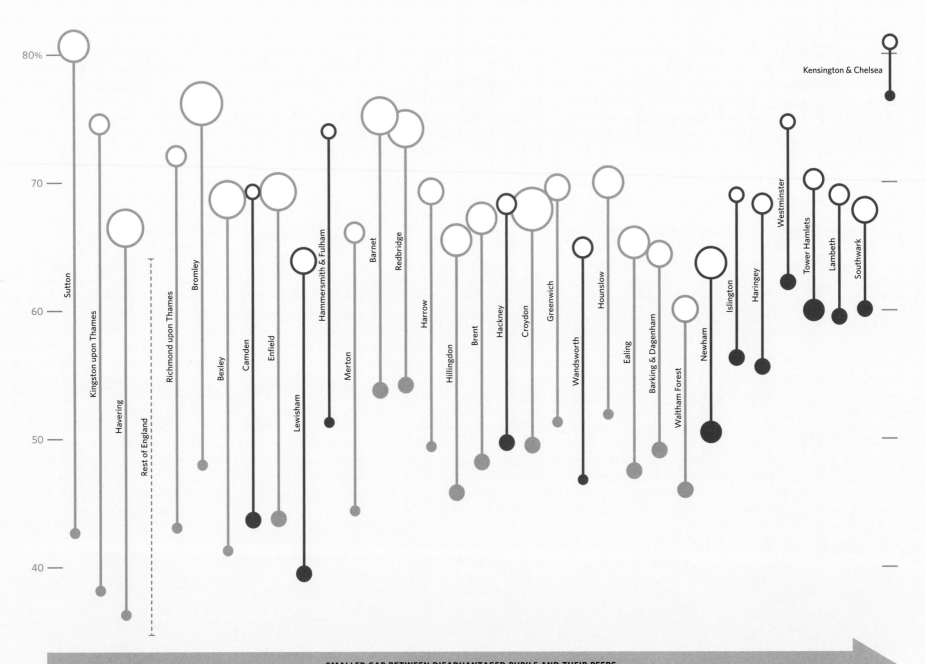

80%

70

60

50

40

Sutton

Kingston upon Thames

Havering

Rest of England

Richmond upon Thames

Bromley

Bexley

Camden

Enfield

Lewisham

Hammersmith & Fulham

Merton

Barnet

Redbridge

Harrow

Hillingdon

Brent

Hackney

Croydon

Greenwich

Wandsworth

Hounslow

Ealing

Barking & Dagenham

Waltham Forest

Newham

Islington

Haringey

Westminster

Kensington & Chelsea

Tower Hamlets

Lambeth

Southwark

SMALLER GAP BETWEEN DISADVANTAGED PUPILS AND THEIR PEERS

Top of the Class

In less than ten years, London's schools have turned around.

Not so long ago, London's schools were a source of national despair. Now, they're an example of progress. Inner London's sixteen-year-olds went from being England's worst performers on GCSE exams to second best, behind only their Outer London peers (see chart, below right). The success story has benefitted children regardless of their backgrounds. The graphic on the left depicts the attainment gap in GCSE results between the capital's disadvantaged children – those who qualify for free school meals – and their classmates. The gap is smallest in Inner London (blue), where all boroughs are exceeding the average for England.

Establishing what's behind the success has been referred to as 'perhaps the biggest question in education policy' since the answer could be replicated for the benefit of children across the country. The Institute for Fiscal Studies (IFS) credit improvements to pupil attainment at younger ages working their way through to GCSE results, whilst the CfBT Education Trust see London's success stemming, in part, from a range of recent public and charitable initiatives. Some say it's with the help of monsters. To learn more about them, turn the page.

Percentage of secondary school pupils achieving grades of A*–C on five or more GCSEs (including English and Maths) by borough, 2012-13

Outer London borough · Inner London borough

Pupils **ineligible** for free school meals

Pupils **eligible** for free school meals

Number of pupils

1,000 · 2,000 · 3,000

Percentage of secondary school pupils achieving grades of A*–C on five or more GCSEs (including English and Maths), 2002-2012

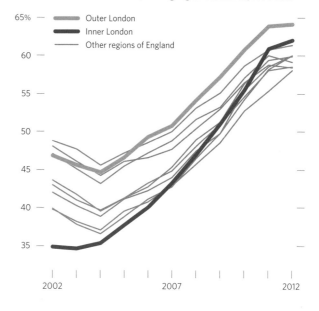

— Outer London
— Inner London
— Other regions of England

65%

60

55

50

45

40

35

2002 · 2007 · 2012

In Their Words

With the help of monsters, children in east London tell their stories.

On the shelves of Hoxton Street Monster Supplies, you'll find impacted earwax, tinned fear and bloodsucker lollipops. Pass through its secret door and you'll find another curiosity: Ministry of Stories (MoS), a creative writing and mentoring centre for young people from the boroughs of Hackney, Islington and Tower Hamlets. Since its launch in 2010, volunteers have helped some 10,000 students to publish three anthologies, a four-part guide to monster housekeeping, a map and a professionally recorded album. Certain themes recur. Of the 36,000 words in those publications, students wrote 'Mum' more than 'Dad', 'zombie' more than 'vampire' and 'ugly' more than 'beautiful'. The more prevalent word in each pair appears in purple.

'There's a great song in the album that was written by this boy, Obie,' says MoS co-director Ben Payne. The lyrics describe a man 'as ugly as a Minotaur' who 'lives in the city of dirt'. In its final verse, *Franky finds the bathroom and turns on the tap / The water is clean and now so is he.* 'When I hear that song,' says Payne, 'you can almost see a lot of the other concerns of children his age encompassed in it.'

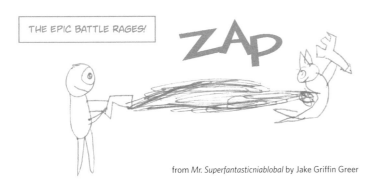

THE EPIC BATTLE RAGES!

ZAP

from *Mr. Superfantasticniablobal* by Jake Griffin Greer

Frequency of words in student writing published by the Ministry of Stories, 2011–13

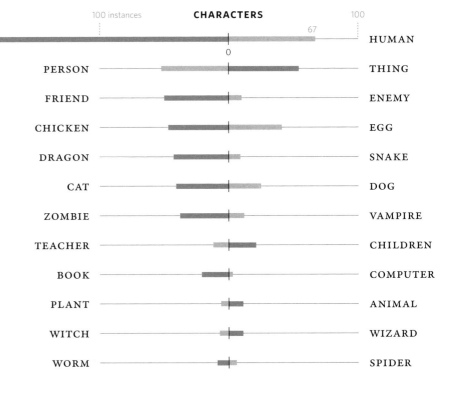

CHARACTERS

100 instances — 100

MONSTER 222 instances	67 HUMAN
PERSON	THING
FRIEND	ENEMY
CHICKEN	EGG
DRAGON	SNAKE
CAT	DOG
ZOMBIE	VAMPIRE
TEACHER	CHILDREN
BOOK	COMPUTER
PLANT	ANIMAL
WITCH	WIZARD
WORM	SPIDER

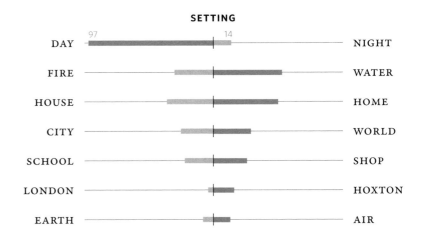

SETTING

DAY 97	14 NIGHT
FIRE	WATER
HOUSE	HOME
CITY	WORLD
SCHOOL	SHOP
LONDON	HOXTON
EARTH	AIR

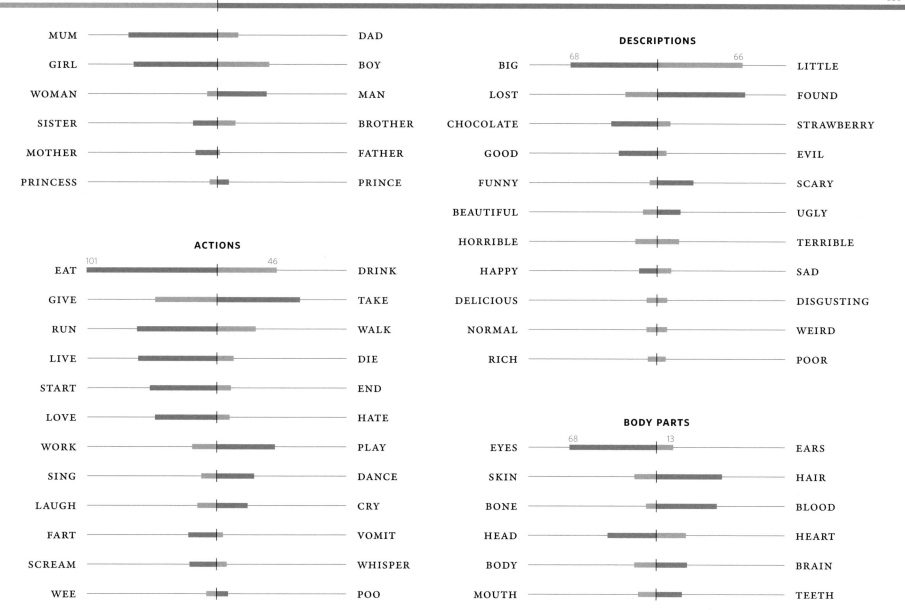

GENERATE

GENDER

SHE 216 instances — 550 HE

MUM	DAD
GIRL	BOY
WOMAN	MAN
SISTER	BROTHER
MOTHER	FATHER
PRINCESS	PRINCE

DESCRIPTIONS

BIG 68 / 66	LITTLE
LOST	FOUND
CHOCOLATE	STRAWBERRY
GOOD	EVIL
FUNNY	SCARY
BEAUTIFUL	UGLY
HORRIBLE	TERRIBLE
HAPPY	SAD
DELICIOUS	DISGUSTING
NORMAL	WEIRD
RICH	POOR

ACTIONS

EAT 101 / 46	DRINK
GIVE	TAKE
RUN	WALK
LIVE	DIE
START	END
LOVE	HATE
WORK	PLAY
SING	DANCE
LAUGH	CRY
FART	VOMIT
SCREAM	WHISPER
WEE	POO

BODY PARTS

EYES 68 / 13	EARS
SKIN	HAIR
BONE	BLOOD
HEAD	HEART
BODY	BRAIN
MOUTH	TEETH

SOURCE: MINISTRY OF STORIES

WHAT WE LIKE

White
Hart Lane

Matchroom
Stadium

Victoria
Road

Emirates
Stadium

Boleyn
Ground

Loftus Road
Stadium

River Thames

Stamford
Bridge

The Den

The Valley

Griffin
Park

River Thames

Craven
Cottage

Selhurst
Park

Kingsmeadow

GREATER LONDON
AUTHORITY BOUNDARY

The Football Tribes

Win or lose, fans of London clubs voice their allegiance on Twitter.

On 22 March 2014, the Chelsea Blues crushed their red rivals 6–0 in a game neither club will soon forget. Arsenal fans took to Twitter to bemoan the loss ('Utterly, woefully, hideously execrable. #afc') while #carefree Chelsea beamed with pride ('There's only one team in London!' #cfc).

In fact, there are thirteen professional football clubs in London. Here, we divided the city into squares, each coloured by the club with the most tweeted hashtag in that area. Taken together, the squares form a mosaic of football loyalties. Chelsea (dark blue) and Arsenal (red) – the London clubs with the most titles in Premier League history (3 each) – dominate on both sides of the Thames; tweets for the eleven other clubs mostly prevail near their grounds.

Chelsea finished the season ahead of Arsenal in the League and in the Twittersphere. The recent #ChampionsOfEurope out-tweeted the Gunners 22,000–19,000. On this map, blue is the colour, indeed.

London's football clubs by popularity on Twitter
August 2013 – May 2014

Each square measures 500 x 500 metres.

A square's colour indicates the football club with the most tweeted hashtag in that area.

PREMIER LEAGUE

■ **CHELSEA** ⌐WINS ⌐LOSSES ⌐DRAWS
Stamford Bridge
2013–14 record: **25-7-6** *(3rd place)*

■ **ARSENAL**
Emirates Stadium
2013–14 record: **24-7-7** *(4th)*

■ **TOTTENHAM**
White Hart Lane
2013–14 record: **21-6-11** *(6th)*

■ **CRYSTAL PALACE**
Selhurst Park
2013–14 record: **13-6-19** *(11th)*

■ **WEST HAM**
Boleyn Ground
2013–14 record: **11-7-20** *(13th)*

■ **FULHAM**
Craven Cottage
2013–14 record: **9-5-24** *(19th)*

FOOTBALL LEAGUE CHAMPIONSHIP

■ Queens Park Rangers
■ Charlton Athletic
■ Millwall

LEAGUE ONE

■ Brentford
■ Leyton Orient

LEAGUE TWO

■ Dagenham & Redbridge
■ AFC Wimbledon

SOURCES: TWITTER; GUY LANSLEY AND MUHAMMAD ADNAN, UNIVERSITY COLLEGE LONDON

**Number of performances
per 100,000 people,** 2012

 —London total

New York **526 performances**
London **415**
Paris **226**

Paris **280**
New York **272**
London **219**

London **146**
New York **135**
Paris **88**

New York **77**
London **35**
Paris **27**

From Shakespeare's Globe
to the O₂ Arena, London
has long been a hub for the
performing arts. In 2012, the
city tore through spools of
tickets at 64,000 theatre,
music, comedy or dance performances. Here we show the
total number of performances
per 100,000 Londoners.

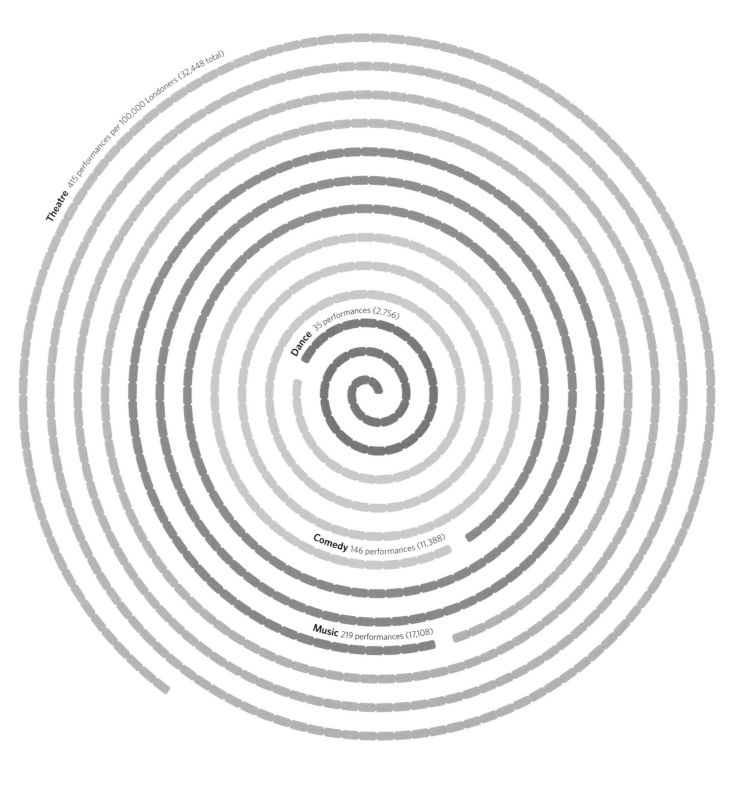

Theatre 415 performances per 100,000 Londoners (32,448 total)

Dance 35 performances (2,756)

Comedy 146 performances (11,388)

Music 219 performances (17,108)

You and your interests are the future of Big Data

In 2013, a company called Renew London installed a dozen 'smart' recycling bins along streets in the City of London. The Wifi-enabled bins automatically logged smartphone data from passers-by, which some feared could have been used to provide personalized ads on the bins' LCD screens. The idea didn't go over so well.

Word soon spread that such data could potentially be used to build a database of people's movements across the city. As former Big Brother Watch director Alex Deane put it, Renew had 'no right to snatch data from the airwaves like this, no matter what [their] ostensible motive and no matter how innocent [their] alleged plans.' His views were widely echoed. The resulting backlash forced Renew to cease and desist. Soon after, they went bust.

Individual-level data collected over airwaves and stored in 'the cloud' is the next frontier of Big Data. You and the gadgets in your pocket are a great, unclaimed territory, rich with resources for both governments and companies. To some, the collected data facilitate unwanted surveillance that infringes privacy; to others,

they offer opportunities for more personalized and inter-active experiences with the city.

Powered by their smartphones, increasing numbers of Londoners are already using apps to collect and manage data about their own lives, including how many tweets they send, how many miles they run, how much they sleep and how they're feeling. Such data are volunteered with an individual's consent. But because these apps are all accessed through a single device, it is hard to draw firm lines between data collected for personal use and those that can be shared with a wider audience. Things become more complex when sharing personal data becomes part of an enjoyable activity like uploading photos (see pp. 206–9) or crafting an online dating profile (see pp. 226-7).

In this final chapter, we choose to focus on some of the more offbeat datasets that are now available. From our football allegiances and fashion forecasts to the wealth of things to do in London (see left), each in their own way reveals 'what we like'. Many of the city's museums and iconic leisure spots are also using data to share their collections online as well as to monitor how we interact with them when we pass through their doors.

With the success of the open data movement in securing access to public information, it may only be a matter of time before the private sector – not least retailers, banks and phone operators – begins revealing the extent of its data stores, too. Currently, these data are deemed too sensitive to share. That may change as the post-millennial generation grows up and demands more control of their data footprints. In this brave new world, Londoners will be able to quantify themselves through a quantified city.

Regent's Canal

London
Zoo

King's Cross
St Pancras

Regent's Canal

Regent's Park

Lord's
Cricket
Ground

SHOREDITCH

Little
Venice

Paddington
Station

OXFORD STREET

St Paul's
Cathedral

SOHO

Hyde Park

Trafalgar
Square

Tower
of London

Tate
Modern

The Serpentine

Borough
Market

London
Eye

THE MALL

Royal
Albert Hall

Buckingham
Palace

River Thames

Palace
of Westminster

Natural
History
Museum

Elephant and Castle

Battersea
Park

0   1 km

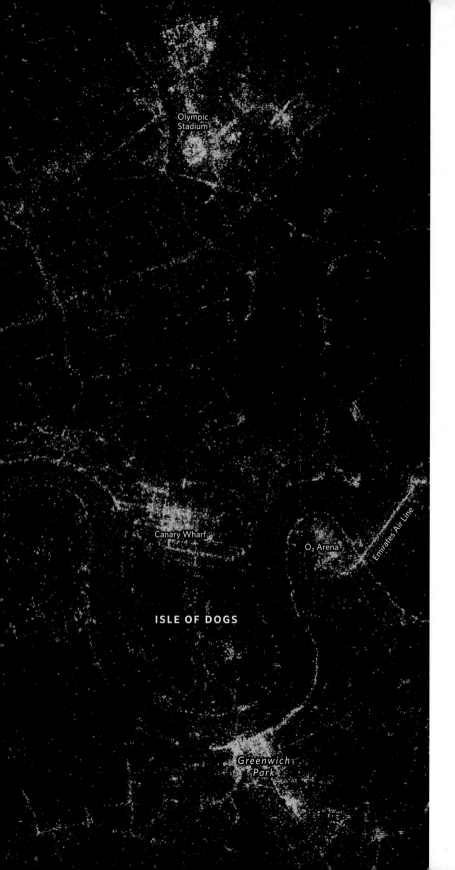

Photogenic Features

Millions of Flickr users capture London's best side.

A sleepy tiger, a blue whale, the Queen's Guards and the arc of the London Eye. To get these shots, leave your guidebook at home and head to spots on this map. Researchers Alexander Kachkaev and Jo Wood at City University London plotted more than 1.5 million pictures taken by 45,000 users on Flickr, the popular photo-sharing site. Like camera flashes in a dark arena, these lines and clusters expose patterns of human activity. Purple dots indicate photographs taken in low light conditions, such as inside a museum or at night; yellow indicates images made in the bright light of day, often in parks and squares or along the Thames, Regent's Canal and The Serpentine. Turn the page to zoom in on Westminster.

Flickr photographs by luminance
January 2008 – June 2013

Day · Outdoor

Night · Indoor

SOURCE: FLICKR

Portobello
Road Market

Paddington
Station

Marble
Arch

NOTTING HILL

Hyde Park

*Kensington
Gardens*

*Round
Pond*

The Serpentine

0 ————————————— 500 m

Thousands of images outline
The Serpentine in yellow
while the museums of South
Kensington create purple
clusters as visitors snap pics
inside them. The Palace of
Westminster and London
Eye inspire shots along the
Thames. Further east on
South Bank, people turn
their lenses towards the
dome of St Paul's and Tate
Modern's Turbine Hall.

Royal
Albert Hall

Harrods

Science
Museum

Victoria and
Albert Museum

Natural History
Museum

SOURCE: FLICKR; ALEXANDER KACHKAEV AND JO WOOD, CITY UNIVERSITY LONDON

British
Museum

OXFORD STREET

Oxford
Circus

St Paul's
Cathedral

SOHO

Covent
Garden

MAYFAIR

REGENT STREET

River Thames

Berkeley Square

Trafalgar
Square

SOUTH BANK

Tate
Modern

PICCADILLY

Green Park

THE MALL

St James's Park

London
Eye

Waterloo
Station

Hyde Park
Corner

Buckingham
Palace

Palace of
Westminster

Imperial
War Museum

Victoria
Station

Okapi **3**

Golden-headed lion tamarin **4**

Pygmy hippo **2**

Rodrigues flying fox **27**

Southern tamandua **2**

Mastigure **4**

Axolotl **13**

Gaboon caecilian **12**

McCord's snake-necked turtle **7**

Mountain chicken frog **37**

Komodo dragon **2**

Number of each species in the 2014 inventory

A True Zoo

The Zoological Society of London (ZSL) counts its creatures, big and small.

ZSL London Zoo's Sumatran tigers, Jae Jae and Melati, made headlines in February 2014 when Melati gave birth to three cubs: Budi, Nakal and Cinta. More tigers means more visitors. Still, the world's oldest research zoo hopes people will find wonder in all 758 of its species. Here we celebrate some lesser-known creatures tallied during the zoo's annual inventory. Whilst keepers monitor animal counts daily,

ZSL London Zoo animal inventory 2014

209 reptiles *(63 species)*

571 mammals   584 birds   684 amphibians   4,903 fish

9,918 invertebrates

59 species   *113 species*   *24 species*   *276 species*

223 species

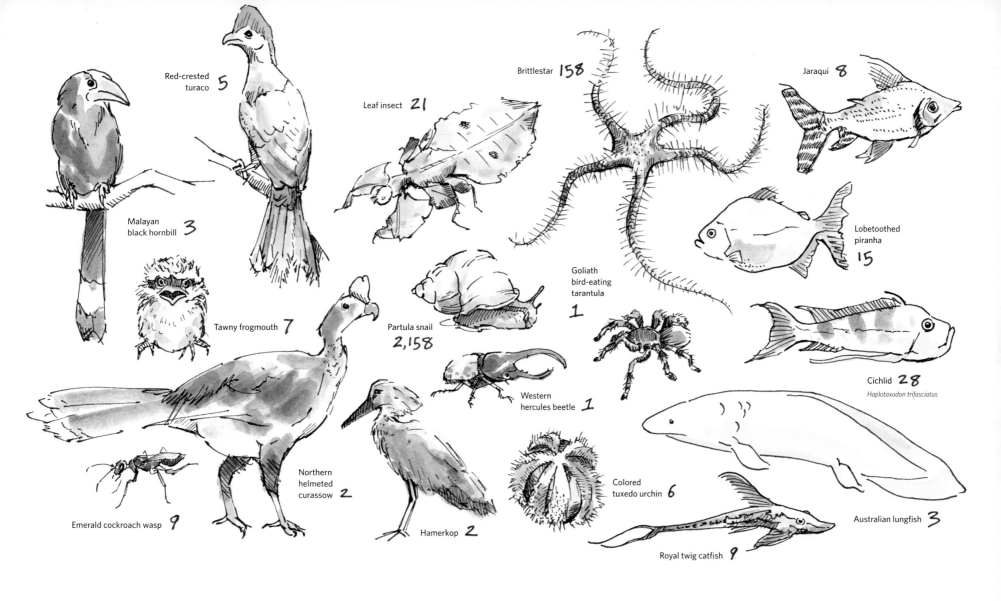

Red-crested turaco 5

Malayan black hornbill 3

Tawny frogmouth 7

Leaf insect 21

Brittlestar 158

Jaraqui 8

Partula snail 2,158

Goliath bird-eating tarantula 1

Lobetoothed piranha 15

Western hercules beetle 1

Cichlid 28
Haplotaxodon trifasciatus

Northern helmeted curassow 2

Emerald cockroach wasp 9

Hamerkop 2

Colored tuxedo urchin 6

Australian lungfish 3

Royal twig catfish 9

the zoo's licence requires them to log an official 'stocktake' into the International Species Information System's global database of 374,000 living animals. This allows ZSL to collaborate with other zoos and governments on breeding programmes for endangered species of all sizes. Thanks to these efforts, three species of Partula snails are back in the trees of Tahiti for the first time since the 1970s.

Nearly 60% of the zoo's animals do not have a backbone. That figure would be much higher if ZSL didn't count its thousands of honeybees and leaf-cutter ants as single colonies.

TOTAL
16,869 animals
758 species

All the Tate's Treasures

Wall space isn't an issue online.

Art lovers rejoice. The Tate art galleries have put all 70,000 works in their collection of British art and international modern and contemporary art online in a database searchable by artist, decade, subject, even emotion. Here we show the 106 artists with at least fifty works in the collection.

No one comes close to J. M. W. Turner, the great painter and Londoner who bequeathed the contents of his studio to the nation in 1851. His bequest includes 280 sketchbooks from his travels and 30,000 preparatory drawings and watercolours like this one. The two large oils he made of this subject hang in museums in Cleveland and Philadelphia, USA. But those are also viewable on the Tate's website.

Artists with 50 or more works in the Tate collection
June 2014

- Painter, printmaker
- Sculptor
- Photographer

YEAR OF BIRTH ▶

Francis Barlow **109**		
Joseph Highmore **79**		
Richard Wilson **66**		
Alexander Cozens **237**		
Susanna Duncombe **76**		
Thomas Gainsborough **158**		
Sir Nathaniel Dance-Holland **169**		
91 Philip James de Loutherbourg		
Heneage Finch **50**		
Sir George Beaumont **62**		
John Flaxman **287**		
Thomas Stothard **215**		
William Blake **180**		
Prince Hoare **64**		
Joshua Cristall **85**		
William Daniell **612**		
Francois Louis Francia **63**		
Thomas Girtin **94**		
John Constable		

1650   1700   1750

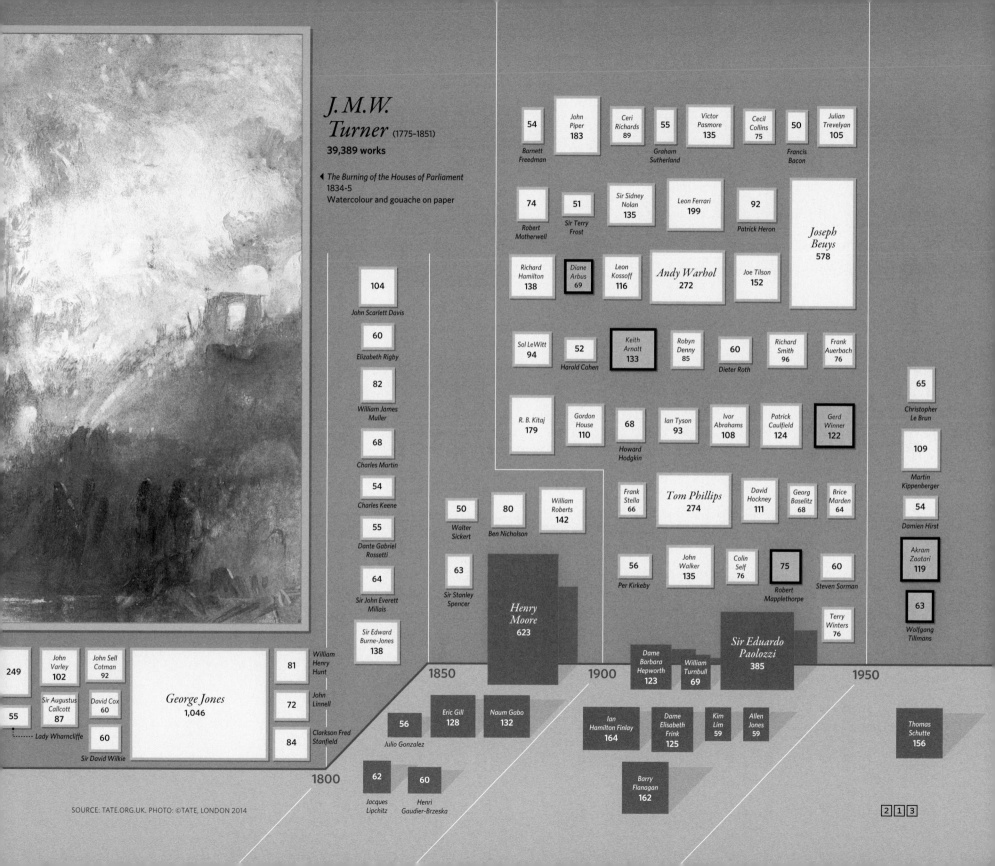

J.M.W. Turner (1775–1851)

39,389 works

◀ *The Burning of the Houses of Parliament*
1834-5
Watercolour and gouache on paper

Barnett Freedman	54
John Piper	183
Ceri Richards	89
Graham Sutherland	55
Victor Pasmore	135
Cecil Collins	75
Francis Bacon	50
Julian Trevelyan	105

Robert Motherwell 74
Sir Terry Frost 51
Sir Sidney Nolan 135
Leon Ferrari 199
Patrick Heron 92
Joseph Beuys 578

Richard Hamilton 138
Diane Arbus 69
Leon Kossoff 116
Andy Warhol 272
Joe Tilson 152

Sol LeWitt 94
Harold Cohen 52
Keith Arnatt 133
Robyn Denny 85
Dieter Roth 60
Richard Smith 96
Frank Auerbach 76

R. B. Kitaj 179
Gordon House 110
Howard Hodgkin 68
Ian Tyson 93
Ivor Abrahams 108
Patrick Caulfield 124
Gerd Winner 122

Christopher Le Brun 65
Martin Kippenberger 109
Damien Hirst 54
Akram Zaatari 119
Wolfgang Tillmans 63

Walter Sickert 50
Ben Nicholson 80
William Roberts 142

Frank Stella 66
Tom Phillips 274
David Hockney 111
Georg Baselitz 68
Brice Marden 64

Sir Stanley Spencer 63

Per Kirkeby 56
John Walker 135
Colin Self 76
Robert Mapplethorpe 75
Steven Sorman 60

Henry Moore 623

Terry Winters 76

John Scarlett Davis 104
Elizabeth Rigby 60
William James Muller 82
Charles Martin 68
Charles Keene 54
Dante Gabriel Rossetti 55
Sir John Everett Millais 64
Sir Edward Burne-Jones 138

Dame Barbara Hepworth 123
William Turnbull 69
Sir Eduardo Paolozzi 385

249
John Varley 102
John Sell Cotman 92
George Jones 1,046
William Henry Hunt 81

Sir Augustus Callcott 87
David Cox 60
John Linnell 72

55
Clarkson Fred Stanfield 84

Lady Wharncliffe
Sir David Wilkie 60

Julio Gonzalez 56
Eric Gill 128
Naum Gabo 132

Ian Hamilton Finlay 164
Dame Elisabeth Frink 125
Kim Lim 59
Allen Jones 59

Thomas Schutte 156

Jacques Lipchitz 62
Henri Gaudier-Brzeska 60

Barry Flanagan 162

1800 **1850** **1900** **1950**

SOURCE: TATE.ORG.UK. PHOTO: ©TATE, LONDON 2014

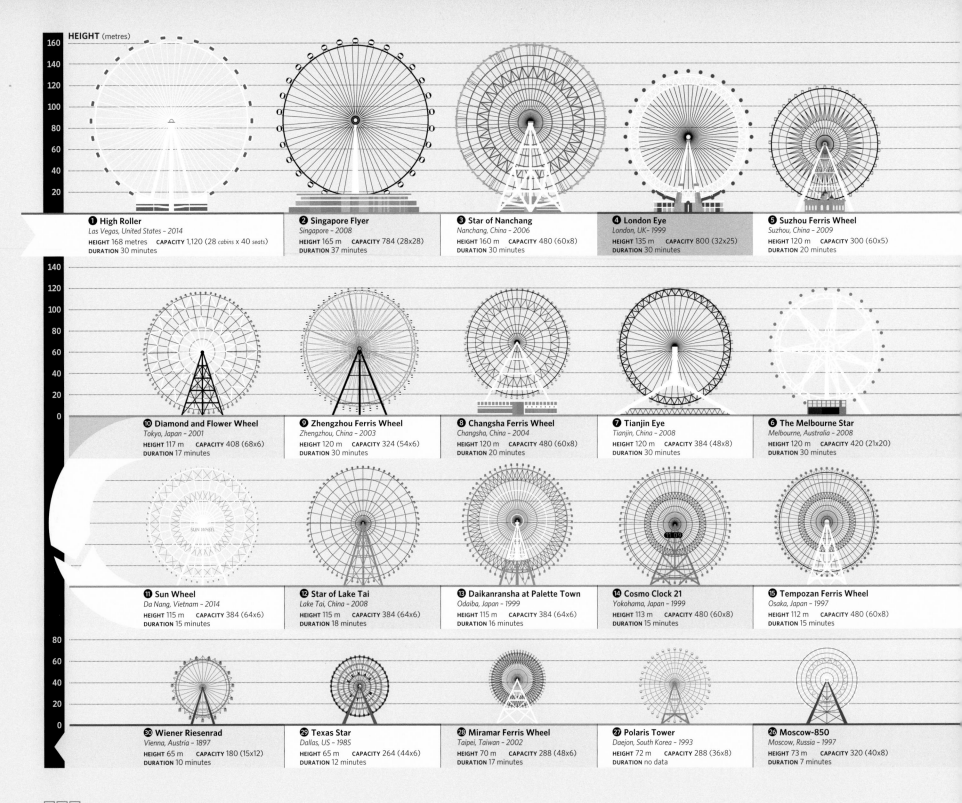

HEIGHT (metres)

160
140
120
100
80
60
40
20

1 High Roller
Las Vegas, United States – 2014
HEIGHT 168 metres   CAPACITY 1,120 (28 *cabins* x 40 *seats*)
DURATION 30 minutes

2 Singapore Flyer
Singapore – 2008
HEIGHT 165 m   CAPACITY 784 (28x28)
DURATION 37 minutes

3 Star of Nanchang
Nanchang, China – 2006
HEIGHT 160 m   CAPACITY 480 (60x8)
DURATION 30 minutes

4 London Eye
London, UK– 1999
HEIGHT 135 m   CAPACITY 800 (32x25)
DURATION 30 minutes

5 Suzhou Ferris Wheel
Suzhou, China – 2009
HEIGHT 120 m   CAPACITY 300 (60x5)
DURATION 20 minutes

140
120
100
80
60
40
20
0

10 Diamond and Flower Wheel
Tokyo, Japan – 2001
HEIGHT 117 m   CAPACITY 408 (68x6)
DURATION 17 minutes

9 Zhengzhou Ferris Wheel
Zhengzhou, China – 2003
HEIGHT 120 m   CAPACITY 324 (54x6)
DURATION 30 minutes

8 Changsha Ferris Wheel
Changsha, China – 2004
HEIGHT 120 m   CAPACITY 480 (60x8)
DURATION 20 minutes

7 Tianjin Eye
Tianjin, China – 2008
HEIGHT 120 m   CAPACITY 384 (48x8)
DURATION 30 minutes

6 The Melbourne Star
Melbourne, Australia – 2008
HEIGHT 120 m   CAPACITY 420 (21x20)
DURATION 30 minutes

11 Sun Wheel
Da Nang, Vietnam – 2014
HEIGHT 115 m   CAPACITY 384 (64x6)
DURATION 15 minutes

12 Star of Lake Tai
Lake Tai, China – 2008
HEIGHT 115 m   CAPACITY 384 (64x6)
DURATION 18 minutes

13 Daikanransha at Palette Town
Odaiba, Japan – 1999
HEIGHT 115 m   CAPACITY 384 (64x6)
DURATION 16 minutes

14 Cosmo Clock 21
Yokohama, Japan – 1999
HEIGHT 113 m   CAPACITY 480 (60x8)
DURATION 15 minutes

15 Tempozan Ferris Wheel
Osaka, Japan – 1997
HEIGHT 112 m   CAPACITY 480 (60x8)
DURATION 15 minutes

80
60
40
20
0

30 Wiener Riesenrad
Vienna, Austria – 1897
HEIGHT 65 m   CAPACITY 180 (15x12)
DURATION 10 minutes

29 Texas Star
Dallas, US – 1985
HEIGHT 65 m   CAPACITY 264 (44x6)
DURATION 12 minutes

28 Miramar Ferris Wheel
Taipei, Taiwan – 2002
HEIGHT 70 m   CAPACITY 288 (48x6)
DURATION 17 minutes

27 Polaris Tower
Daejon, South Korea – 1993
HEIGHT 72 m   CAPACITY 288 (36x8)
DURATION no data

26 Moscow-850
Moscow, Russia – 1997
HEIGHT 73 m   CAPACITY 320 (40x8)
DURATION 7 minutes

Following the Leader

Cities around the world have been eyeing up the London Eye.

When the London Eye opened in 2000, it was the tallest observation wheel in the world. Over the course of a 30-minute ride, the thirty-two cars lift passengers to a height of 135 metres for unprecedented views of Westminster and beyond. The wheel became an instant symbol of prosperity. Every major world city wanted one. The Eye was eventually topped by the Star of Nanchang in 2006 and then the Singapore Flyer in 2008. Plans for at least five larger wheels in Beijing, Berlin, Dubai, Jeddah and Orlando were scrapped, leaving London's in the top three until the 168-metre High Roller opened in Las Vegas in March 2014.

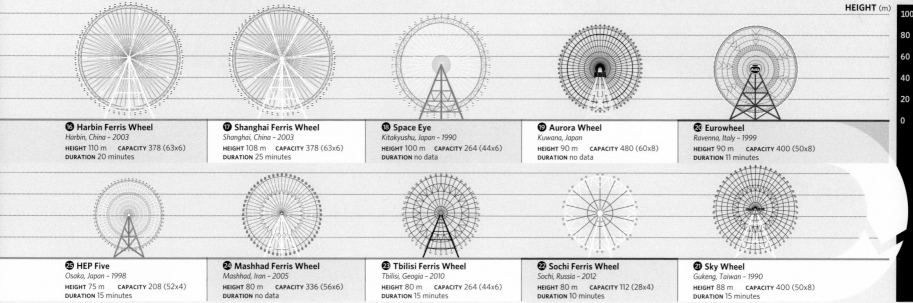

HEIGHT (m)

❶❻ **Harbin Ferris Wheel**
Harbin, China – 2003
HEIGHT 110 m   **CAPACITY** 378 (63x6)
DURATION 20 minutes

❶❼ **Shanghai Ferris Wheel**
Shanghai, China – 2003
HEIGHT 108 m   **CAPACITY** 378 (63x6)
DURATION 25 minutes

❶❽ **Space Eye**
Kitakyushu, Japan – 1990
HEIGHT 100 m   **CAPACITY** 264 (44x6)
DURATION no data

❶❾ **Aurora Wheel**
Kuwana, Japan
HEIGHT 90 m   **CAPACITY** 480 (60x8)
DURATION no data

❷⓪ **Eurowheel**
Ravenna, Italy – 1999
HEIGHT 90 m   **CAPACITY** 400 (50x8)
DURATION 11 minutes

❷❺ **HEP Five**
Osaka, Japan – 1998
HEIGHT 75 m   **CAPACITY** 208 (52x4)
DURATION 15 minutes

❷❹ **Mashhad Ferris Wheel**
Mashhad, Iran – 2005
HEIGHT 80 m   **CAPACITY** 336 (56x6)
DURATION no data

❷❸ **Tbilisi Ferris Wheel**
Tbilisi, Geogia – 2010
HEIGHT 80 m   **CAPACITY** 264 (44x6)
DURATION 15 minutes

❷❷ **Sochi Ferris Wheel**
Sochi, Russia – 2012
HEIGHT 80 m   **CAPACITY** 112 (28x4)
DURATION 10 minutes

❷❶ **Sky Wheel**
Gukeng, Taiwan – 1990
HEIGHT 88 m   **CAPACITY** 400 (50x8)
DURATION 15 minutes

GRAPHIC: FRANCESCO FRANCHI, ALESSANDRO GIBERTI, *IL SOLE 24 ORE*. ILLUSTRATIONS: LAURA CATTANEO. ADDITIONAL SOURCE: OBSERVATION WHEEL DIRECTORY

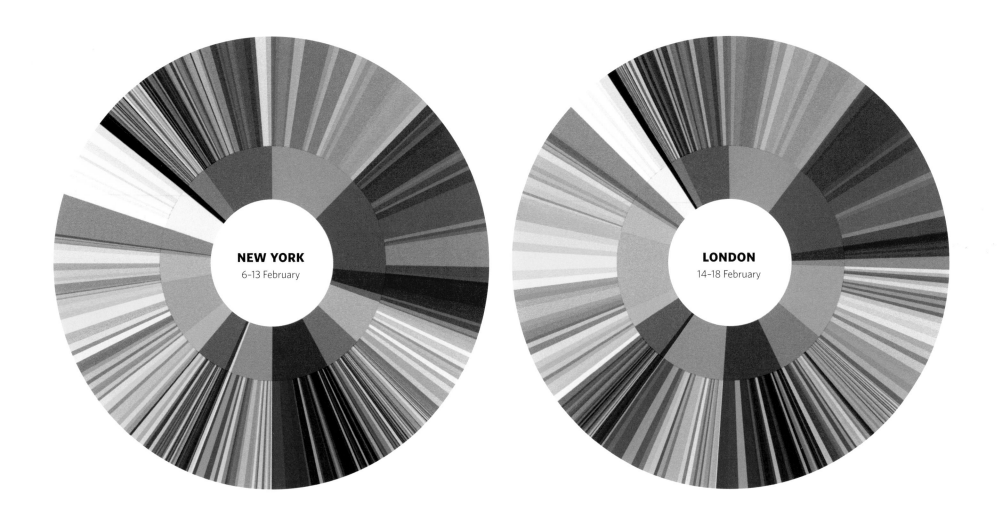

NEW YORK
6–13 February

LONDON
14–18 February

Fashion Cycles

The London fog appears to be lifting.

The world's top designers are preparing for another blustery winter. Warmth and comfort are in. Oversized parkas, turtlenecks, quilting, shaggy furs, layers and leopard prints dominated the runways during international fashion month in February 2014. Style and fit weren't the only effects of the cold. The world's colour palette shifted, too. EDITD, a London-based fashion analytics firm, extracted colour data from photographs of every garment shown at each of the four

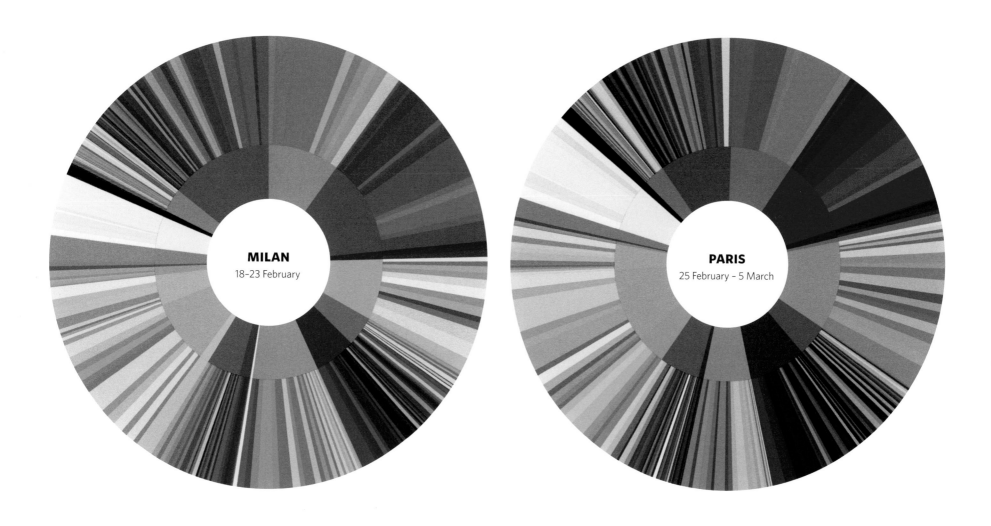

MILAN
18–23 February

PARIS
25 February – 5 March

fashion weeks in New York, London, Milan and Paris to create the wheels above. In addition to glacial blues, forest greens and the drinkable tones of red wines, the Autumn-Winter 2014 palette features unseasonably vivid colours to brighten moods on dreary days. Of the four fashion capitals, London can look forward to the least muted palette. Nearly a third of the looks cleared away the dreary greys in favour of sunshine hues.

Percentage of garments shown during each international fashion week by colour
Autumn-Winter 2014

New York and Paris bookended the month with support for the pastels that were popular in the spring lines. Milan elected for the most muted palette, opting for more shades of coffee, oatmeal and granite than the other cities.

They Came,
They Saw,
They Spent

In terms of spending per visitor, Arab tourists reign.

If the 2012 Olympics were supposed to be an elaborate marketing campaign for the capital, it worked. 16.8 million overseas visitors came to London in 2013, the highest recorded total since 1961. Continuing a 43.5% rise in international visits since 2003, the banner year unseated Paris (16.6m) as Europe's most visited city. Backpackers on a shoestring these were not. Altogether, they dropped £11 billion.

The Olympics can't claim all the credit though. For the past five years, Ramadan – the Muslim month of fasting – has coincided with the heat of summer. Before it begins, millionaires from Gulf Arab states like Saudi Arabia have been escaping to London for a few weeks. While American tourists spent the most as a country, as we show to the right, they can't compete with Saudis in terms of spending per visitor. The average American spends £800 on a trip to London. The average Saudi will spend over triple that. Many retailers are now hiring Arabic-speaking staff to welcome them.

Number of overseas visitors in thousands, 2012

EACH TOURIST SPENDS THIS MUCH

At the time of publication, the most detailed country breakdown available was from 2012. As was the case in 2013, more Americans visited than any other nationality. France, Germany, Italy, Spain, Netherlands, Ireland and Sweden each sent more than half a million tourists, but they do not appear on this chart because each visitor spent less than £500.

Top 20 nations by spending per visitor to London, 2012

25,000 visitors

£100 spent per visitor

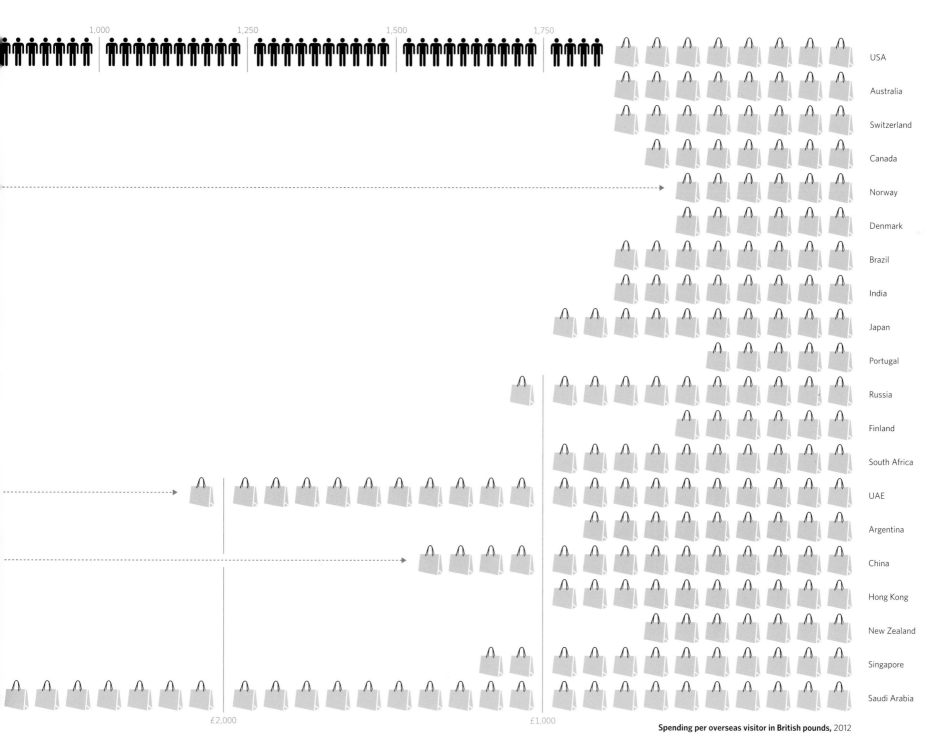

1,000   1,250   1,500   1,750

USA
Australia
Switzerland
Canada
Norway
Denmark
Brazil
India
Japan
Portugal
Russia
Finland
South Africa
UAE
Argentina
China
Hong Kong
New Zealand
Singapore
Saudi Arabia

£2,000   £1,000

Spending per overseas visitor in British pounds, 2012

Shop Window

London's supermarkets fragment the city.

In this graphic, we drew a line halfway between every major super-market or convenience store and its next nearest to show how far Londoners have to travel for their closest shop. What emerges is a stained-glass window of consumer choice.

Though people don't always use their closest store, they won't go too far out of their way to visit a competitor. This distance varies with transport mode. Relatively few people have cars in more central areas. They shop locally and often to avoid carrying too much. Stores in outer boroughs tend to be bigger and offer large car parks to their customers, who will travel a little further for a big 'weekly' shop.

Supermarkets, April 2014

- Waitrose
- Tesco
- Sainsbury's
- Morrisons
- Asda
- Iceland
- Co-Op
- Lidl   • Supermarket
- Aldi

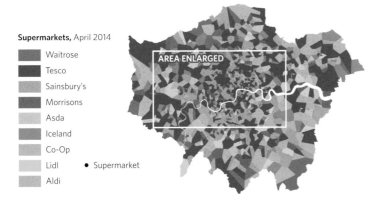

AREA ENLARGED

We all forget the milk from time to time, so big brands like Sainsbury's (orange) and Tesco (blue) have been sticking smaller convenience stores near Tube and train stations to attract commuters on their way home. Waitrose (green) is popular with the wealthy set; Aldi (light blue) and Lidl (yellow) can be found in less affluent areas.

SOURCES: FOOD STANDARDS AGENCY; OSM

HARROW

EALING

HOUNSLOW

RICHMOND
UPON THAMES

HARINGEY

WALTHAM
FOREST

CAMDEN

HACKNEY

BRENT

ISLINGTON

NEWHAM

TOWER
HAMLETS

CITY

River Thames

KENSINGTON & CHELSEA

WESTMINSTER

HAMMERSMITH & FULHAM

GREENWICH

SOUTHWARK

LAMBETH

LEWISHAM

WANDSWORTH

0   1 km

HEIGHT
(metres)

1,915 m
London only

3,390 m
National circulation

2,450 m

1,729 m
THE TIMES

1,717 m

1,500

1,000

6 Shards

5 Shards

4 Shards

Who Says Print is Dead?

Londoners love newspapers.

Despite the growing prevalence of digital news, millions of pages of newsprint still appear in London every morning. Veteran papers like the *Guardian*, *The Times* and the *Daily Telegraph* maintain loyal readerships, but more Londoners get their news from free dailies than any other paper. They read the *METRO* on their morning commutes and the *London Evening Standard* on their rides home. In fact, so many *METRO* papers are delivered each day in the capital that if stacked they would tower 1,915 metres above the city – more than the height of six Shards!

National daily circulation, March 2014

8,000 metres

25 Shards — 7,748m

4,451

3,390

ENLARGED BELOW

6 Shards

4,000

500

Sun
Daily Mail
METRO
Daily Telegraph
The Times
Evening Standard
Financial Times
Guardian
Independent

820 m

3 Shards

2 Shards

520 m

310 metres

100 metres

Tower heights multiply circulation by the approximate thickness of each paper.

Independent	Guardian	Financial Times	London Evening Standard	The Times	Daily Telegraph	METRO	The Shard
66,500 papers	208,000	234,000	687,000	384,000	545,000	766,000	

WHAT WE LIKE

The Buzz About Town

The capital's premier blog keeps Londoners in the know.

Since 2004, *Londonist* – originally titled *The Big Smoker* – has covered both the serious and slightly quirkier sides to the capital. Contributors report on breaking news as well as how to queue for the Wimbledon Championships, 'weird facts you probably didn't know' and the ever-popular 'Free & Cheap' things to do in the capital. They 'tag' each post with searchable terms like 'Boris Johnson' or 'frugal fun'. Below, we took every tag used more than fifteen times between 2008 and 2013 and grouped them by theme. We then charted the number of times they were used to see what London was talking about each month. Christmas chatter increased each year, whilst the Olympics quickly became old news.

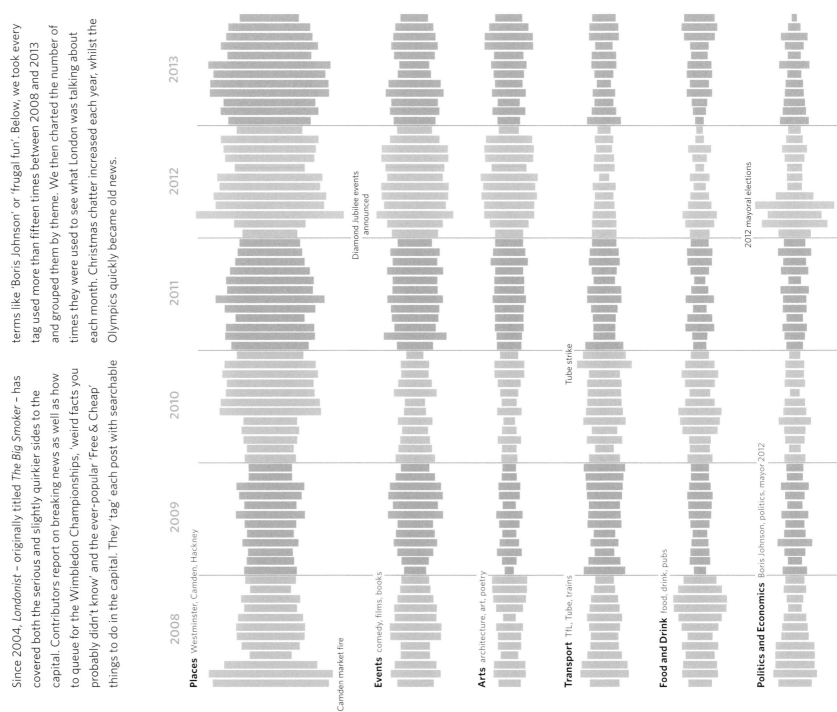

2008   2009   2010   2011   2012   2013

Places Westminster, Camden, Hackney

Camden market fire

Events comedy, films, books

Diamond Jubilee events announced

Arts architecture, art, poetry

Transport TfL, Tube, trains

Tube strike

Food and Drink food, drink, pubs

Politics and Economics Boris Johnson, politics, mayor 2012

2012 mayoral elections

Theatre and Cinema cinema, Sadlers Wells, National Theatre

London film festival

Things to Do Things To Do, whats on, stuff to do

Museums exhibition, Museums & Galleries, Tate Modern

Olympics Olympics, 2012, London 2012

Beijing 2008

London 2012

Photography Flickr, Photo of the Day, seasonal photo

Sport sport, cycling, football

Free Free & Cheap, cheap, frugal fun

Crime and Terrorism crime, police, Metropolitan Police

Riots

Science science, weekly geek listings, geek

Seasonal Christmas, santa's lap, Christmas 2013

Christmas

Maps maps, hand-drawn maps of London

Launch of hand-drawn maps competition

Royalty royal wedding, Queen, Prince George

Royal Wedding

Queen's Diamond Jubilee

J F M A M J J A S O N D J F M A M J J A S O N D J F M A M J J A S O N D

WHAT WE LIKE

Looking for Love

Who wants who online.

Searching for a soulmate can feel like fumbling around in a dark room: you can only see what's in the beam of your torch. Online dating sites like *lovestruck.com* offer a wider beam. Yet most users choose to narrow theirs to a desired age range spanning around fourteen years. The question then becomes not how wide is the beam but in what direction is it pointing? Younger or older?

On the right we show the average desired age ranges of Londoners of four sexual orientations at five different ages: 22, 32, 42, 52 and 62. Brighter areas show the most desired ages where multiple searchlights overlap. In general, twenty-two-year-olds tend to have the narrowest search, with the exception of gay men who were open to dating men more than ten years older. As straight men get older they continue to look for increasingly younger partners, but (surprise!) so do straight women. Fifty-two-year-old gay men cast the widest searches; by 62 though, they begin to search among their peers. Older gay women also cast a wide net, but overall, age appears less important to them; sixty-two-year-old gay women were the only demographic in our sample searching for companions in their seventies.

2,700

MEN *seeking* MEN

54,000

MEN *seeking* WOMEN

70,000

WOMEN *seeking* MEN

Average desired age ranges of approved Lovestruck profiles in London, April 2014

In 2012, the Office for National Statistics asked 180,000 respondents to its Integrated Household Survey about their sexual identity at the time. 2.5% of Londoners answered gay, lesbian or bisexual adult, the highest percentage in the UK. There aren't many same-sex searches on Lovestruck because other dating services dominate those markets.

1,200

WOMEN *seeking* WOMEN

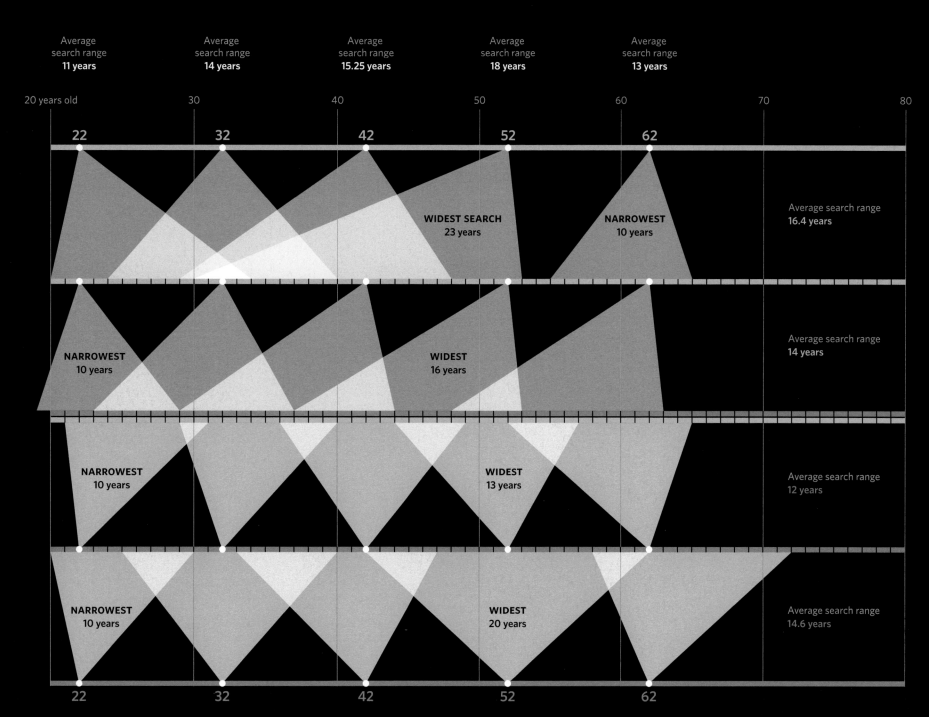

Average
search range
11 years

Average
search range
14 years

Average
search range
15.25 years

Average
search range
18 years

Average
search range
13 years

20 years old   30   40   50   60   70   80

22   32   42   52   62

WIDEST SEARCH
23 years

NARROWEST
10 years

Average search range
16.4 years

NARROWEST
10 years

WIDEST
16 years

Average search range
14 years

NARROWEST
10 years

WIDEST
13 years

Average search range
12 years

NARROWEST
10 years

WIDEST
20 years

Average search range
14.6 years

22   32   42   52   62

Happy Times

Cheer increases as the day progresses.

In 2010, George MacKerron, now a lecturer at the University of Sussex, set out to gauge the nation's happiness. His idea was simple: create an iPhone app that 'pings' people a few times a day to ask how happy they are and what they are doing at the time. He thought he would be lucky if a thousand people signed up. One year later, more than 40,000 people had shared several million answers to his questions, making 'Mappiness' one of the largest ever surveys of subjective well-being.

Londoners make up about twenty per cent of the app's user base. Their responses are shown here. From left to right the time of day runs from 8 a.m. to 10 p.m.; from top to bottom the day of the year runs from 1 September 2010 to 31 August 2011. The stripe pattern highlights the city's mood swings. Weekends and holidays make people happy (yellow); weekday mornings find them feeling blue.

London's happiness, September 2010 – September 2011

UNHAPPY ▬▬▬▬▬▬▬▬ HAPPY

A swathe of yellow in late April shows Londoners enjoying a national holiday for the Royal Wedding between Prince William and the then Kate Middleton.

Large splashes of yellow appear in late December and mid-April during the Christmas and Easter breaks. Note the very happy period late on New Year's Eve.

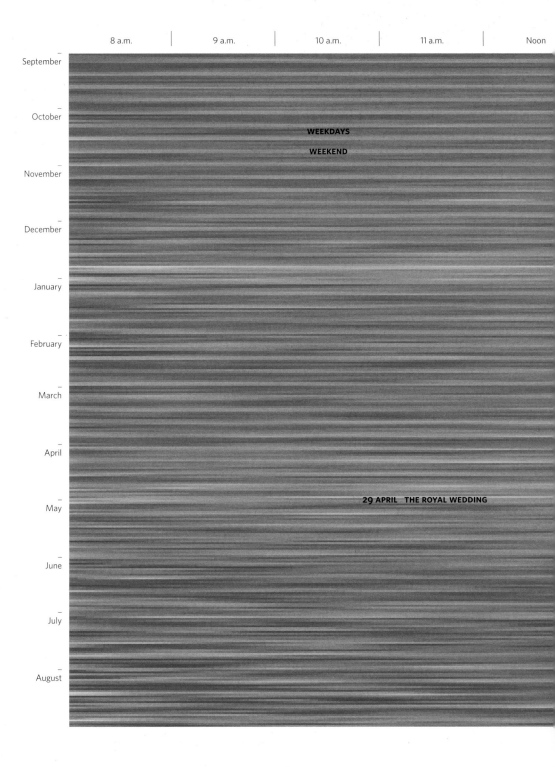

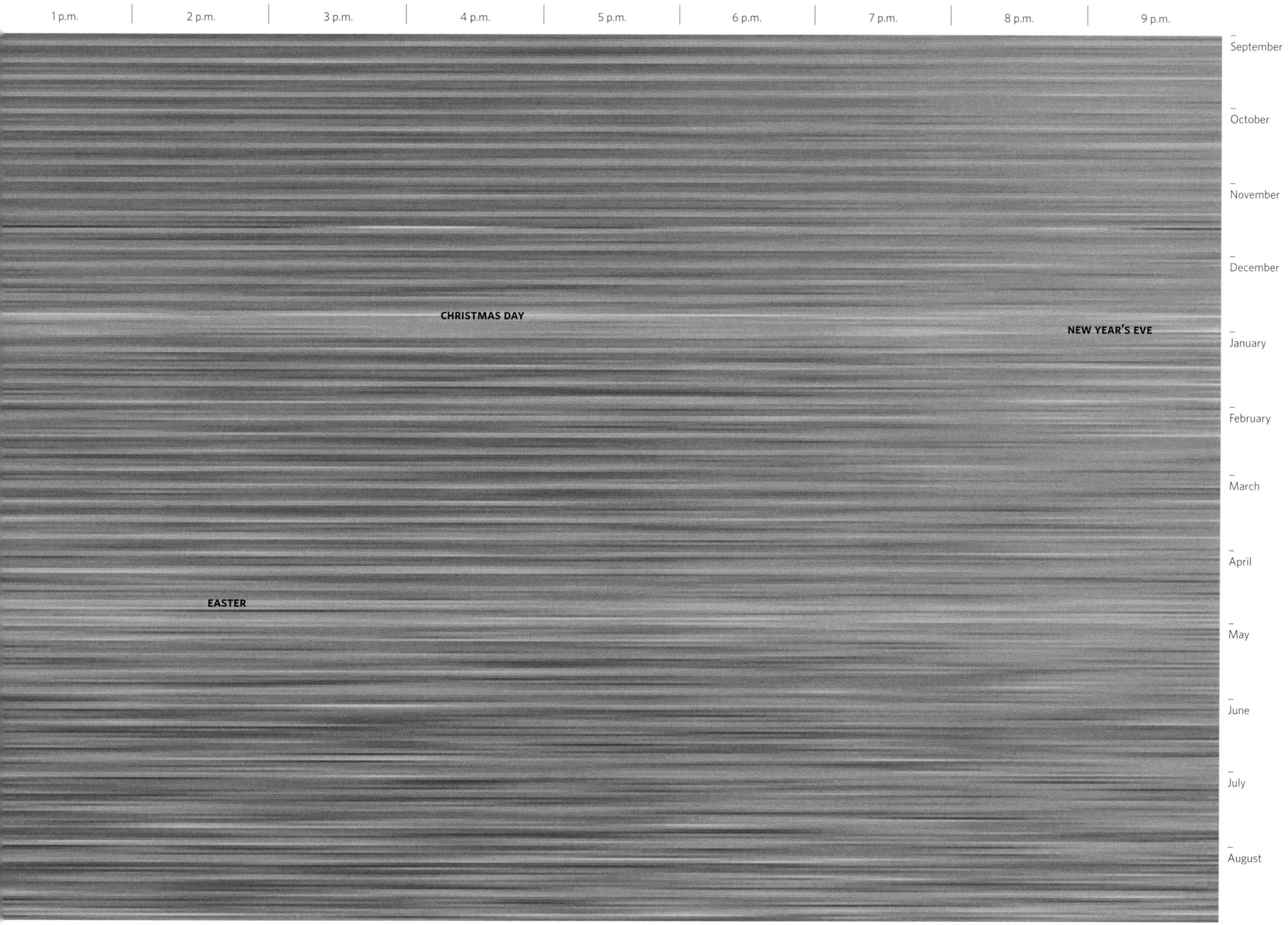

1 p.m.   2 p.m.   3 p.m.   4 p.m.   5 p.m.   6 p.m.   7 p.m.   8 p.m.   9 p.m.

September

October

November

December

CHRISTMAS DAY

NEW YEAR'S EVE

January

February

March

April

EASTER

May

June

July

August

Further Reading

ON LONDON

One of the joys of creating *London: The Information Capital* has been getting to know the city better through its great books and websites. These have provided us with inspiration and much needed context to the graphics we have created.

London: The Biography by Peter Ackroyd (2001) offers the most in depth introduction to the past life and times of the city and augments the visual introductions offered by *London: The Illustrated History* (Cathy Ross and John Clark, 2008) and the excellent *Times History of London* (Hugh Clout, 1999). Map addicts will thoroughly enjoy *London: A History in Maps* (Peter Barber, 2012) and the wealth of historic maps in the British Library's Crace Collection online gallery (*www.bl.uk/onlinegallery/onlineex/crace*). The Mapping London blog (*mappinglondon.co.uk*) regularly posts more up to date cartographic representations of the capital as does Londonist (*londonist.com*).

To get to know Londoners past and present, we would recommend Steven Johnson's *The Ghost Map* (2006) that details how John Snow took on cholera, and the BBC TV series and associated book entitled *The Secret History of Our Streets* (2012) that compares Charles Booth's London with the contemporary city. Craig Taylor's *Londoners* (2011) shares the personal stories of those who have made the city their home and reminds us that behind every data point is a person.

Finally, the ultimate reference book for London is *The London Encyclopaedia* (Ben Weinreb, Christopher Hibbert, Julia Keay, John Keay. 3rd Edition, 2010). Hours could be spent jumping from one entry to another and the sheer volume of information it contains is worthy of a graphic by itself.

If you have been inspired to create your own graphics, the London Datastore (*data.london.gov.uk*) is the best place to start for any data you might need.

ON INFORMATION GRAPHICS & DESIGN

There are many great instructional books on information graphics. To save yourself time and shelf space, start with *Cartographies of Time* (Daniel Rosenberg and Anthony Grafton, 2010), *The Functional Art: An Introduction to Information Graphics and Visualization* (Alberto Cairo, 2013) or *Visualize This: The FlowingData Guide to Visualization, Design and Statistics* (Nathan Yau, 2011).

Any discussion about the process of making maps and graphics must include the writings of Edward Tufte. Our 'Causes of Death' graphic pays homage to his 'sparklines', while the principles outlined in his classic trio – *Envisioning Information* (1990), *Visual Explanations* (1997) and *The Visual Display of Quantitative Information* (2001) – guided our thinking throughout the book.

For designers in search of the perfect typeface for their next project, we highly recommend *The Anatomy of Type: A Graphic Guide to 100 Typefaces* (Stephen Coles, 2012). If you are looking for inspiration, new graphic forms or best practices, pick up the latest copy of the *Guardian, National Geographic* or *The New York Times*. The data teams at those three publications continually raise the bar for what we can communicate through visuals.

ON MAPS

Infinite Perspectives: Two Thousand Years of Three-Dimensional Mapmaking (1999) shows how maps can literally jump off the page. *How to Lie with Maps* by Mark Monmonier (1996) is a classic amongst cartographers seeking to produce maps that don't mislead, and Denis Wood's *Rethinking the Power of Maps* (2010) is a reminder that maps can be extremely influential in the right (or wrong) hands.

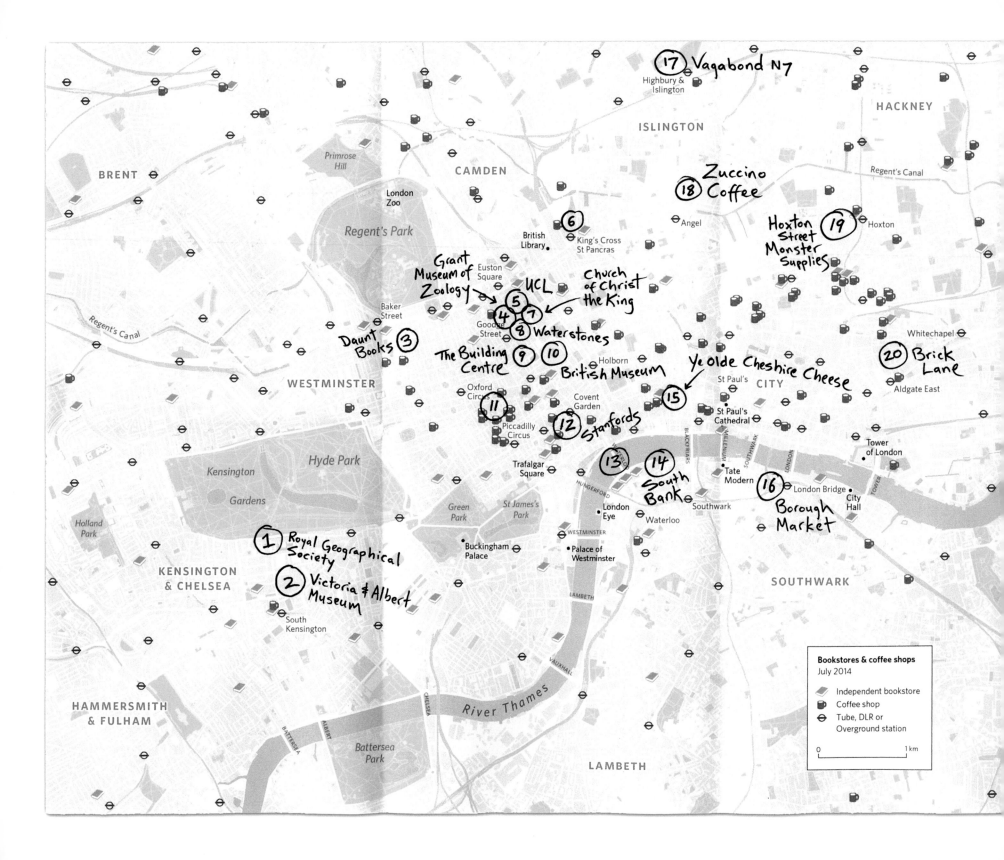

㉗ Vagabond N7
Highbury & Islington

HACKNEY

ISLINGTON

Regent's Canal

CAMDEN

⑱ Zuccino Coffee

Angel

⑲ Hoxton Street Monster Supplies
Hoxton

London Zoo

Primrose Hill

BRENT

Regent's Park

⑥ King's Cross St Pancras

British Library

Grant Museum of Zoology

Euston Square

UCL ⑤

Church of Christ the King

④ ⑦

⑧ Waterstones

Goodge Street

Baker Street

Regent's Canal

Daunt Books ③

The Building Centre ⑨ ⑩

British Museum

Holborn

Ye Olde Cheshire Cheese
St Paul's

CITY

Whitechapel

⑳ Brick Lane
Aldgate East

WESTMINSTER

Oxford Circus

Covent Garden

⑮

St Paul's Cathedral

⑪

⑫ Stanfords

Piccadilly Circus

Trafalgar Square

⑬ ⑭ South Bank

BLACKFRIARS

Tate Modern

SOUTHWARK

Tower of London

Kensington Gardens

Hyde Park

Green Park

St James's Park

London Eye

Waterloo

Southwark

⑯ Borough Market

London Bridge
City Hall

Holland Park

WESTMINSTER

Buckingham Palace

Palace of Westminster

① Royal Geographical Society

② Victoria & Albert Museum

KENSINGTON & CHELSEA

South Kensington

LAMBETH

HAMMERSMITH & FULHAM

Battersea

Battersea Park

CHELSEA

River Thames

VAUXHALL

LAMBETH

Bookstores & coffee shops
July 2014

Independent bookstore
Coffee shop
Tube, DLR or Overground station

0   1 km

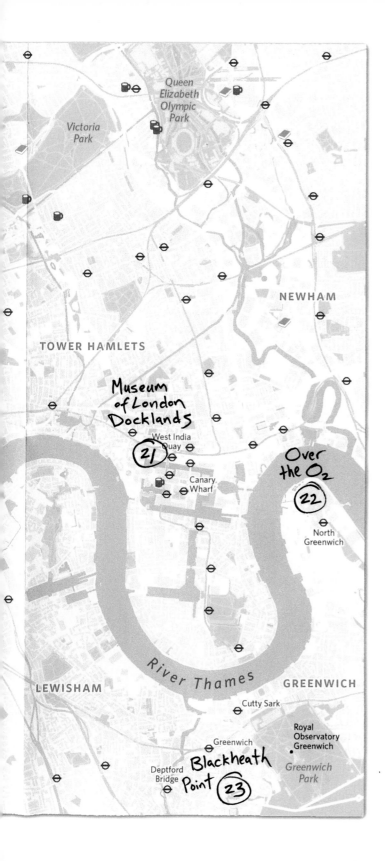

Books, Coffee, etc.

When Oliver came to London, I drew him a few maps to find his way around.
We decided to do the same for you. Here are a few spots to fuel your mind.

1 Royal Geographical Society
The heart of geography in the UK hosts Monday night lectures by explorers and academics alike as well as excellent, and often map-based, exhibitions during the year.

2 Victoria and Albert Museum
Get lost among 2.4 million objects spanning art, design, fashion and architecture. Then find yourself in the museum's Victorian café.

3 Daunt Books Marylebone
An Edwardian bookshop focusing on non-fiction and literature.

4 Grant Museum of Zoology
Home to a jar of moles, skeletons and an extensive collection of bisected animal heads, it's not for the faint-hearted!

5 University College London
Jeremy Bentham's dressed skeleton and wax head (with his real hair) is on display. To this day, 'Bentham' attends the occasional UCL Board meeting.

6 John Betjeman Statue
St Pancras station offers the grandest gateway into London. Betjeman helped to preserve it and is rewarded with its best view.

7 Church of Christ the King
Oliver's parents were married there in 1970 when it was the church for London's universities.

8 Waterstones Gower Street
Housed in Gower Street's most elaborate building, this bookshop has an excellent London section alongside a huge collection of second-hand books and remainders.

9 The Building Centre
Head here to view a giant 3D model of central London.

10 British Museum
Did you know it has a Prints and Drawings collection with rare linocuts by Picasso?

11 John Snow Pub
Epidemiologists, historians and geographers make pilgrimage to this pub across the street from the infamous pump its namesake identified (see pp. 30–31).

12 Stanfords Bookshop
The world's biggest travel bookshop was our first port of call for books and maps about the capital.

13 Waterloo Bridge
The view is unparalleled.

14 South Bank
This cultural hub makes for a nice evening stroll from the London Eye to Tower Bridge.

15 Ye Olde Cheshire Cheese Pub
Dickens frequented this pub off Fleet Steet and sent characters there to dine in *A Tale of Two Cities.*

16 Borough Market
Start a Saturday morning sampling fruits, cheeses, bread and coffee – if you can stand the crowds.

17 Vagabond No. 7
When you've been caught in a downpour, the espresso and eggs here will warm you up.

18 Zuccino Coffee
Along Camden passage in Angel, its small garden is the place to sip a flat white on sunnier days.

19 Hoxton Street Monster Supplies
Running low on heebie-jeebies? Stop by this shop on Hoxton Street. All purchases support the Ministry of Stories (see pp. 198–9).

20 Brick Lane
Curry houses. Enough said.

21 Museum of London Docklands
The best place to connect with London's nautical past and learn how the East End is changing.

22 Over the O$_2$
With the Thames on three sides and Canary Wharf opposite, the roof of the O$_2$ Arena offers a stunning panorama of London.

23 Blackheath Point
You can take in a dramatic sunset from this Protected Vista (see pp. 68–73) without the crowds of Primrose Hill or Greenwich Park.

SOURCES: BOOKSELLERS ASSOCIATION; LONDON COFFEE GUIDE; OSM

Notes

Open data from the Office for National Statistics (ONS), Ordnance Survey (OS), and OpenStreetMap (OSM) have been essential to this book. We abbreviated their credits on graphics; we include it in full here:

ONS: Office for National Statistics licensed under the Open Government Licence v.2.0.

OS: Contains Ordnance Survey data © Crown copyright and database right 2014

OSM: © OpenStreetMap contributors CC BY-SA

Any additional data sources are credited as fully as possible at the bottom of each graphic or in their associated text.

All the URLs listed below were live in August 2014.

INTRODUCTION (pp. 20-33)

For more on Phyllis Pearsall and the creation of the first *A to Z*, see: *designmuseum.org/design/phyllis-pearsall*

For more on Henry Beck's Tube map – and many others – see Mark Ovenden's *Metro Maps of the World* (London: Capital Transport Publishing, 2nd Ed. 2005).

The Open Data Rankings come from the *2013 Open Data Barometer*: *www.opendataresearch.org/dl/odb2013/Open-Data-Barometer-2013-Global-Report.pdf*

The conversation between Gordon Brown and Sir Tim Berners-Lee is quoted from the *Guardian*: *www.theguardian.com/commentisfree/2010/nov/06/google-david-cameron-copyright*

Francis Maude, Minister for the Cabinet Office, frequently talks about the British Government's commitment to open data: *www.gov.uk/government/speeches/francis-maude-speech-on-transparency.* This follows the government white paper entitled *Open Data: Unleashing the Potential*: *data.gov.uk/sites/default/files/Open_data_White_Paper.pdf*

The UK's Open Government License is detailed here: *www.nationalarchives.gov.uk/doc/open-government-licence*

More on the Information Commissioner's Office and Freedom of Information Requests appears here: *ico.org.uk/for_organisations/freedom_of_information/guide*

More on the Ordnance Survey can be found here: *www.ordnance-survey.co.uk/about/overview/activities.html* and a history of the census in England and Wales can be found on the ONS's website: *www.ons.gov.uk/ons/guide-method/census/2011/how-our-census-works/about-censuses/census-history/index.html*

For additional research on Booth's work, see the London School of Economics's online archive: *booth.lse.ac.uk*

The Science Museum has a brief biography of William Farr: *www.sciencemuseum.org.uk/broughtto-life/people/williamfarr.aspx*

The Ghost Map (Steven Johnson, London: Penguin, 2006) details the work of John Snow.

WHERE WE ARE

Contours of the City (36-7)

The origin of London at the lowest convenient crossing point of the Thames is outlined on p. 494 of *The London Encyclopedia* (Weinreb, Hibbert, Keay, Keay. London: Macmillan, 2008).

We checked our historic rivers against the *Times History of London* (Hugh Clout, 1999) and the *Atlas of London* (Emrys Jones and Daniel Sinclair, 1968).

What we talk about when we talk about London (38-9)

Peter Ackroyd's full quote from p. 779 of *London: The Biography*

(London: Vintage, 2001) reads: 'London goes beyond any boundary or convention. It contains every wish or word ever spoken, every action or gesture ever made, every harsh or noble statement ever expressed. It is illimitable. It is Infinite London.'

The origins of Ealing, Greenwich and Arsenal come from their entries in *The London Encyclopedia* (Weinreb, Hibbert, Keay, Keay. London: Macmillan, 2008)

Hub for the World (40-41)

Heathrow Airport has its full history outlined here: *en.wikipedia.org/wiki/History_of_London_Heathrow_Airport*

Heathrow was ranked first in terms of international passenger traffic in 2013 by Airport Councils International: *en.wikipedia.org/wiki/World's_busiest_airports_by_international_passenger_traffic*

From Home to Work (42-3)

The commuting time data are taken from the ONS's *Commuting to Work* report from 2 June 2011: *www.ons.gov.uk/ons/dcp171776_227904.pdf*

The estimate for London's wider metropolitan area was taken from EPSON, but there are others. See here: *en.wikipedia.org/wiki/List_of_metropolitan_areas_in_Europe*

Hot Spots (46-7)

For more on the urban heat island effect, see *National Geographic*'s online entry: *education.nationalgeographic.co.uk/education/encyclopedia/urban-heat-island*

Seeking Shade (48-9)

For more on London's trees, see *The Mayor's Street Tree Programme Final Evaluation Report* published in 2012 by the Mayor of London: *www.london.gov.uk/sites/default/files/archives/mstp_evaluation_winter_2012.pdf*

The Urban Wild (50-51)

The Daniel Raven-Ellison quote was taken from a press release promoting the start of the Greater London National Park campaign. For more details: *www.greaterlondonnationalpark.org.uk*

Holding Back the Tide (52-3)

London's Victorian embankments were built by Sir Joseph Bazalgette to house sewers taking effluent downstream out of the city. See p. 272 of *The London Encyclopedia* (Weinreb, Hibbert, Keay, Keay. London: Macmillan, 2008) for more information.

The BBC has a good article on the 1928 flood of London: *www.bbc.co.uk/news/magazine-26153241* and the GLA has details from the 1953 flood: *www.london.gov.uk/mayor-assembly/mayor/london-resilience/london-prepared-blog/2013/01/remembering-the-1953-floods*

For more on how the Thames Barrier works and its use at the start of 2014, see: *www.gov.uk/the-thames-barrier*

The London Assembly Environment Committee published a report in April 2014 entitled *Flood Risks In London*: *www.london.gov.uk/sites/default/files/14-04-*

07-Flood%20risk%20slide%20pack%20-%20FINAL_0.pdf

What Lies Beneath (56-7)

To produce our text and drawings, Crossrail gave us access to their image library and Archaeological Sites summary, but there's plenty of good info available to the public at *www.crossrail.co.uk*

Back From the Blitz (62-3)

The BBC has a detailed account of the Blitz and its death toll: *www.bbc.co.uk/history/events/germany_bombs_london*

(Un)Affordable Flats (66-7)

The 'more billionaires than any other city' statement is drawn from the *Sunday Times* Rich List reported here: *www.channel4.com/news/london-sunday-times-super-rich-list-billionaires*

For more on the dynamics of people buying or renting their homes, see here: *www.ons.gov.uk/ons/rel/census/2011-census-analysis/a-century-of-home-ownership-and-renting-in-england-and-wales/short-story-on-housing.html*

We based our mortgage affordability on this advice: *www.which.co.uk/money/mortgages-and-property/guides/mortgage-deposit-explained/how-much-deposit-do-i-need-for-a-mortgage*

Our median income calculation is based on 2013 figures from the ONS quoted here: *www.ons.gov.uk/ons/dcp171778_335027.pdf*

13 Views Worth Protecting (68-73)

Each protected vista is detailed in the London View Management Framework published by the GLA in 2012: *legacy.london.gov.uk/ mayor/strategies/sds/docs/spg-views-final-all.pdf*

As of Spring 2014, 230 skyscrapers were planned for London according to the *London's Growing Up!* report by New London Architects. *www.newlondonarchitecture.org/dls/TB_B1.pdf*

WHO WE ARE

Why it's worth knowing who we are (78-9)

The quote from the Royal Statistical Society is taken from its response to the consultation on the census and the future provision of population statistics in England and Wales, published December 2013: *www.rss.org.uk/uploadedfiles/userfiles/files/RSS%20Beyond%202011%20consultation%20response%20December%202013.pdf*

The threat of cancelling the 2011 Census was detailed in a letter to the Chair of the UK Statistics Authority. His response can be viewed here: *statisticsauthority.gov.uk/reports---correspondence/correspondence/letter-from-sir-michael-scholar-to-francis-maude-mp---20-may-2010.pdf*

In July 2014, the UK government announced there would be a census in 2021. They also said, 'It is the government's ambition that beyond 2021 the decennial census would not be undertaken. Instead, more regular and timely administrative data would be used to produce statistics.' *www.ft.com/cms/s/0/4313fd34-1586-11e4-9e18-00144feabdc0.html#axzz-38kdBejkX*

Similarities Attract (80-81)

For more on the London Output Area Classification, see: *Longley, P.A. Singleton, A.D. London Output Area Classification (LOAC). Census Information Scheme, GLA Intelligence, London.*

Life and Death (82-3)

ONS predicts London's population will reach 9 million by 2021: *www.ons.gov.uk/ons/rel/snpp/sub-national-population-projections/2012-based-projections/stb-2012-based-snpp.html*

Professional Networking (86-7)

For a full list of the occupation types collected by the 2011 Census, see here: *www.nomisweb.co.uk/census/2011/qs606ew*

High Streets (88-9)

London's high streets are a priority for the GLA. Through Design for London, they funded Gort Scott to undertake the study used here: *www.gortscott.com/project/high-street-london*. For more information on the GLA's most recent initiatives, see: *www.london.gov.uk/priorities/regeneration/high-streets*

There's a Guild for That (90-91)

The colours and dates of London's livery companies were cross-referenced between John Kennedy Melling's *Discovering London's Guilds and Liveries* (Oxford: Shire Publications, 2003) and *The London Encyclopedia* (Weinreb, Hibbert, Keay, Keay. London: Macmillan, 2008). More information on the individual companies can be found via *liverycompanies.com* or the City of London: *www.cityoflondon.gov.uk/about-the-city/working-with-and-for-others/Pages/city-livery-companies.aspx*

Moving In, Then On (94-5)

Research by the estate agency, Hamptons International, suggests that most moves out of London are around 26 miles. *www.hamptons.co.uk/news-research/press-releases/dec-02-2013*

The migration statistics were drawn from the ONS's Statistical Bulletin entitled *Internal Migration by Local Authorities in England and Wales, Year Ending June 2012* (published June 2013).

Increasingly Eastern (96-7) Passports, Please (98-9)

The data and analysis for both of these graphics were derived from a series of 'Census snapshots' published by the GLA: *Diversity in London; Passports held; Country of birth, Passports held and National Identity* – all of which are downloadable from the London Datastore: *data.london.gov.uk*

Page 5 of *Passports held* notes that 7.5 million Londoners held 7.8 million passports because some people held two or more. Tallies of passports count people twice, which is why we used tallies of passport *holders* for our graphics.

EthniCity (100-101)

London's waves of migrants feature in almost every history of the capital. We took our contextual information for this graphic from *London: The Illustrated History* (London: Penguin, 2008) for this graphic.

Greetings from London (104-5)

The statistic that over 300 languages are spoken in London is widely quoted. The original source may be the book *Multilingual Capital* (Philip Baker, John Everseley. London: Battlebridge Publications, 2000).

Who London Inspired (108-9)

For the most comprehensive guide to London's Blue Plaques, see *Lived in London: Blue Plaques and the Stories Behind Them* (Emily Cole. London: Yale University Press, 2009).

We excerpted Van Gogh's quotes from *The Letters of Vincent Van Gogh* (Mark Roskill, ed. New York: Antheneum, 1963).

WHERE WE GO

There is order and beauty in the chaos of your commute (114-5)

TfL log around 24 million journeys a day across the network: *www.tfl.gov.uk/corporate/about-tfl/what-we-do?intcmp=2582* and release a business plan each year detailing their future plans and how they are seeking to squeeze more capacity from their infrastructure: *www.tfl.gov.uk/cdn/static/cms/documents/tfl-business-plan-december-2013.pdf*

Untangled on Arrival (116-9)

Wikipedia has a good article on wake turbulence from aircraft: *en.wikipedia.org/wiki/Wake_turbulence* and NATS have produced an infographic that explains the need for stacking at Heathrow and other large airports: *nats.aero/blog/2013/06/infographic-why-do-aircraft-hold-at-heathrow-airport*

The quote 'It's about Britain's place in the world' appears on p. 3 of Heathrow Airport's report entitled *A New Approach: www.heathrowairport.com/static/Heathrow/Downloads/PDF/a-new-approach_LHR.pdf*

Thames Gateway (120-123)

The headline statistics for the Port of London Authority are taken from here: *www.pla.co.uk/assets/infographicplaporttrade-standard-quality-0.5mb.pdf*

The 'River Thames Whale' has its own Wikipedia entry: *en.wikipedia.org/wiki/River_Thames_whale*

The full quote from John Burns is 'The St Lawrence is water, the Mississippi is muddy water, but the Thames is liquid history'. *Daily Mail* (25 January 1943)

Fiona Rule's *London's Docklands: A History of the Lost Quarter* (London: Ian Allen, 2009) offers detailed insights into the origins and history of the docks that provide important context to the area we know today.

For a more detailed history of many key landmarks along the Thames, we recommend the final section (pp. 401-47) of Peter Ackroyd's *Thames Sacred River* (London: Vintage, 2007), from which we drew information for our captions on Isle of Dogs and Hope Reach.

The first chapter of Terry Farrell's book, *Shaping London*, (Chichester: Wiley, 2010) explains how the Thames influenced the development of the capital and provided some useful context to this graphic.

Getting to Work (124-5)

TfL quote 2.4 billion bus journeys in 2013/14 here: *www.tfl.gov.uk/info-for/media/press-releases/2014/may/annual-passenger-journeys-on-london-s-buses-top-2-4-billion*

For bus fares, see: *www.tfl.gov.uk/fares-and-payments/fares/bus-and-tram*

The 2010 *Future of London Buses* report details the importance of buses as affordable transport: *www.london.gov.uk/sites/default/files/buses-future.pdf*

To and Fro, on the Tube (126-7)

Page 937 of *The London Encyclopedia* (Weinreb, Hibbert, Keay, Keay. London: Macmillan, 2008) offers a good overview of the conception and creation of London's railways both above and below ground.

The population of the Victorian world was taken from here: *www.un.org/esa/population/publications/sixbillion/sixbilpart1.pdf*

A Week on the Underground (128-9)

The Tube ridership record was broken on 2 August 2012 with 4.32 million journeys: *www.tfl.gov.uk/info-for/media/press-releases/2012/august/london-2012-games-bring-busiest-days-in-tubes-history*

Around the World in 10 Lines (130-131)

Data in this graphic came from the *London Underground Performance Almanac*, which is updated each month: *www.tfl.gov.uk/corporate/publications-and-reports*

Disrupted (132-3)

We obtained the statistics on delays and suicides through two Freedom of Information Requests to TfL: *www.whatdotheyknow.com/request/causes_of_delays_london_undergro* and *www.whatdotheyknow.com/request/suicide_statistics_13*

The changeover time of 218 seconds for Victoria Line drivers is quoted from this article: *www.therailengineer.com/2013/05/08/squeezing-more-from-the-tube*

A summary of the transport improvements implemented in the run up to the 2012 Olympics is outlined in the House of Commons Standard Note SN3722 entitled *London Olympics 2012: Transport*. For more on the legacy of this, see the London Assembly's report entitled *London 2012 and the Transport Legacy* (published February 2013).

The Tube Challenge (134-5)

The rules of the Tube Challenge can be found here: *www.tubeforum.co.uk/rules.html*

For more on *Labyrinth*, Art on the Underground's collaboration with artist Mark Wallinger, see here: *art.tfl.gov.uk/labyrinth*

Mental Maps (138-141)

We obtained our 'Knowledge' runs from 'blue books' issued by Taxi Trade Promotions in Spring 2014: *www.taxitradepromotions.co.uk*.

The first study to identify larger hippocampi in taxi drivers was published in 2000: Maguire, E., Gadian, D., Johnsrude, I., Good, C., Ashburner, J., Frackowiak, R. and Frith, C. 2000. *Navigation-related structural change in the hippocampi of taxi drivers. PNAS. 97, 8: 4398-4403.*

Minicab Corridors (142-3)

For the full methodology behind Ed's community detection see: *Manley, E. 2014. Identifying functional urban regions within traffic flow. Regional Studies, Regional Science. 1, 1: 40-42.*

Lost & Found (144-5)

We gathered the data for lost property at Heathrow Airport through a search on *missingx.com* for 1 January to 31 December 2013. For simplicity, some categories on the site were combined.

We obtained statistics from TfL on the number of returned items using a Freedom of Information Request: *www.whatdotheyknow.com/request/lost_property_returns*

The Morning Ride (146-7)

Cycling to work increased 155% in London between the 2001 and 2011 Censuses. Reasons for such an increase were reported by *The Times*: *www.thetimes.co.uk/tto/public/cyclesafety/article3706006.ece*

There is no guarantee that all the 'Cycle Superhighways' proposed and shown in the graphic will ever be built. For the latest information, see here: *www.tfl.gov.uk/modes/cycling/routes-and-maps/barclays-cycle-superhighways*

Exhausting Rides (150-151)

For the EU recommendation on air pollution limits, we consulted Directive 2008/50/EC of the European Parliament and of the Council of 21 May 2008 on ambient air quality and cleaner air for Europe. *www.euro.who.int/__data/assets/pdf_file/0020/182432/e96762-final.pdf?ua=1*

Our source for estimates of air pollution deaths is the Public Health England report published in 2014 entitled *Estimating Local Mortality Burdens Associated with Particulate Air Pollution*: *www.hpa.org.uk/webc/HPAwebFile/HPAweb_C/1317141074607*

Cycling is still one of the healthiest ways of getting around the capital as this article in the *British Medical Journal* shows: *www.bmj.com/content/348/bmj.g425*

Cable Car to Nowhere (152-3)

The data for this graphic were found in two existing Freedom of Information Requests: *www.whatdotheyknow.com/request/emirates_air_line_user_figures* and *www.whatdotheyknow.com/request/emirates_air_line_user_numbers*

There has been a steady stream of negative headlines about the Emirates Air Line. Boris Johnson's latest (at the time of writing) attempt to defend it involved hosting his monthly radio phone-in show from one of the gondolas: *www.itv.com/news/london/2014-07-01/boris-insists-underused-cable-car-is-a-howling-success*

Why Not Walk It? (158-9)

The Mark Mason quote is taken from page 4 of his excellent book *Walk the Lines* (London: Random House, 2011)

Tube journey times are taken from TfL's journey planner: *journeyplanner.tfl.gov.uk*

HOW WE'RE DOING

Islington Has Issues (162-3)

The data used in this graphic were taken from the ONS's Statistical Bulletin *Personal Well-Being Across the UK, 2012/13*. The statistics themselves remain experimental, which means they will be tweaked in the future before reaching the gold standards of national statistics such as the census.

It was the best of times, it was the worst of times (164-165)

Written by Charles Dickens, *A Tale of Two Cities* was published in 1859 and is set in both London and Paris.

For more on the recent trends and changes in the distribution of poverty in London, see the report entitled *London's Poverty Profile 2013* published by Trust for London and New Policy Institute.

We quote John Snow from his 1854 report entitled *The Cholera Near Golden Square and at Deptford* in the *Medical Times Gazette. 9: 321-322.*

Lives on the Line (166-7)

For details on how this graphic was created, see this research paper: *Cheshire, J. 2012. Lives on the Line: Mapping Life Expectancy Along the London Tube Network. Environment and Planning A. 44 (7)*

The London Health Observatory first used the Jubilee Line to chart life expectancy. The diagram they used to do it can be found here: *www.lho.org.uk/LHO_Topics/National_Lead_Areas/HealthInequalitiesOverview.aspx*

The 32 Stops (Danny Dorling, London: Penguin, 2013) takes each station along the Central Line and details the social inequalities between those living around them.

The Shape of Obesity (170-171)

For more information on studies of childhood obesity, see Public Heath England's National Child Measurement Programme: *www.gov.uk/government/news/latest-phe-national-child-measurement-programme-figures-available*

The GLA Intelligence Unit also published a report in 2011 entitled *Childhood Obesity in London*: *www.london.gov.uk/sites/default/files/glae-childhood-obesity.pdf*

Causes of Death (172-3)

ONS released these rankings at the request of Clean Air in London: *cleanairinlondon.org/hot-topics/first-ever-rankings-of-top-10-death-rates-for-every-london-borough*

The information on John Graunt comes from Edward Tufte's *The Cognitive Style of PowerPoint* (Graphics Press, 2004) and the *Oxford Dictionary of National Biography*: *www.oxforddnb.com/view/article/11306*

Quit Dates (174-5)

For more on Stoptober, see Public Health England's press release: *www.gov.uk/government/news/stoptober-challenge-reaches-new-high-as-countrys-biggest-mass-quit-attempt*

Scientific American has a link to the science behind Monday quit days: *www.scientificamerican.com/podcast/episode/mondays-top-quit-smoking-google-sea-13-11-12*

To make this photoillustration, we combined four stock images by photographer Dmitry Maslov.

Pill Boxes (176-7)

The prescription data were a major open data release and one that identified millions of pounds of potential savings for the NHS. *www.economist.com/news/britain/21567980-how-scrutiny-freely-available-data-might-save-nhs-money-beggar-thy-neighbour*

Call 999 (178-9)

For a history of 999 – which first launched in London – see here: *www.bbc.co.uk/news/magazine-18520121*

The £3.5 billion cost statistic comes from Public Health England's October 2013 report, *Alcohol Treatment in England 2012-13: www.nta.nhs.uk/uploads/alcohol2012-13.pdf*

For more on booze buses: *www.londonambulance.nhs.uk/news/alcohol-related_999_incidents.aspx*

Top Crimes (182-3)

'54% of Newham residents' refers to Question 13 from the September 2013 MPS Public Attitude Survey: 'To what extent are you worried about crime in this area?'

You Can't Hide (184-5)

We obtained these flight data through an FOI request: *www.whatdotheyknow.com/request/3_months_of_mps_asu_flight_logs*

To view their photos, follow @MPSinthesky on Twitter. To see videos of their thermal camera in action, check out *content.met.police.uk/Site/airsupportunit*

Sound the Alarm! (186-7)

The #fiftyshadesofred campaign data came from correspondence with the London Fire Brigade as well as their 29 July 2013 press release entitled *Number of people trapped in objects like handcuffs and toilet seat rises: www.london-fire.gov.uk/news/C92C30A17C5547278C728EF-4B9A8B530_2807201320.asp#.U9hU3IBdUZA*

Safer Drivers (188-9)

For more detailed analysis of road safety trends in London, see TfL and the Mayor of London's *Safe Streets for London – London's Road Safety Plan 2012* report published in 2013: *www.tfl.gov.uk/cdn/static/cms/documents/safe-streets-for-london.pdf*

The results from Operation Safeway were reported in *Cycling Weekly: www.cyclingweekly.co.uk/news/latest-news/over-14000-penalised-by-police-in-london-road-safety-operation-19177*

How Cyclists Get Hit (190-191)

This graphic is an adapted version of the diagrams included in a September 2011 Transport for London Surface Transport report entitled *Pedal cyclist collisions and casualties in Greater London*. It also draws from the *Safe Streets for London* action plan: *www.tfl.gov.uk/cdn/static/cms/documents/safe-streets-for-london.pdf*

The ban on unsafe lorries is reported here: *www.theguardian.com/uk-news/2014/jan/30/unsafe-lorry-ban-cyclists-london-m25*

Journalist Olaf Storbeck keeps a tally of severe cyclist crashes in this Google Doc: *docs.google.com/spreadsheet/ccc?key=0AuEt-gCUuVBDUdHZqbEZ1NVctVTBVe-FRqTmNVbGZnbXc&hl=de#gid=0*

Street Views (192-3)

Data for this graphic were taken from the 2013/14 CHAIN Annual Report: *www.broadwaylondon.org/CHAIN/Reports/S2h2014/S2H%20full_2013-14%20final.pdf*

The Unconnected (194-5)

Data for this graphic come from responses to a question in the 2013 Labour Force Survey: 'When did you last use the Internet?' *data.london.gov.uk/datastore/package/internet-use-borough-and-population-sub-groups*

Top of the Class (196-7)

The quote 'perhaps the biggest question in education policy' is from Sam Freedman, Director of Research, Evaluation and Impact at the education charity Teach First: *samfreedman1.blogspot.co.uk/2014/06/the-london-schools-effect-what-have-we_28.html*

The Institute for Fiscal Studies report cited was published in June 2014 and entitled *Lessons from London Schools for Attainment Gaps and Social Mobility: www.gov.uk/government/uploads/system/uploads/attachment_data/file/321969/London_Schools_-_FINAL.pdf*

CfBT Education Trust's *Lessons from London Schools* was published the same week as the above: *cdn.cfbt.com/~/media/cfbtcorporate/files/research/2014/r-london-schools-2014.pdf*

The BBC's education correspondant, Sean Coughlan, wrote a comprehensive review of both reports here: *www.bbc.co.uk/news/education-28003851*

In Their Words (198-199)

We scraped the word counts for this graphic from nine Ministry of Stories publications: *Green Wobbly Things, Dancing* (2011); *Plenty of Petrol for 106 Miles* (2011); all four volumes of *The Awfully Bad Guide to Monster Housekeeping* (2011); *Detective Flatley's Mysterious and Monstrous Map of Hoxton* (2012); *A Story You Never Tasted Before* (2013); and *Share More Air* (2013).

WHAT WE LIKE

The Football Tribes (202-3)

We used the 'official' hashtags of the football clubs. Chelsea's, for example, is #cfc and #chelseafc.

You and your interests are the future of Big Data (204-5)

The graphic takes data from the *World Cities Culture Report* published in 2013 by the Mayor of London: *www.london.gov.uk/sites/default/files/WCCR2013.pdf*

The BBC reported on the smart bins: *www.bbc.co.uk/news/technology-23665490*

The Alex Deane quote comes from his post on Big Brother Watch: *www.bigbrotherwatch.org.uk/home/2013/08/bin-snooping-weve-been-here-before.html*

A True Zoo (201-11)

Press releases about the tigers and Partula snails were found on ZSL's website: *www.zsl.org*

'374,000 living animals' refers to ISIS's Zoological Information Management System (ZIMS): *www2.isis.org/products/Pages/default.aspx*

All the Tate's Treasures (212-3)

The Tate Collection make it easy to download all their catalogue data from here: *github.com/tategallery/collection*

Following the Leader (214-5)

An earlier version of this graphic originally appeared in *IL Magazine #14* in November 2009. We updated it to include wheels that have been built since then.

For reference, we consulted photographs, the Observation Wheel Directory *www.observationwheeldirectory.com* and Wikipedia: *en.wikipedia.org/wiki/List_of_Ferris_wheels*

Fashion Cycles (216-7)

Each season, EDITD offers 'Digital Trend Reviews' from the four fashion weeks: *editd.com/resources*

They Came, They Saw, They Spent (218-9)

The ONS calculates passenger spending using their International Passenger Survey: *www.ons.gov.uk/ons/guide-method/method-quality/specific/travel-and-transport-methodology/international-passenger-survey/index.html*

The 2013 visitor numbers came from here: *www.ons.gov.uk/ons/rel/ott/travel-trends/2013/sty.html*

GLA Economics published a working paper in 2012 (#53) entitled *Tourism in London* that details the growth in visitor numbers and how much they spend: *www.london.gov.uk/sites/default/files/wp53.pdf*

Who Says Print is Dead? (222-3)

We measured the newspapers as they were stacked in their stands and made back-of-the-envelope calculations to establish their approximate thickness.

Our circulation figures come from Wikipedia: *en.wikipedia.org/wiki/List_of_newspapers_in_the_United_Kingdom_by_circulation*

Looking for Love (226-7)

Headline results from the ONS's *2012 Integrated Household Survey* are available here: *www.ons.gov.uk/ons/rel/integrated-household-survey/integrated-household-survey/january-to-december-2012/info-sexual-identity.html?WT.mc_id=74d8bdd269c255d-06715cf7e3ff9352c&WT.z_taxonomy=pop&WT.z_format=draws%20you%20in&WT.z_content=interactive&WT.z_trigger=proactive*

Happy Times (228-9)

For more about *Mappiness*, watch an interview with George MacKerron: *www.theguardian.com/technology/2011/feb/13/bright-idea-mappiness-happiness-app* or visit: *www.mappiness.org.uk*

About the Authors

Dr James Cheshire is a geographer with a passion for London and its data. His award-winning maps draw from his research as a lecturer at University College London and have appeared in the *Guardian* and the *Financial Times,* as well as on his popular blog, *mappinglondon.co.uk.* He is a Fellow of the Royal Geographical Society.

Oliver Uberti is a visual journalist, designer, and the recipient of many awards for his information graphics and art direction. From 2003 to 2012 he worked in the design department of *National Geographic,* most recently as Senior Design Editor. He has a design studio in Ann Arbor, Michigan.

Estimated number of data points in this book

Each ● represents 66,000 data points.